FACILITATING
CHANGE
IN
GROUPS
AND TEAMS

FACILITATING
CHANGE
IN
GROUPS
AND TEAMS

A GESTALT APPROACH TO MINDFULNESS

PAUL BARBER

LIBRI
PUBLISHING

Copyright © Libri Publishing 2012

ISBN 978 1 907471 68 1

A CIP catalogue record for this book is available from The British Library

Cover design by Helen Taylor

Design by Carnegie Book Production

Printed in the UK by Ashford Colour Press

Libri Publishing
Brunel House
Volunteer Way
Faringdon
Oxfordshire
SN7 7YR

Tel: +44 (0)845 873 3837

www.libripublishing.co.uk

Acknowledgements

A thank you to all those students and clients who challenged and confronted me over the past thirty years – especially the more difficult and challenging ones! You know full well who you are.

I would like to express appreciation to my many facilitative influences: Oscar Rowley at Northwich College of Art; Joe Quinn, Gunnar Dietrich and Professor Annie Altschul in my nursing career; John Heron and Dr James Kilty within the Human Potential Research Group at the University of Surrey; Dr Stuart Whiteley, Pat McGrath and Norman Vella from my days with the Association of Therapeutic Communities; Professor Petruska Clarkson, Sue Fish, Marriane Fry and Professor Malcolm Parlett from my Gestalt psychotherapy training; and more recently, Joseph Zinker.

The warmest of thanks to Anna, my partner, for initially encouraging me to write and my son, Marc – the former who nourished my imagination and exercises my compassion, and the latter who keeps me attuned to the transpersonal.

Contents

Introduction

Hesitant like one wading a stream in winter;
Timid like one afraid of his neighbours on all sides;
Cautious and courteous like a guest;
Yielding like ice on the point of melting;
Simple like an un-carved block…

(*Tao Te Ching*)

Chapter one

Orientation to the Text
and Underpinning Models

i)   The Origins of My Journey and this Book

In the early 1970s, I attended a 10-day workshop at the Henderson Hospital focussed upon Therapeutic Community Practice (see Chapter 3). Within this programme, John Heron from the Human Potential Research Group delivered Gestalt-like encounter groups heavily biased towards humanistic psychology and Stewart Whiteley from the Henderson Hospital's Therapeutic Community facilitated the large group in a gentle, analytic way. We started the day in a morning community group, decanted to small analytic groups, joined together in Therapeutic Community fashion cleaning and cooking groups, all while living communally together. After lunch we attended seminars and humanistic workshops before coming together in plenary. Some years later while training in Gestalt I ended up running a Certification in Therapeutic Community Practice with the Association of Therapeutic Communities prior to being recruited to the Human Potential Research Group. In this way, I trod in the footsteps of my facilitators! The twin influences of humanistic psychology (see Chapter 2) and group analysis (see Chapter 5) – cemented by Gestalt – made a big impression upon me and inform me still. This is how I got started in holistic facilitation and consultancy; this book says a little of what I have learnt since.

ii)   Core Influences in this Text

This work illuminates a multiple-reality model of facilitation infused by the following influences:

- *Physical/sensory reality* as evidenced through our bodily engagements (gathering data and attending to cognitive and biological aspects of environment)

- *Social/cultural reality* as conventionally taught and intellectually constructed (engaging and analysing the cultural context, values and norms)

- *Emotional/biographical reality* as felt in reference to earlier experience (charting biographical influences and releasing emotional blocks)

- *Imagined/projective reality* as conjured up via images projected outwards onto the world (exploring metaphor and the effects of unconscious bias)

- *Intuitive/transpersonal reality* as intuitively and symbolically created (exploring unknown potentialities and surfacing spiritual values) [Figure 1].

The above overlapping influences are fluid and constantly in flow, emerging and dissolving as we attune to our external and internal environments. They don't stand alone. In this perspective, holistic reality is a river with five ever-swirling currents. I tease out these influences in the following chapters so that we might better appreciate methods of working with each modality so as to appreciate how our facilitative massaging of each can influence the whole.

Figure 1. Contents and Themes of this Text

Chapter 2 (Sensing)

Physical/sensory reality as evidenced through our bodily engagements – gathering data and attending to cognitive and biological aspects of environment

Interventions and consultancy/coaching addressing: physical and biological change; health and burnout; Need Theory and motivation; behaviour and cognition; the Gestalt contact–withdrawal cycle; active listening; action learning; observation skills; embodied learning; task-centeredness; functional power, biological and organic models of group development; orientation to resolution; developing attention and perceptive awareness

Chapter 3 (Thinking)

Social/cultural reality as conventionally taught and intellectually constructed – engaging and analysing the cultural context, values and norms

Interventions and consultancy/coaching addressing: social and cultural development, individual and communal power-relationships; Alpha and Servant Leadership; redressing the status quo; authentic communication; dialogical inquiry; authoritative and facilitative intervention styles; the interplay of social attitudes and ethics; the Therapeutic Community; culture building; conflict resolution; from pseudo to real community

Chapter 4 (Feeling)

Emotional/biographical reality as felt in reference to earlier experience– charting motivational patterns and releasing emotional blocks

Interventions and consultancy/coaching addressing: emotions; transference and counter-transference; biographical and historical influence; group, teams and organisational patterns; psychological and emotional defences; emotional atmosphere; psychodramatic influences; emotional phenomena and prior emotional learning/transference; semi-conscious and unintended influence; analytic models of change; co-creation

Chapter 5 (Imagining)

Projective/imagined reality as conjured up via projected images from the self – exploring metaphor and the effects of unconscious bias and meaning

Interventions and consultancy/coaching addressing: the imaginative power of ideas; unconscious communication; group/teams dynamics; projection and mirroring; the personality of teams and organisations; 'presence' and 'being'; projective identification; shadow dynamics; group and institutional defences; self and selfhood; regression and ego defence mechanisms

Chapter 6 (Intuiting)

Intuitive/transpersonal reality as intuitively and symbolically created – exploring unknown potentialities and surfacing spiritual values

Interventions and consultancy/coaching addressing: archetypes; Dharma and higher purpose; the authentic and spiritual self; field theory and the phenomenological field; 'I–Thou' and 'Thou–Thou' relationships; transpersonal and cosmic forces; spiritual and cosmic laws; envisioning; heuristic inquiry; mindfulness; the causal body; notions of soul and love; the knowing field; Tantric Yoga and Taoism

Alongside and complimenting interventions in each of the above is a developmental process within the facilitator–client relationship which travels through the following phases:

1) **Orientation** (*initiating*): a client-centred phase where the facilitator (be they a coach or consultant) and client (be this an individual, group or organisation) meet together, build trust and *orientate* to each other's world-view and emotional presence while beginning to form a working alliance (*Winter* – before relational life has sprung);

2) **Identification** (*planning*): an issue-centred phase where facilitator and client identify possible problem areas and prospective strategies, sketch an initial contract and raise to awareness the purposes and tasks of facilitation and consider the nature of the researcher–client relationship in which they will engage (*Spring* – as relational buds begin to sprout);

3) **Exploration** (*implementing*): an implementation-of-strategy phase where facilitator and client work together to implement actions, raise hypotheses and modify these in the light of feedback, and speculate upon the future steps the coaching or consultancy might take (*Summer* – as the relationship bears fruit);

4) **Resolution** (*debriefing*): an evaluation phase where facilitator and client evaluate outcomes, review follow-up as necessary and complete the present contract while working towards a positive ending of their current relationship (*Autumn* – when relational energies wane).

Occasionally in this text, I refer to pre-contact and post-contact phases in the facilitative relationship to capture the wider field. This evolving relationship plus the laminations of reality described are cemented together by Gestalt and a practitioner–client relationship which pays attention to how we perceive and attribute meaning, while exploring the whole of what we experience, including:

- Contact

- Excitement

- Need fulfilment

- Self-empowerment

- What is currently unfolding

- Moment-to-moment awareness

- The energetic cement that shapes events

- Assumptions that influence current behaviour

- Interruptions to our organic flow and movement

- What we sense and feel and project out upon the world

- Creating an authentic dialogical relationship

- Distortions and limitations to awareness

- How awareness is being shaped

- What is of greatest interest

- Experiential inquiry

- Interrelatedness

- Self-support

- Joy

In short, Gestalt seeks to illuminate 'the total pattern' of our awareness.

Gestalt reminds us that when we are most fully aware and authentically connected in the moment and that through an illumination of awareness 'change' happens naturally! In these terms, a Gestalt practitioner doesn't 'do change' but rather cultivates an environment where clients might be changed through a raising of consciousness.

So, on first impression, how does this holistic model, with multiple levels of reality and developmental phases held together by Gestalt, impact you?

iii) What is Meant by 'Change'?

A Gestalt coach, group facilitator or consultant does not 'plan' or 'employ strategic interventions' in the business-school tradition, but rather seeks to liberate restrictions to awareness – they interfere with the interference! Personally, I have learnt the hard way that the more you push for change, the more others resist. I find truth enough to support Gestalt's 'paradoxical theory of change' (Beisser 1970), which suggests that change:

- Best occurs when you become more fully 'what you *are*' rather than when you 'try to become what you are not'

- Does not occur through force or pressure but through abandoning what you would like to become and being more fully appreciative of how you maintain your world view

- Is resisted when a person has two warring voices in them saying 'what they believe they should be' and 'what they are' and shifts continually between two warring identities.

Thus, in this work 'change' is seen as a process of co-creation within the facilitator–client relationship where awareness is raised to the degree that transformation flows from the inside out.

iv) What is Facilitation and What Do Facilitators Do?

'Facilitator' is a generic term which includes all who inquire through dialogue with a view to influencing the world of their clients; the facilitation they perform informs consensual styles of leadership, therapy and collaborative forms of research.

Practically, Carl Rogers (1967/87) suggests facilitators draw from their personally acquired store of skill, knowledge and intuitive wisdom with the aim of:

- Setting the initial culture and trust for exploration

- Helping to elicit and clarify purpose

- Acting as a flexible resource

- Responding to expressions, intellectual content and emotional attitudes while endeavouring to give to each individual the time and attention they warrant

- Taking the initiative in sharing themselves and their thoughts and feelings in ways which do not impose, but rather represent an invitation to take or leave what is on offer

- Accepting and openly acknowledging their own limitations.

Gestalt facilitators, specifically, add to this mix by focusing and illuminating: the human condition; free will and choice; experimentation and engagement; experiential learning; the whole of experience and everything that percolates into awareness; cultivating alertness to processes of social engagement and 'contact'; clarifying emerging needs and personal responsibility; the authority of what is being experienced now rather than the 'right answer' so as to:

- Generate individual and group understanding

- Liberate and refine new experiential knowledge

- Raise personal and social awareness

- Educate and empower all involved.

Last but not least, who am I to lecture you on facilitation and what kind of facilitator am I? As a facilitator, I conduct holistic inquiry while role modelling relational health and sharing my human vulnerability. As a human being in my own right I seek to facilitate creativity alongside rigor. I want 'the process' of my inquiry as much as 'what results' to make a positive contribution. *I reason that, as life is developmental and as humans are by turns clear and chaotic, focused and defuse, I must respect these qualities in my facilitation and inquiry.* I also endeavour in a research-minded and humanistic way to:

- Enact a co-operative group inquiry into what is current and happening now

- Surface the tacit hypotheses behind our beliefs and actions for practical testing

8

- Put into active form what is being passively imagined or thought

- Keep the spirit of play and active experimentation continually alive and fresh

- Question everything including the influence of myself and the implied politics and influences of my facilitative role

- Draw attention to how we do things and what we are taking for granted

- Illuminate blind-spots

- Support and challenge by turns

- Work towards personal and systemic health

- Enliven and embody transparency and authenticity.

I bring to bear upon the above a life informed by mental health, the martial arts (Aikido and Iaido), training to Gestalt and Humanism, plus group analysis and Taoism, as well as learning I've amassed from designing and delivering master's programmes in change and management consultancy, but most importantly a love of people and the human condition and a profound respect for Nature.

v) So Why Facilitate Holistic Development in People and Organisations?

Zen cites many paths for the development of 'mindfulness'. In Japan they call such routes to awareness 'do', or 'ways', as in Judo and Aikido. This text looks at 'work-do' – ways to mindfulness through work-based relationships. As for what it is like to work in organisations that fail to account for the development of the human spirit and mindfulness, consider this:

> Often a person's identity, that wild inner complexity of soul and colour of spirit, becomes shrunken into their work identity. They become prisoners of their role. They limit and reduce their lives. They become seduced by the practice of self-absence. They move further and further away from their own lives. They are forced backwards into hidden areas on the ledges of their hearts. When you encounter them you meet only the role. You look for the person, but you never meet him.
>
> (O'Donoghue 1997, pp.187–8)

Holism, akin to the Gestalt notion of field theory (Lewin 1952), invites individuals and organisations to dialogue with what is spiritual and developmental as well as the physical and mundane. A consultant or coach in this tradition attends to an individual or organisation's energetic field, their whole ecology. For instance, in this text I dialogue not just with Gestalt but psychoanalysis to illuminate wisdoms from the Tavistock school of consultation and notions of the unconscious and organisational shadow, plus spiritual sources of knowledge and being. But although every level of reality is valued, nevertheless there is recognition that healthy adaptations foster self-support whereas dis-at-eased ones limit awareness and adaptation, for instance in relation to 'work':

- When we anchor ourselves in **physical–sensory reality**, work may be seen as an exercise for body and mind where physiological energies are generated and exchanged; here we may lose ourselves in our instincts and habits – *or heighten our awareness and contact through sensory engagement with the moment.*

- When we attune to **social–cultural reality**, we relate via rules and intellectual maps and engage with work through conventional roles and rituals; here we may become like ghosts trapped in a machine – *or through heightened communication develop a positive sense of community and enrich ourselves through relationships with others.*

- When we encounter **emotional–biographical reality**, work re-stimulates bits of our emotional history as yet unresolved, to the degree we may negatively enact family roles or blindly act out earlier conflicts – *or can raise to awareness the patterns that entrap us and negotiate beyond them.*

- When we engage **projective–imagined reality**, work can become a mirror of ourselves, where in a negative fashion we become lost in a self-generated ego trip as we act out our own movie – *or through mindful observation we can transcend our self-serving desires to meet with a more authentic sense of being.*

- When we open up to **intuitive–transpersonal reality**, work is integrated into the universe and we may feel ourselves submerged or overwhelmed by uncontrollable and containable energies – *or can allow a more subtle intelligence to guide us upon a spiritual journey which fulfils our true destiny.*

In this light, a Gestalt-informed coach or consultant draws attention to potentially negative patterns while supporting healthy ones. As our natures are complex and multi-faceted so too are the relationships and organisations we co-create.

So at work do we revert to being animals in a concrete jungle fighting for survival? Do we promote I–It relationships and become akin to human cogs in a great social machine endeavouring to run smoothly? Do we enact an emotional drama which chains us to our past? Surrender our responsibility and act like dependent children in the organisational family? Are we self-absorbed and driven by inner desires to win at all costs? Do we become work-heroes? Do we search for a higher sense of meaning and purpose while mindfully moving towards self-actualisation? Are we seeking to serve mankind? These multiple influences and facets of reality constantly shape behaviour. Better to raise such influences to awareness than to act them out blindly. Then again, the world is a far simpler place when you remain within the confines of physical reality and live life as you are socially taught to! A 'surrender to ignorance' is all too common in the workplace.

It is not easy walking towards our fears, but 'growth' necessitates discomfort and a meeting with vulnerability born of releasing control and moving beyond our comfort zone. Take risks and your territory grows; play safe and it shrinks!

Lastly I leave you with these thoughts. Whatever we concentrate on grows stronger; what we withdraw energy from grows weaker and dies. And our fears, along with other emotions can't be walked around – they have to be met and lived through to be resolved!

vi) So Why Did I Bother Writing this Text?

This book celebrates the fruits of my practitioner research. It is an act of self-appraisal and an integration and celebration of learning. I attempt to share what workshop participants, clients and I have found useful while drawing you into dialogue about what constitutes excellence in facilitation. To this end, I brainstorm you with options, tie together multiple influences and challenge you to think and feel outside the world you habitually inhabit. Many of the reflections that I offer for your response, I also respond to. I hope that from this synthesis of theory, practice and reflection you will build your own picture or 'gestalt' of what facilitation means to you.

Underpinning this work is an intention to 'heal' or 'to make things whole'. I believe this text has much to offer not only organisational consultants and coaches but all people-facing professionals. As for my political motives in writing this work, I believe Gestalt is too important an influence to be isolated to therapy and so attempt to illuminate its educative and developmental potential.

Lastly, a caution: don't read this book slavishly from cover to cover but rather flip through it playfully. Dip into it, review the examples of interventions at the close of each chapter, flit between reflections, digest the text when something interests you but challenge everything save that which resonates with experiences of your own.

Paul Barber
Redhill, Surrey, on a cloudy November morning

Reflections upon this Introduction

With a developmental model of the facilitative relationship (orientation–identification–exploration–resolution) plus multiple realities at play (physical, social, emotional, imagined, transpersonal):

- What thoughts are stimulated by this mapping?

- What is your 'felt sense' of the model?

- How might you use this model to profile your own facilitation?

If qualities associated with an analytic approach to facilitation and a humanistic one are positioned on a continuum (as below):

Analytic:	*Humanistic:*
Withholds self	Shares self
Limits engagement	Uses engagement
Agenda mostly hidden	Agenda mostly overt
Adopts an opaque stance	Stays open and transparent
Works from outside the relationship	Works within a relationship

• Where on this continuum would you place yourself?

If we go one step further and extend a continuum from Humanism to Gestalt:

Humanistic:	*Gestalt:*
Shares self	Works as I–Thou
Uses engagement	Remains authentic
Agenda mostly overt	Lets agendas unfold
Stays open and transparent	Remains here and now
Works within a relationship	Co-creates relationship

• Where on the above would you place yourself now?

(Come back to this page to re-position yourself again after reading this text.)

• So, what biases are enshrined in the approach to facilitation described here?

• Having read this introduction, what notion might you carry through the text to keep you critical of what is being presented?

Exploring and Illuminating Energetic Currents in the Field

As things are completed – they have their distinct forms, which we call shapes. Shape is the body preserving within it the spirit – and each shape and spirit has its own innate nature.

(Chuang Tzu)

Chapter two

Raising Awareness
to Physical and Sensory Influences

Competition stifles creativity, reduces the options and limits our thinking. Worse still, in striving to be better than others we reduce life to a game.

2.1   To Heal or to Grow? –
Building a Healthy Foundation for Transformation

At the sensory level of engagement, a facilitator attends to physical aspects of systemic health to consider how biological needs, instincts and physiological energies contribute to the organic development of relationships and the organisation's field. In this chapter we also consider motivation and embodied learning, organic rhythms of change and developmental phases of relationship.

Within this plane of awareness, attuned to their senses, facilitators endeavour to soak-in sensory information while remaining physically grounded, for without clear and concentrated sensory contact how can they collect the necessary data or cultivate the grounded presence demanded for facilitative excellence? The embodiment of learning and physical apparatus of mindfulness emanate from this position, for at root our body never interprets or lies – it just is! Remember, a bodily generated 'felt-sense' does much to ground our intuition and appreciation of the energetic field we work within. Simply, we must learn to read and to employ our bodies as a facilitative antenna.

Before I intervene in a client-system, I consider not only 'client readiness' but 'organisational health', to gauge whether there is enough free energy to support the 'change' a client envisages. Health in this context is an ability to let go of the tried and tested, to deepen contact and risk a meeting with 'difference' – a prompt for freedom to learn. I also monitor my own 'physical health', for to be effective I deem it necessary to embody sufficient physical robustness and energy for my message to be believable. After all, if as facilitators we fail to care for ourselves what are we role modelling to others? Moreover, if we give clients something we desire for ourselves, our compassion will be flavoured with resentment? Wounded carers enact a perverse sort of care, and needy facilitators who make use of facilitation to meet their own needs will likely foster 'learnt dependence' and 'learnt helplessness'.

A tired and spent individual or team will not welcome change, and any amount of facilitation, re-training or motivational reinforcement will be wasted if people are too physically depleted to adapt. Those in organisations or communities that are approaching burnout experience a dearth of free energy and cling onto the tried and tested as if their very lives depend upon it. They do not cling to 'what is familiar' because this is the best option, but because they feel unable to summon the energy necessary to address what is 'unfamiliar'.

I recall stories of concentration camps where victims shrank back from moving through newly opened gates; children that suffer abuse who are torn kicking and screaming from their abusing parents – so strong is the habitual pull of what is familiar. Threaten a person's existent physical and psychic supports, even when these are dysfunctional, and we risk pushing clients further into burnout. Indeed, in my experience, too much 'undigested change' and 'ungrounded enthusiasm' exacerbates burnout! As for the 'environmental supports' people need at work, here are a few my clients have reported:

- Role and job security

- Established friendship patterns

- Feeling a part and a core member of a work team

- Knowing the ropes so you can negotiate around obstacles

- Having established expertise from doing a job well for a number of years

- Being identified with certain specialist activities which others come to you for

- Being trusted or accepted in your present position to the extent that you are left in peace

- Having mates around who will cover for you should you slip out for a while

- Working in a job which is self-directed and self-supervised

- Familiarity with the ways things are done here

- Having an ally in high places

- Predictability.

Threaten or otherwise interfere with these physical habits-cum-'supports' and you will have clients 'climbing the walls' in no time. In unsafe environments survival skills predominate and experimentation is feared; consequently, people withdraw into themselves to avoid the energy drain new learning demands. When people stop learning they stop developing and their capacity for 'change' ceases; in this regard John Heron (1990) makes the distinction between 'living as survival', 'living as learning' and 'living as learning to learn'. Where would you position yourself and your clients on this scale?

To summarise, when we feel insecure and vulnerable we are apt to grip too tightly onto the practicalities, to focus upon details and to place an inordinate degree of effort on maintaining the status quo. Scared people seek certainty and predictability and require a firm outline around everything. When our security emanates from tangibles and well-designated roles there is no space for abstract conceptual reflection. So what might we do as facilitators to foster 'health' in such climates as these? Perhaps merely illuminating what is, sensitising people to their pain while cultivating a review of the options and what might be done differently is a worthy beginning.

i) Burnout – Symptoms of Dis-at-ease in the Individual and System

Sometimes, to open dialogue about the costs of work and to assess systemic health, I invite clients to check if these responses associated with burn-out, below, resonate with them – and if so, how often:

Commonly/Occasionally/Rarely/Never

- Constant neck tensions and headaches
- Feeling trapped and unable to change
- Recurrent absenteeism and sickness
- No time for a hobby you cherish
- Excessive smoking or drinking
- More hours needed in the day
- Acting on emotional impulse
- Early morning awakening
- Preoccupation with work
- Inability to concentrate
- Extreme defensiveness
- Memory disturbances
- Little sexual energy
- Addicted to stress
- Life feels a fight
- Short-tempered
- Loss of energy
- No time to eat
- Dread waking
- Mood swings
- Cannot sleep
- Exhaustion
- Depression
- Irritability

Three or more ticks in the common column and I might suggest it would be advisable to consider slowing down, stepping back and building-in extra self-support via the services of a counsellor or coach. A similar profile in the workplace could indicate that a team or organisation is generative of burn-out and an unfit home for the human spirit, let alone in place to benefit from the change agenda I am supposed to facilitate! They might need healing through such options as team-building first. But I don't use the above list to diagnose, so much as to stimulate reflection and open discourse on the cost of what we are doing and our need for further support. Cultivating a healthy and 'learning to learn' environment where individuals can be heard and feel valued is often my first step in a consultation.

So how common are the above symptoms within groups and organisations you frequent? What if the above features are not pathological but part of an organisation's character, its personality, as it doesn't know any better – then what might you do? Perhaps, in terms of illuminating 'healthy functioning', we could start by considering the reverse of the above qualities, say by inviting a group to reflect upon how they might convert being 'short-tempered with others' towards becoming 'accepting of others' and what they would need to implement an attitudinal change such as this. From this beginning it is but a small step to implement an appreciative inquiry (Bushe 1998; Cooperrider 1990) into when people felt most creative and content in the workplace and what conditions supported this working high. Sometimes, an examination of how such conditions of efficiency and health might be seeded in managerial policy arises. It's all too easy to surface organisational discontent; but turning this discontent around into a celebration of attitudes and events that value people and community health, this is the trick.

Facilitating for Health – A Multidisciplinary Investigation into the Workplace Experience

Within a three-hour team reflection run on appreciative inquiry lines, focussing upon the experience of the working environment within a health trust, the following arose:

'What is it like to work here?'

- 'Compared to how it was prior to Trust status – and even to merely three years ago – the pace is much faster and demands are much greater than they were previously'

- 'These days chasing petty details such as paper-work and form filling tends to subtract from time spent delivering specialist treatments and quality patient care'

- 'Protocol seems directed to chasing "stars" or abstract performance targets rather than improving practice'

- 'There is no time to reflect or plan as we are constantly drawn into fire fighting'

- 'Managerial policy often conflicts with quality care and undermines clinical policy'

- 'As crisis management rules "I have to make a crisis to be heard – although I don't like myself for what I have become in my effort to be heard'

- 'Management seems to fault-find and criticise and constantly implies we should always give more but never says what we are doing well'

- 'I just wish that at times when I've stood in for senior staff or worked extra hours to cover clinical needs someone would just say thanks'.

Generally, the group recognises that if things go on as they are in the current climate of crisis management, with crises becoming thicker and faster with ever more resources being withdrawn, then 'if something drastic doesn't happen soon, care will deteriorate and the system will collapse'. In the meantime, it appears that more balanced feedback and an occasional 'thank you' would go a long way to improving the working climate.

'What has been an especial low point at work over the last year?'

- 'Having 25 deaths over the two weeks of Christmas and receiving no recognition for what I was going through, plus being pressured and chased at this time to fulfil protocol by maintaining the flow of forms on time';

- 'Working one's heart out and receiving no thanks for "going the extra mile"';

- 'Having a manager appointed who didn't know the current up-to-date ways of clinical practice although they acted as if they did';

- 'Having to fight for basic recognition of patient needs';

- 'Being instructed to answer the phone within three rings – and this being given priority over much more crucial care provision and clinical criteria'.

Working at full stretch and without thanks seems commonplace within the clinical culture. Without balanced feedback and recognition by seniors of what they are doing well, staff naturally enough feel unvalued. Add to this the reality of remote decision-making, where the Chief Executive is never seen and would not be recognised even if he walked on site, and the sense of powerlessness grows even more acute.

'What in the workplace encourages you to stay and raises your spirits?'

- 'The intimate and warm relationships enjoyed through close contact with clients';

- 'The way staff pulled together during a crisis and helped across the disciplines';

- 'The peer support, banter and good will expressed by fellow staff even when under pressure';

- 'When for one day 'the system ran as it should' rather than frustrated professional activity';

- 'Working nights or out-of-office hours when petty management issues were relaxed and staff could use their professional expertise and authority without having to fight to do the same'.

Indeed, it was almost as if a Blitz mentality, a sort of 'we have to draw together and sort things out ourselves' prevails, as 'management can't be relied upon for support'.

'What would you like to happen if you had something akin to a magic wand?'

- 'To slow down the system so we can catch up with ourselves and reflect where we are going';
- 'Clinical power to maintain a realistic bed policy';
- 'Managerial recognition of what I am doing well'.

Simply, the above wish list seems to support the observation that 'we just want to be let get on with our jobs' without undue outside interference.

'So what do we appear to have learnt from this inquiry?'

- 'It is not just me who feels frustrated and caused to deliver a service where I can't give of my best, we all do, so I need not blame myself nor feel myself a failure';
- 'We now have a place where we can share our frustrations, be heard and witnessed, and experience the support of peers;
- 'As my professional problems appear to be shared by others and experienced by other disciplines, it appears the system may be at fault';
- 'If existing policies and managerial strategies are seen to be causing us similar difficulties, perhaps we can join together to make a multidisciplinary case for supporting positive change'.

Hopefully future groups will help us to express, identify and form strategies for better dealing with frustrations of the workplace, while fostering the degree of empowerment necessary to add value to ourselves and our clinical functions.

So, by starting with a reflection on current dis-at-ease, surfacing awareness upon what was in place when health flourished, while all the time cultivating a climate in which people can be seen and heard while surfacing their needs – much can be achieved. But how does this listening approach, where a consultant plays a sort of organisational healer role, sound to you? Is it a bit too pink and fluffy for your blood? After all, this 'consultant as listener' challenges the old chestnut of a consultant as saviour, task-leader or macho redeemer! And what exactly is the health we are seeking to cultivate by working in this person-valuing way?

ii) A Humanistic Vision of Super-health

During the 1950s, humanistic psychology arose as a reaction to two dominant influences upon the psychological thinking of the time: psychoanalysis, with its notion of the unconscious, and behaviourism, with its emphasis on conditioning. Humanistic psychologists countered these pessimistic influences by championing human potential and individual choice and by a focus upon personal growth and self-actualisation. In 1962, Abraham Maslow published *Toward a Psychology of Being*, in which he described humanistic psychology as the 'third force' in psychology. Gestalt was part of this melting pot. Yet as a Gestalt practitioner, I do not see psychoanalysis or behaviourism as competing schools, so much as contributions to a holistic understanding of the human condition.

Humanistic psychology expanded its influence throughout the 1970s and '80s and continues to rebuff scientific approaches to psychology, which it views as dehumanising and incapable of capturing the richness of conscious experience. Humanistic psychology has contributed to modern thinking in three ways: the provision of a new set of values for understanding human nature and human kind; an expanded horizon of qualitative methods for inquiry into the study of human behaviour; a broader and increased range of effective person- and process-centred methods in the practice of psychotherapy.

The beliefs of humanistic psychologists resonate with much of Gestalt and its existential foundations, namely:

- To be mentally healthy, individuals must take personal responsibility for their actions, regardless whether those actions are positive or negative

- Each person, simply by 'being', is inherently worthy, for although they may act negatively such actions do not cancel out their value as a person

- The ultimate goal of living is to attain personal growth and understanding, for only through constant self-improvement and self-understanding can an individual ever be satisfied and actualised.

Humanistic psychology supports Gestalt's stress upon *holism*, *autonomy*, *experiential learning* and *democracy*. These working principles discussed further below, I suggest, provide an 'ethical base' for the practice of Gestalt facilitation:

- **Holism** suggests that a person's mental, physical, intellectual, emotional and spiritual qualities are integral to 'everything they do' and 'all they are'. Consequently, an individual is best approached as a whole mind–body–spiritual being rather than reduced to one or more of their parts. As everything is multi-faceted and multi-influenced, we are cautioned that there are no easy answers or simple solutions to human problems. *In the practice of Gestalt I am encouraged to approach groups as organic entities, which, though composed of conscious and unconscious elements of the individuals within them,* *nevertheless express a life of their own. With individual clients I likewise look to the wider dynamic field they are embedded within and influenced by.*

- **Autonomy** supports the notion that, given opportunity and resources, individuals are best placed to diagnose and resolve their own problems, for they know more about themselves than I or anyone else ever will. *As a Gestalt practitioner I watch and listen very carefully to what groups and individuals present, follow what emerges and share my observations while inquiring into the dynamics we create. In this way I attempt to act as a flexible resource who works alongside clients on their journey towards autonomy, personal responsibility and self-empowerment.*

- **Experiential inquiry**, in service of personal development, encourages us to meet life in an open and inquiring way, to attend to the unique nature of our present relationships and to experiment with becoming the whole of ourselves. *As a consultant I encourage people to take nothing for granted and to question everything. Through a focus upon 'what is unique' coupled with on-going inquiry into our perceptions, beliefs and relationships, I seek to illuminate through experiential inquiry insight born of experience.*

- **Democracy** supports the notion that we are interdependent rather than independent, and suggests that reason and negotiation should inform all our decision making and debate. In this vein, rather than authoritative imposition and covert agendas, transparency comes to inform our social actions. *Holding this in mind, I work to negotiate a client-centred menu where everyone is involved in forming the 'how' and the 'what' of the experience on offer. Democracy also keeps me alert to the need for healthy 'I–Thou' relationships and causes me to be watchful of communication that slides towards an ego-centric 'I–I' or a reductionist 'I–It' stance to life, the self or others.*

But why bother? What greater purpose does working in this way serve? Well, personally I see Gestalt's humanistic manner of working as conducive to 'self-actualisation', a state that enables people to maintain peak performance and to distinguish themselves in their careers – a worthy aim commensurate with the notion of 'super-health'! In his study of human potential, Maslow identified the following characteristics of 'self-actualisation' – namely an aptitude to:

- Perceive reality efficiently
- Tolerate uncertainty
- Accept oneself and others for what they are
- Be spontaneous in thought and behaviour
- Maintain a good sense of humour
- Be problem-centred rather than self-centred
- Be highly creative

- Be resistive to en-culturalistion but not purposely unconventional
- Demonstrate concern for the welfare of mankind
- Be deeply appreciative of the basic experiences of life in a child-like way
- Establish deep, satisfying relationships with a few rather than court the friendship of many
- Look at life philosophically and objectively.

(Maslow 1967)

This is the nature of the 'health' to which I aspire and seek to advance in clients.

Reflections

* Which of the personal support systems of 'job security', 'friendship patterns', 'team membership', 'established expertise', 'being seen as self-directed and self-supervising' and 'familiarity with the ways things are done' are important to your own sense of security? And what others might you add to the list? *(I think 'friendship patterns' figure large in my world, plus 'established expertise'. Without something to offer others, I guess I'd feel less worthy. As for what I would add, I think 'creativity', 'novelty' and 'challenge' are potent drivers for me.)*

* Contemplate the qualities you associate with 'growth' as opposed to 'survival', and the kinds of facilitative intervention those caught in a 'living as survival' mode might benefit from. *(For me, 'growth' promises challenge and change, while 'survival' conjures up routine, 'the daily slog' and having to endure rather than enjoy.)*

* Consider also the notion of 'consultant as healer' and what this implies for the business community and coaching. *(It's interesting, as if the phrase 'consultant as healer' softens the macho image of 'the consultant' and the 'authoritative expertise' one associates with such notions as 'flawless consulting'. It also suggests that organisations – and perhaps even the business community itself – may be 'sick' and in need of 'care'.)*

* In terms of the following humanistic principles – holism, experiential learning, autonomy and democracy – how humanistic is your practice? Where are you strong and where are you weakest?

* From the list of self-actualising principles cited below, which might you single out as providing suitable learning goals for yourself?

- To perceive reality efficiently
- To tolerate uncertainty
- To accept oneself and others for what they are

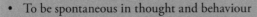

- To be spontaneous in thought and behaviour
- To maintain a good sense of humour
- To be problem-centred rather than self-centred
- To be highly creative
- To be resistive to en-culturalistion but not purposely unconventional
- To demonstrate concern for the welfare of mankind
- To be deeply appreciative of the basic experiences of life in a child-like way
- To establish deep satisfying relationships with a few rather than court the friendship of many
- To look at life philosophically and objectively.

2.2 Needs and Intrinsic Incentives – Towards 'Meaningful' Motivation

I find that most managers have in their 'organisationally fashioned heart' a belief that they need to motivate a diverse and unpredictable group of people, and to this end look to coaches and consultants to do their dirty work for them. But what does motivation really entail? If we are arrogant enough to become facilitators we have a duty to reflect long and hard upon the 'politics', 'ethics' and 'health' of our own actions or we may find ourselves used as tools of control or persecution fashioned to promote the self-same behaviours we desire to correct. Perhaps it is best endowing 'health' as our primary client rather than those who pay the fee!

Half a century ago, Abraham Maslow suggested that unsatisfied needs create tensions which release energy towards need-quenching behaviours; recognised that unfinished business bred frustration; and demonstrated that we are better internally motivated than externally coerced. But although unmet physical needs have influence, this is not the whole story. Herzberg produced evidence that goals associated with 'ego-status' and 'self-actualisation' had more relevance to on-the-job motivation, and that 'belonging' and 'safety' merely kept frustration from creeping in. His field studies (Herzberg 1966) drew attention to '*hygienic factors*', components that prevented dissatisfaction but had little effect upon everyday motivation, such as: salary, job security, working conditions, status, company procedures, quality of supervision and the quality of interpersonal relationships. In contrast, factors which maintained self-support and clear boundaries, so-called '*intrinsic satisfiers*' or '*strong motivators*', were found to include: achievement, recognition, responsibility, advancement, 'the work itself' and the possibility of 'growth'. As for de-motivators, not feeling valued or heard figures huge in those who leave or otherwise absent themselves from organisational life.

At the physical level, it seems the spirit or ghost that inhabits the physiological machine has a far greater influence than biological needs. Indeed, Herzberg showed how the same factors could be interpreted by subjects as good or bad motivators depending upon the situation. Here we find field conditions are a defining influence, and that 'perceived meaning' rather than 'conventional reward' shape behaviour.

I am reminded here of those who undergo physical deprivation and hardship for ideological reasons or to uphold a personal ethic; hunger strikers who hold personal values preferential to biological survival. It would appear that 'actualisation of the self' and identification with a higher value is a much more powerful than a desire for physical comfort and safety – though we would never know this from most organisational literature! Even though the field trials of Hackman and Oldham's (1980) 'Work Design Model' long ago identified 'experienced meaningfulness of work', 'experienced responsibility for the work and its outcomes' plus a 'knowledge of results and performance feedback' as most significantly impacting worker satisfaction, the business community, by and large, still attempts to motivate the greater proportion of its members through 'hygienic factors'.

One of Gestalt's most distinguishing features is its emphasis upon the role 'awareness' plays in motivation and adaptation. Whatever they are delivering – coaching, teambuilding, training or culture change – Gestalt practitioners help the client and client-system to develop a deeper, more holistic appreciation of 'what is happening' and 'what is needed' with a view to fostering 'intrinsic satisfaction'. Mind you, we are cautioned by Saner (1999) that awareness does not take place in a vacuum but influenced by the social milieu or 'Zeitgeist of the moment' (Saner 1999, p.6). For instance, he observes that cultures which 'support individual effort' and employ 'awareness' vary greatly from those that 'focus on others', and that cultures which 'value action' will encourage a faster discharge of 'energy into action' than ones where reflective practice is seen to bring its own reward. We are reminded that 'the organisation's energetic stamp' will greatly affect each and every intervention we make.

In light of the above, we need to remember that facilitative interventions will serve little purpose unless they 'add meaning', 'empower individuals' and contribute towards a 'culturally sustainable system of quality feedback'. This leads me to suggest that we can best encourage meaningful change through a dialogical approach to consultation which:

- Illuminates a client's current needs

- Generates self-support while building clear boundaries

- Rattles-and-shakes a client's beliefs through quality feedback

- Considers at depth the conditions that best support clients in giving their best
- Experiments with and promotes systems which enable clients to assume greater responsibility
- Seeds an appreciation of the workplace as a living and learning community
- Co-creates solutions that work best for clients within the system in which they are embedded
- Promotes a client's development and growth.

All of which raise awareness while simultaneously creating conditions for genuine motivation.

Reflections

* Bring to mind a work group or community with which you are familiar and list the 'intrinsic satisfiers' and 'hygienic components' present – also consider which features it might be wise to preserve. *(I have in mind a previous workplace, an academic climate where my 'intrinsic satisfiers' were my face-to-face delivery of workshops and student feedback, and the 'hygienic component was flexi-hours.)*

* How do you imagine a consultant in the group or community you have in mind might facilitate with a view to increasing 'the experienced meaningfulness' of the work, engender a 'shared responsibility for work outcomes' and build-in 'knowledge of results and performance feedback'? *(In the department I worked within, very little cross-fertilisation of ideas or team-teaching occurred, so I guess community envisioning of our future offerings or the co-creation of a departmental mission statement would have been useful.)*

* What needs does your role as a facilitator meet for you? Given that much learning is tacit and unconsciously acquired, what do you role model to your clients as a facilitator?

2.3 Losing Our Mind to Come to Our Senses – Transforming from Moment to Moment

Personal development cannot be separated from professional development for each is wed to the other. Show me how well you share of yourself, understand your own interpersonal process and are able to communicate this to others and I'll have some measure of how good a facilitator you are. But more than this, excellence in facilitation demands that you learn to dance on a moving carpet, for at the last we have no choice but to make 'change' a friend and close companion.

Nothing is forever and nothing is permanent; all is in flux. Physics tells us that in the real world beyond our senses, energies dance and constellate before us and that what we perceive as solid mater at the quantum level is 99.9% space! Nature never rests. We have long been taught to believe and to place our trust in control and permanence – but change is the norm. We rarely contemplate our own death – the ultimate change process awaiting us – or comprehend 'our reality' as a momentary grasping at an ever-flowing experience. We are 'change' personified. But letting go of old tried-and-tested ways and surrendering ourselves to uncertainty can be very hard work – especially when we resist!

'Change', according to Charles Handy (1991), is unique and should be seen as a discontinuous rather than continuous process. Change, he says, is confusing and disturbing, especially to those in power, and is often brought about by minute events – for instance small differences concerning how our work is organised can make major differences to our lives. Change is irregular and unpredictable and demands non-rational, upside down thinking if we are to adapt to its influences creatively. To illustrate this point further, Handy shares a reminiscence of some thirty years ago when he first worked for a world-famous multinational company, which to encourage him produced a suggested outline of his future career. He recalls that the career profile he was offered ended with his promotion to 'the chief executive of a particular company in a far-off country' (Handy 1991, p.5). He observes that 'the job', 'the company' and even 'the country' picked for him no longer exist! Global, organisational and individual fields are ever changing.

Today, in most areas of our life there are no longer guarantees; we cannot expect 'more of the same'. This has always been so, but change is now recognised as so rampant that we cannot retain the delusion of permanence that supported our forefathers. Change is the only reality, the only guarantee. Welcome it or fight it, we remain subject to it.

Change is 'up-tight and personal'; it is physically threatening though paradoxically value neutral. Its meaning and effects are shaped by the values and emotions we attach to change. We might just as well attempt to stifle our breathing as try to avoid change; it is not a question of 'what we do with it' or 'how we deal with it' – but more how we accept it as a 'given' of our lives.

As for what happens when we resist change: we find ourselves denying reality and alienated from the environment; retreating into dogma or authoritarianism; longing for a romanticised past or focussing upon a hoped-for golden future; attempting to reason it away; ritualising our life so that our historically patterned behaviours decide for us; in sum, vainly refusing to be the authors of our life in a changeable world.

Paradoxically, even if we resist it, we still undergo change – but in less than healthy ways which cause us to be out of step with the environment. Losing sight of alternative strategies may also plunge us into ever-deepening regret for what can never be. So, what behaviours and attitudes are conducive to healthy adaptation? Well, I dare to suggest a few:

- Accepting transitional 'growing pains' such as embarrassment and vulnerability as a necessary part of our movement through life

- Releasing ourselves from having 'to know the answer' or 'to predict the outcome'

- Accepting our feelings as informative energies rather than things to be controlled

- Giving ourselves permission to learn through mistakes

- Endeavouring to move beyond our defences

- Experimenting with new and novel ways

- Walking towards our fears.

Such attitudes as these support a willingness to keep in dialogue with what is changing, re-constellating and unfolding around and within us – now.

Self-observation can help us discover a little about how gentle adaptation to moment-to-moment change is a subtle requirement of our everyday life. For example, if I break off from writing this passage to focus upon my thoughts, sensations, feelings and intuitions (my perceptive organs and their associated impressions), the following cycle of awareness unfolds:

- Focusing on my *thoughts*, I'm aware of speculating upon the possible direction to next steer this chapter, mentally sifting through its themes to date while attempting to map a strategic way forward to bring the work to a meaningful conclusion.

- Focusing on my current tactile and visual *sensations*, I'm aware of being warmed by the bodyheat of Chen, my Siamese cat, who is stretched out on my lap; as I watch the rise and fall of her rhythmic breathing I glimpse a grey sky outside and find my attention being caught by flakes of snow falling gently past the window.

- Focusing on my *feelings*, I notice that I'm feeling low in emotional and physical energy, satisfied with my progress so far – but a little introverted and emotionally flat.

- Focusing upon my *intuitions* and fantasies, an intuition comes to mind that I need a rest from this work and desire a little more fun; an image flashes to mind of a local pub, a blazing log fire and a foaming pint of beer – this daydream lingers and takes some time to clear!

Through reflection on my moment-to-moment perceptions, I gain a richer sense of myself and an increased awareness of my existence now. Attending to my senses somehow grounds me more soundly in the present. For instance, the diagnosis of my tiredness was only possible when I stepped out from my head and into my body. This recognition of becoming tired was the catalyst that changed me. Indeed, the speculative solution and the creation of 'a strategy' stemmed from increased self-awareness. Awareness is freeing and it is also a potent agent of change, but we have to stop, still ourselves and undo our behavioural and social habits before this can be appreciated. Change, in this scenario is an ever-present subliminal process my physiology enacts, responds to and embodies.

I have found the reflective technique described above, of sharing with a partner your current awareness of what you are *thinking*, *sensing*, *feeling* and *imagining*, to be a powerful facilitative tool for developing holistic consciousness.

Unless we develop an ability to distinguish between our sensations and intuitions we remain unable to decode whether we are interpreting or observing, or yet again mapping external data or drawing on internal reactions. This is a sad state of affairs for the 'average Joe' – but disastrous for a facilitator. Many people likewise fail to differentiate between sensory data and imaginative interpretation; they report their projections and thoughts rather than 'what is' and in consequence they weaken their potential and effect.

If our thinking overlaps with our sensing, prejudice results as unexplored, untested and invalidated bias leaks in to colour our sensory and physical reality. When sensing overlaps with feelings and intuitions, we become deluded as emotions and imagination intermingle with sensed data. Likewise, unclear boundaries between thinking and intuition can flood our intellect with irrational fears.

In this light, the thinking–sensing–feeling–imagining cycle exercise becomes a practical vehicle with which to 'become response-able' – a tool to help us appreciate where we are drawing our evidence from so that we might better understand our decisions and co-create more appropriate responses.

Our sensate world has much to teach us. As I enter a workshop or consultancy, I turn to my body for guidance. I observe where in my body I resonate with the group. Sometimes I feel heavy as if the group is difficult to digest, other times my head feels light and busy; as we begin to engage I check if I am breathing 'in' the group or breathing it 'out'. Whenever my emotions threaten to overwhelm me or my thoughts clamour for attention, I return to my breathing. Observing my breathing out and breathing in, breathing in for a count of one and breathing out for a count of two never fails to ground me. In this way I loosen my mind to attend to my senses. I watch and listen very carefully to all around me; soaking in how others move and where their energy appears blocked or focussed. Some present a head, others enter with stiff knees and necks; many seem hyper-alert while others drift away inwards lost in their internal worlds – as individuals appear in body, so often they later present in mind. Some don't see me and appear to fling aspects of themselves upon me – I observe but say nothing. As I absorb my surroundings, my breathing deepens and a sense of belonging grows. When my body settles, the whole of me lands and I feel ready to work. Getting our clients to land, orientate to the occasion and 'to really be here' is a prerequisite of the authentic dialogical consulting I favour – this is my Gestalt bias speaking here.

Reflections

* In terms of sensing, feeling, thinking and intuition, which of these do you predominately attune to in your everyday life? Which do you generally under-use? *(My growth as a person and as a facilitator was like a letting go, a release of my rigidities, preconceived ideas and ego defences – as if by unclogging my pre-conceptions I began to learn. My intellect is seemingly full of old redundant knowledge and by releasing its hold I awaken to my senses and what is current now.)*

* Pick a partner. Take it in turn to share the thoughts, sensations, feelings and intuitions that arise as you one another take turns to say:

> *I am aware of thinking…*
> *I am aware of sensing…*
> *I am aware of feeling…*
> *I am aware of imagining…*

Keep repeating the above cycle, alternatively with your partner, until you have exhausted your store of perceptions.

Opening up Thinking

- Practice putting your beliefs and judgements on hold so as to cultivate a beginner's mind unfettered by conclusions and answers – then see what thought provokes;

- Attempt to discriminate between the facts, assumptions, fantasies, sensed data and beliefs that litter and shape your moment to moment thinking;

- Play devil's advocate by rattle-and-shaking the substance of an idea or theory you are entertaining or firmly committed to – then entertain the opposite.

Opening up Feeling

- Explore just what your feelings are saying about what is happening now, magnify the emotion that prevails, make a non-verbal sound that expresses this emotion;

- Spend time each evening surfacing emotions you earlier held in check throughout the day, bring them to mind and re-experience them – see what then remains;

▶ • Attempt to recognise the emotional messages and historical re-stimulations that drive you – notice how your past sometimes drives you.

Opening up Sensing

• List your pleasures and delights, choose one and allow yourself time to re-experience it, paying particular attention to the type of sensory stimulation that gives you pleasure;

• Take time with a partner to explore sensory delights, foods, smells, caresses, music and notice the quality of your attention and awareness before, during and after this exercise;

• Experiment with sifting out from your thoughts and feelings what you actually see and hear right now – attend to your breathing and notice where your breath leads you.

Opening up Intuition

• Stop to look at images and scenes that catch your eye, quietly soak them in and see what emerges in terms of memories, bodily sensations and imaginative imagery;

• Relax and let the day's events float before you, see what stands out, give today's activities a title and reflect on what this title means for you at this stage of your life;

• Sit quietly and ask yourself what in your life is preventing you from being content; observe what images and intuitions flow fleetingly past you.

2.4 Organic Rhythms of Change – Facilitating Contact with a Field's Energetic Flow

In Gestalt, 'experience' is seen as richest on the 'contact boundary' between an individual and their environment. Clean and clear contact is the basis of our 'sensing of the world' and 'action', and physical contact is the primary reality for this enactment. In this way we 'make sense of ourselves' and 'sense ourselves'. All this negotiation takes place on the contact boundary where we make choices about which bits of the world we consider important and interesting while we simultaneously identifying with sensations we perceive to be 'me' or 'not me'.

Gestalt practitioners sometimes refer to the 'contact–withdrawal' cycle' as an example of how we reach out to the environment or yet again interrupt our ability to meet and contact our environment. This perspective assumes that human beings are stimulated into environmental contact and awareness by their emerging needs, which in turn evoke the following sequence:

> **Sensation**: an acknowledgement of a need or environmental opportunity which draws us into sensory experience which in turn concentrates...

> **Awareness**: a surfacing and alertness to feelings, ideas and potential actions which stimulates an emotional reaction which generates...

> **Mobilisation of energy**: a dawning emotional motivation and accompanying sharpening focus for the quenching of a felt need and so to...

> **Excitement**: the engagement of physiological energy which then leads to...

> **Action**: an act of concentration and behavioural response which stimulates movement towards...

> **Contact**: which brings us into a robust exchange with our environment inclusive of self or others until satisfaction is achieved, leading to...

> **Withdrawal**: a natural sense of completion and rest from the current unease until the next need emerges.

An interruption to this cycle frustrates natural flow – in people and organisations alike. Granted, both individual and organisation are energetically connected and influence each other; but can they really be equated? The individual is a conscious being, the organisation a mere phenomenological consequence of people coming together. Nevertheless, in the contact cycle we have a metaphor that draws our to attention to the importance of need fulfilment and the possible conflicts that emerge when this movement towards need fulfilment is blocked. Some consultants, such as Critchley and Casey (1989), have used this device to suggest a direction consultancy and coaching may take to facilitate more healthy and satisfactory contact:

1. Interruptions between Withdrawal and Sensation

Example – The Suppressed Organisation

When a group or company is unable to swing from withdrawal into sensation, they are suggested to experience a disconnected state akin to coma which requires radical life-saving measures. People and groups here rarely show feelings as they have withdrawn into themselves and become increasingly isolated. Relationships are cold, inapt and uninfluenced by events, structured by rules and mechanistic controls. Government departments and total organisations such as the army and prison service plus well-established city banks can sometimes fall into this category.

* **Remedy?** *Try to anchor the client-system in the sensory world by raising awareness to sights, sounds and other physical stimuli while inviting people to move, explore, to follow their curiosity and to actively engage.*

2. Interruptions between Sensation and Awareness

Example – The Hysterical Organisation

Blocked between sensation and awareness, people in organisations such as this experience sensations but 'don't know what their sensations and awareness means', 'what to do with them' or 'how to organise them into meaningful patterns'; they experience acute anxiety but have no idea about what to do about it. Arrested at this point, individuals habitually respond with excitability and get overwhelmed by sensations and carried away by emotions. Being ungrounded they easily attach grandiose meanings to experiences; energy and emotions run high but self-awareness remains low. Artistic, fashion-driven, theatrical companies and advertising agencies have been seen to fall into this category.

** **Remedy?** Work at developing sensitivity and insight into the relationship between sensation, physiology, physical effects and dynamics. Endeavour to ground people. Show the relationship between environmental causes and psychological effects, while encouraging speculation and consideration of future experiments.*

3. Interruptions between Awareness and Mobilisation of Energy

Example – The Intellectually Aware and Angry Organisation

When groups or organisations are unable to move from awareness to mobilisation, emotional energies are blocked and depression sets in. Although much preparatory intellectual rumination occurs there is no follow-through; i.e. 'I know what I should do but I haven't the strength'. Energy is often blocked for fear of unleashing powerful emotions that threaten intellectual control. Irritation and anger is turned inwards rather than used to meet external challenges or to fuel healthy competition. Procrastination replaces action. They know their problems, have a good intellectual grasp of the situation but always find reasons for avoiding action. Policy is constantly refined and re-worded but nothing changes. Organisations composed of civil servants, academics or representative of minority groups can exhibit these symptoms.

** **Remedy?** Encourage people to feel and to release their emotional energies positively, to recognise the usefulness of emotional perception and to consider how feelings might be used to motivate experimental action and a more robust contact with the here-and-now; build in sufficient support for them to face and put to test their hypotheses.*

4. Interruptions between Mobilisation of Energy and Action

Example – The Fearful Organisation

Everything comes to a standstill here; wheels spin at a great rate but, as those involved are unable to act on impulse, nothing gets done. This impotent state may result in paralysis and wasting as inner tensions cause a short-circuiting of the internal infrastructure. Groups and people arrested in this phase are aware of what they want or need but cannot settle to a plan of action. They seek to play safe and because change includes 'risk'. The general impression is one of teetering on the brink of action – but forever holding back. Meetings proliferate but serve as defences against risk rather than to firm-up decisions. Universities and legal establishments often fall into this category.

** **Remedy?** Offer emotional support and encourage clients to identify their needs and to test out their ideas through action rather than through passive rumination; put in place a commitment to behaviour strategies and support individuals as they tentatively risk active engagement.*

5. Interruptions between Action and Contact

Example – The Task-fixated Organisation

Individuals here feel diffused and unclear regarding physical boundaries. A person thus afflicted may do and express a lot but is unable to assimilate experience or experience effective contact, as emotional diffusion renders concentration shallow and engagement superficial. The person and group's experience of itself is essentially one of unreality, where no matter what is done nothing satisfies. This is like having a thirst that cannot be quenched. People and organisations here are obsessed with thinking and performing tasks to perfection and place great attention upon detail. Persons influenced in this way take themselves very seriously, are dutiful and have high output but have little idea of what they are doing well, as there is little time for reflection. Management consultancies that do a class act by producing excellent technical solutions that clients can't use are an example, as are local authorities and health trusts where operations are deemed a success – but patients and services fail to thrive.

** **Remedy?** Help clients to localise and to act with awareness, build up their sense of self-identity and help them practise self-control and mindful self-expression; challenge them to locate themselves in the wider picture and to envision what they need to feel better supported right now.*

6. Interruptions between Contact and Withdrawal

Example – The Burn-out Organisation

Individuals and teams here cannot turn off; although striving for more contact they never reach satisfaction as they are addicted to maintaining a continuous stress-inducing high. People have been at full production for far too long and stress has become chronic. As far too few periods of relaxation have been created, exhaustion threatens. Stuck in movement, players are condemned to remain in action and to perform as if in a constant state of war. Individuals here fail to appreciate when something is finished and it's time to move on. The police and emergency services during times of unrest and companies under a permanent threat of closure can end up in this position.

*** Remedy?** *Focus upon the stress and strains that have resulted from lack of rest, raise awareness to what needs to happen to bring activity to a successful conclusion; develop support, encourage relaxation while building awareness to 'what can' and 'can't be done'; consider ways of de-briefing and de-stressing the system.*

So, are the above energetic fields produced by the people within them or do they arise due to the cultural conditions and so persist? If it's due to the organisational level, this is a mindless process for the organisation is without mind. But organisational cultures nevertheless develop, may become sick and thus sickness inducing! Again, I don't use the contact–withdrawal cycle as a diagnostic tool so much as a reflective trigger, a metaphor to solicit richer metaphors and symbols from the client's lived experiences.

In teambuilding or training events, I will sometimes circulate a hand-out of the aforementioned blocks and invite participants to consider where our current learning community seems to experience difficulty. This usually occasions much debate and heightens awareness to the energy and resistance at play, while suggesting what we might do to augment our experience.

Groups and communities travel through many energetic cycles during their lifetimes, endure many climates and multiple energetic highs and lows. One day a group may be creative, only to revert to being destructive the next (Randall and Southgate 1980). All have their seasons. So what does this imply for the facilitation of coaching, consultancy or organisational change? Well, an intervention that works one day may fail dismally the next, just because our timing is out or we misperceive how the field or wider context has moved on. Facilitators must learn to gauge individual and community readiness and match the energy of their intervention to that of the client-system. Sounds easy, but timing and appreciation of a system's moment-to-moment energetic readiness only comes with practice; it is acquired experientially and employed intuitively.

I'm not a great fan of the contact–withdrawal cycle but I appreciate that it helps some to intellectually approach themes otherwise too abstract to entertain. Groups are like lasers: they collect individual energies, concentrate and focus them and project them towards the facilitator. Perhaps the contact–withdrawal cycle in this context may help us speculate upon the needs of groups which we have labelled as troublesome. Those that whelm if not overwhelm us!

We will next explore models that help us grasp and map the organic development of groups.

Reflections

* Next time you are in a pub, canteen or meeting, see if the above energetic cycle holds water – if groups evidence organic features of moving towards need fulfilment or not.

> * Observe where you personally experience difficulty upon the sensation–withdrawal cycle, and if there is any point where you habitually interrupt your flow?
>
> * In terms of consultancy and coaching activities such as 'initiating', 'negotiating', 'developing a unifying theme', 'identifying a current need', 'raising awareness to the options' and 'designing a strategy for moving forward', at what stage do you experience the most resistance within your own facilitative 'sensation to withdrawal cycle'? *(Sometimes at the beginning of a consultancy or coaching session I catch myself frozen between sensation and awareness. Overwhelmed by the information before me I can feel a responsibility to make sense of things for others – and interrupt my own flow this way.)*

2.5 State Appropriate Facilitation – Appreciating Developmental Patterns

Raising awareness can bring its own problems, especially with beginners who are but dimly aware of their deficits, those travelling through a phase of 'conscious incompetence' when shame may inadvertently be provoked. At any one time, individuals meet with the following resistances and mindsets as they develop from novice to expert:

Stage 1. **Unconscious Incompetence** (Novice): Here we are *unaware* of 'what we don't know', 'ignorance is bliss' and we have little incentive to learn. We might say to ourselves 'I'm fine as I am' or 'Why change things?' 'It wouldn't be me to do things differently'. *(Rooted by habit and blind to our own potential we need to be confronted with the consequence of our lack of knowledge and challenged if we are to move on.)*

Stage 2. **Conscious Incompetence** (Beginner): Now, as we become aware of our skill deficits and begin to learn, we recognise we do not yet 'have the hang of it' and may say to ourselves 'I'm trying to do this but it doesn't feel like me doing it'. Sometimes fear of failure can keep us stuck here. *(We need support and encouragement at this stage if we are to continue to experiment and learn without fear of criticism.)*

Stage 3. **Conscious Competence** (Advancing Student): With practice our competence grows. We begin to recognise the gains we are making; no longer feel embarrassed but need concentration to maintain our skill. Here we may say to ourselves: 'I can do this now, it is becoming a part of me'. In this phase we need to be trusted to monitor ourselves. *(It can be helpful here if we are encouraged to coach or teach others in those self-same skills we are currently developing.)*

Stage 4. **Unconscious Competence** (Expert): Having internalised our learning, our skill is now automatic; we may now say to ourselves 'Doing this comes naturally to me'. *(We now need to be challenged afresh to unpack what we do if we are to refine our skill further, to deconstruct ourselves and re-engage afresh with incompetence all over again to rise to the next level.)*

Obviously, it is important that a coach or consultant tracks the above, for each position clearly requires very different support. Awakening our clients from 'unconscious incompetence' and guiding them towards 'unconscious competence' is a prime objective in training and raising awareness alike.

Change always includes risk – and taking risks arouses energy. Pulling risks off in positive and creative ways breeds confidence. Failing, and indeed sometimes we must fail, provides us with a further challenge. Simply – we 'win' or we 'learn'. But if we give of our best and endeavour to do no harm to others there is nothing more to be done.

I have found it useful over the years to map the facilitative territory I plunge myself and my clients into via the two facilitative exercises cited below, which surface and map the energetic stamp of an evolving group. Many quote Tuckman's (1965) well-known USA Navy task-orientated model of group stages, consisting of:

Forming: where we ask 'Can I belong and is it really for me?'

Storming: where we ask 'Where exactly do I fit and can I meet my needs?'

Norming: where we ask 'What can I do and what can I not do in this group?'

Performing: where we ask 'How come it took so long to get here and how can it go on longer?'

Mourning: where we ask 'So whatever next?'

However, personally, I find the following more relational and person-centred framework better suited to my field-led and emergent style:

Orientation – *laying the groundwork for a relationship:* warming-up to the presence of another and establishing/re-establishing social contact; providing space to share spontaneously what is foremost to mind; placing attention upon 'what is currently being said' and 'how it is being said'.

Identification – *surfacing and focusing your own and the client's awareness:* focusing upon mutual interests/needs while identifying a unifying theme; balancing consensus with challenge so as to build trust and to appreciate difference; illuminating the potential and interactive territory available in the unfolding relationship.

Exploration – *locating and meeting with the client's energy and interest:* widening personal and social awareness through active exploration with the arising issues; engaging emotional energy and activities of mutual interest; focusing upon an arising purpose and fulfilling specific needs.

Resolution – *debriefing for insight and completion:* raising awareness to the options and choices we co-create; deciding how best to proceed further with what has been begun; celebrating and addressing 'endings'; envisioning a strategy for applying what we have learnt to 'life'.

The above framework is extended in Figure 2.

Figure 2. Phases of the Client–Consultant and Facilitator–Group Relationships

Pre-contact: An imaginative impression forms and, with no evidence to hand, projection fills the gaps. *(Envisioning – here individuals seek to address the question 'So what might happen next?')*

Orientation: The potential relationship and the working partnership are considered. *(Acclimatising – here the imagined relationship is compared to the actual one that begins to unfold; each orientates to the reality and world view of the other; the potential for empathy and trust are assessed and individuals attempt to answer the question 'So can we work together?')*

Identification: Tasks are defined and a working contract is created. *(Planning – here rapport is established and rules of engagement are negotiated; problems and tasks are identified; working hypotheses are posed and approaches are suggested and agreed upon and individuals raise to mind 'How might we work together?')*

Exploration: Experience is engaged and experiments performed. *(Acting and Observing – here boundaries are laid and tested and a safe environment is created; awareness is raised towards a developing theme and engaging practical experiments; support is mobilised, fantasies are checked and awareness of the moment is heightened and individuals seek to answer the question 'What needs to happen now?')*

Resolution: Findings and results are evaluated. *(Debriefing and Evaluating – here earlier working hypotheses are appraised; a debriefing of events and their prospective meaning is performed; mapping of the inquiry to date is made and future routes are considered; and individuals address the question 'What were the gains and costs of this relationship?')*

Post-contact: Out of contact with the real experience, memory and interpretation of earlier events is left to shape what the relationship means. *(Remembering – here individuals reflect upon the question 'So what did this experience mean to me?')*

I find that much coaching and consulting is task driven and dashes into the 'identification' of 'the problem' at the drop of a hat, skipping over the 'grounding' and 'trust building' of the orientation phase. I caution against haste and ask you to give your clients a 'good listening to' rather than a 'good talking to'. Attend to the organic development of your relationship. But it would be remiss of me to suggest that each of these phases (orientation through to resolution) progress smoothly of their own volition; for each facilitative event encompasses its own unique birth pains. So when citing developmental theories of group development such as this, always hold close the following cautions:

- Though groups change over time, they do not proceed in predictable or sequential ways

- As group membership and contexts differ, every group is unique and defies categorisation

- There is no right or ideal way for groups to develop over time

- A group's 'external field' or context frame impacts greatly upon its life.

(Harris 1998)

In this regard, John Bernard Harris's suggestion that we attend to both sides of a group's boundary, its inner membership and external context, makes good horse sense, as does his equally valuable suggestion that we need to attend to a 'vertical' sense of 'how things change over time' and pay attention to 'the patterns that arise in the here-and-now' (Harris 1998). In this way, facilitators are cautioned to explore 'group gestalts' or patterns that arise within and outside its boundaries and look to 'what is happening now' rather than 'prescribe what ought to be happening'. Hopefully, the relational model suggested in Figure 2 is better able to honour these conditions. In groups, although social, emotional and projective energies course together, it is the physiological root that informs the energy behind 'fight-or-flight' responses and it is often at the bodily level that 'support' is best experienced.

i) Sociogramatic Mapping

When seeking to acquire physical evidence of the energetic play of relationships, I find the sociogram (Moreno 1951) a useful tool for mapping and making more tangible an emerging group dynamic. To construct a sociogram, we progress through the following stages:

- First, draw a series of small circles in a circular pattern on paper to represent those present (perhaps identifying individuals by their initials)

- Second, draw an arrow from the current speaker in the direction of the recipient towards whom they are directing their comments (placing group members on paper in a circular formation with a hollow centre space allows me to capture comments to the group as a whole by arrows pointing to the hollow centre)

- Third, keep thickening the arrows to and from people and to the centre of the group as communication builds.

After about fifteen minutes, you should end up with a map of thick lines for those who speak frequently, a much thinner arrow denoting those who speak infrequently, and no arrows at all from silent members. Perhaps those who speak regularly to 'the group as a whole' with lines of communication radiating to the centre are attention-hungry, seeking to control or competing for leadership! But whatever, with a sociogram to hand we have a visual representation of the group's energetic communication pattern to draw further inferences from. I have also found it useful to construct a separate sociogram for each fifteen-minute period. With a series of time-lapse sociograms, I feel better equipped to report a group's evolving shape. I sometimes map eye contact in a similar way, which can differ greatly from the verbal representation, for although verbal communication is seemingly being addressed to one individual (X) the eyes may stray to another (Y) whose opinion is courted and audience cherished! The more interconnections between members and the less isolates, the healthier and more self-sustaining the group. Sociograms, I suggest, can do much to foster appreciation of what is being dynamically configured plus a group's changing relational constellation over time.

ii) Relational Sculpting

On occasion, I work in a live physical mapping mode, inviting individuals to stand in the centre of the room then encouraging other members of a team or learning community to position themselves, without dialogue, at a distance from the subject indicative of how near or close they feel to them, either to the position they have adopted or to the person themselves. When this has been done, I ask the subject to gaze around to observe who is nearest and furthest from them, to take this in but to resist dialogue until later. When numerous others have taken the risk of receiving feedback in this way, we discuss our impressions. This simple non-verbal exercise can rapidly provide an impression of who is supporting or distancing themselves from us and where we really stand at any one moment in a group's life.

Sometimes I undertake this exercise myself to glean an unspoken impression of how I am being received and my support within a group or workshop. Stripped of dialogue and the need to rationalise their position, participants will often take risks they could never verbalise. For instance, mild-mannered, smiley participants have been known to place themselves in the furthest corner from me – or just outside a classroom door! I don't question this at the time, but may repeat the exercise sometime later to see if their position relative to me has changed.

iii) Physical Enactment

When massaging through a group's cultural armour, I will sometimes invite members to stand up and mill around together without words, as the spirit takes them. I might invite them after a few seconds to observe how they are moving, where they feel alive and flexible in their bodies and where they tense up. A little later I might suggest they make eye contact and see how this affects them and the

42

flow of their movement – all the time without words. On occasion I will act out being a parental figure and in a loud voice say 'stop', or some other injunction, then ask participants where in their bodies this instruction landed. Later in debrief, participants often notice how injunctions such as this are experienced as stiffness in their necks and shoulders, a blow to the guts, or a postural freezing. Earlier memories sometimes surface. Subsequently we may explore where in our body we somatise or hold our responses to anger, love, resentment, shame, joy. Sometimes individuals are able to identify their habitual patterns of holding and storing stress, anger, fear or resentment. A very fruitful exercise, I find, is to invite participants to form pairs, stand facing each other and to join together in pushing hands while one partner says 'yes' and the other says 'no'. Following which, they change roles. Subsequent discussion unpacking when they felt strongest – whether whilst saying 'no' or saying 'yes' – or whether they competed and tried to win or merely held the energy can produce very rich and insightful feedback indeed.

Reflections

In terms of the following positions:

Unconscious Incompetence: when someone says 'I'm fine as I am, why change things?'

Conscious Incompetence: when someone says 'I'm trying but it doesn't feel like me'.

Conscious Competence: when someone says 'I can do this now, it is a part of me'.

Unconscious Competence: when someone says 'I know I can do it but I'm not sure how'.

* How might your facilitative style differ within each of the above phases and what kinds of interventions may be most suited to each phase? *(I can see a link between blocks to contact described within the Gestalt contact–withdrawal cycle and the above phases of learning. Perhaps in the unconscious incompetence phase an individual could benefit from interventions geared to awakening them to their sensations and to a wider field of awareness.)*

* How do you consider a facilitator's style might need to differ in the 'orientation' stage of group life from that of the 'exploration' stage? *(Broadly, I believe I'm most attentive and gently questioning in the orientation phase, as if I'm easing myself in and dancing with the energies. In the exploration phase, I experience myself as permissive and encouraging; I feel like a resource, a tool of exploration or inquiry, someone others will use when necessary.)*

▶

* While going about your everyday duties, say in a team meeting or group gathering, construct a sociogram and see what results.

* Would you consider using sculpting or physical enactment? If not, why not? And if you would, in what circumstances might you consider it appropriate?

2.6   Towards an Embodiment of Learning – Awakening our Bodily Wisdom

Kepner (2003) has suggested that most of us have an impoverished appreciation of our bodily nature and consequently our ability to delve deeply into our embodied life remains under-developed. As a result, we remain but dimly aware of the visceral and somatic links that root us into our 'being-in-the-world'. When facilitating individuals through particularly difficult events, say ones which re-stimulate earlier emotions and associated memories, to help ground and anchor them in current physical experience I may invite them into one or more of the following exercises:

- To stay in eye contact and attune to what arises when they give themselves full permission to 'see' and be 'seen'

- To list what they are seeing, hearing, physically sensing and otherwise experientially aware of in the present

- To attend to their perceptive functions and how these inform their awareness and moment-to-moment contact

- To focus upon their physical supports such as breathing, posture and movement with a view to bettering their environmental support

- To pay attention to any physical blockages or resistances which are currently repeating themselves

- To give a running commentary upon their moment-to-moment sensations plus what they are seeing and hearing

- To locate where in their body they perceive any muscular tension or other manifestation of armouring or resistance

- To bring to mind their current needs and to reflect on how these might be met at the present time in the available circumstances.

This looking to body, exploring our physicality, magnifying its reactions and opening ourselves to its physiological message is common to Gestalt, especially when an attempt is made to counterbalance notions of 'self as intellect'.

This disconnection of bodily life from the identified 'I' is deeply embedded in Western religious, philosophical and cultural life. Our culture has reified the intellect as the 'self', leaving emotions and embodiment as distinct and separate realms. The roots of our Western relational tradition, reflected in Descartes' dictum, 'Cogito ergo sum', deeply reinforces our belief that our thinking equals self-existence. Daily life also confirms this. Our interactions, our conversation with others and our self-reflection includes little of our bodily experience. It is difficult enough to go against our own personal restrictions and lack of connection to our body experience, but it is even more challenging to climb uphill against the larger social field.

(Kepner 2003, p.7)

Kepner reminds us that we should hold an awareness and appreciation of the body as intrinsic to all human processes, inclusive of social, mental, emotional and spiritual phenomena. Simply, the body is a pool in which all else is reflected. But to work in an embodied way as a facilitator you need to attune to your own physiology and its store of experiential learning.

All groups and organisations I enter thrust upon me their energetic stamp. Some literally evoke a viscous sense of swimming in treacle; others seem to enrol me into a light-heartedness of being; a few throw up a wall of tiredness. Each contains its own unique tonal blueprint. Indeed, grounding a group physically and supporting its members towards a fully embodied sense of the present is often my first facilitative duty.

Personally, be it in the role of facilitator or immersed in the daily business of life, I have sometimes found it more fruitful to ask my body a question rather than my intellect. My intellect is steeped in the archaic 'world as taught' historical information – my body is for 'now'. When information is insufficient for my highly schooled reason to deal with I ask my body. Eventually I get a clear 'gut' response. A 'no' I equate with a 'sense' of 'fullness' or general sickliness; a 'yes' with a physical light-ness and a sense of 'opening' within my chest. Physiologically, my body never lies! Plainly, the bodily end of my 'body–mind' has proven more trustworthy to me.

It is through primordial experience that we explain how the body has been given a knowledge of the world that is not ordinarily accessible to my thinking, and it is upon this body-knowledge that my thinking is founded.

(Kennedy 2003, p.82)

As a facilitator I attune to my body to sense the group field. I note how my posture, breathing and bodily held tensions seem to be echoing others in the group, or energetically expressing a deeper and hidden dynamic. Fight and flight and fears in all their forms are 'sensed' this way. My first physiological impressions, I find, are especially useful to help me catch up to speed when I enter a new group or established team.

Reflections

* In relation to embodiment, Kepner (2003) cites the following features: embodied listening; embodied empathy; embodied language and gesture; embodied energy. How useful is the notion of embodied learning, do you feel, and how might you get it to work for you? *(The next time you enter a group, scan your bodily response, observe where in your body the group tends to impact you – that is to say, which muscle areas tense up? how does your rate of your breathing alter? etc. Note which part of you relaxes and what behaviours in the group manifest subsequent to these physical reactions; in this way, build up a catalogue of the various responses you initially embody and the meanings these acquire in the light of later engagements. Indeed, perhaps consider any bodily responses that may have been stimulated by your reading of this chapter.)*

Reflections upon Chapter 2

* You are contracted by an executive team to initiate an action-learning approach to the development of team leadership skills:

- How might you set about establishing the organisational readiness for this intervention?

- What questions might you ask?

* Given that the organisation has sufficient cultural support and health for facilitative inquiry:

- What interventions might you employ in the orientation through to identification phase?

- How might the intention behind your interventions differ within the various phases?

* Having entered a consultancy and found there to be a lukewarm reception for leadership training by middle managers, on whom your facilitation is to be focussed, how might you use the information of this chapter to:

- Better motivate and prepare the workforce you are intending to engage?

- Develop their sensory perception, attention and listening skills?

- Provide a rationale for your intended consultancy interventions?

▶

- What shape might your interventions take at this stage?

- Which subsequent responses would suggest to you that progress is being made?

* In terms of your ability to enhance and to work with the following phenomenon: sensation (alertness to environment); awareness (surfacing feelings and needs); mobilisation (raising motivation); excitement (directing energy); action (concentrating movement); contact (meeting robustly); and withdrawal (enabling completion):

- Where are you most skill and least skilled?

- Within which phase do you find your attention most and least alerted and focussed?

(*Personally, I find I'm most energised at the awareness, mobilisation, action and contact phase, but least impacted by the sensation and withdrawal phase. I believe this is because the latter two require a less-robust presence – I'm more Yang in nature and warm to challenge.*)

The physical world of form and phenomena is the totality of the known manifested in the infinity of the unknown manifest consciousness.
I do nothing.
Being manifests, and living happens.
I am that consciousness.
You are that consciousness.
All that exists is consciousness.

(Deepak Chopra 1996)

Chapter three

Raising Awareness
to Social and Cultural Influences

The most ardent block to new ideas is a limiting belief or untested assumption. Take nothing at face value – test everything, especially yourself if you want to avoid fossilising around a cherished notion.

3.1 From Common to Postmodern Sense – Cultural Influences within Consultation

At the socio-cultural level we review facets of 'the world as taught' and the influence of our wider cultural heritage. Here history, power and leadership figure, as do comparisons between authoritative and facilitative interventions. In this chapter, we explore ways of working with and through gamey and pseudo communication in the search for real community and authenticity.

As most traditional approaches to organisational consultation operate within a context defined by socio-cultural reality, it is here I locate the history of consultation. This level is also what most have in mind when they refer to 'the real world' – although the so-called 'real world' they inhabit is usually an imagined one informed by self and imagination, where social interaction is reduced to a strategic encounter. No space in this so-called real world for authentic communication and genuine relating, as instrumental 'I–It' relationships, rather than respectful 'I–Thou' ones, are far too often the norm in corporate cultures.

Many accounts in managerial literature convey a simple message: if leaders would only state clearly and forcibly what they want and prescribe 'the necessary values and behaviours', then 'all would be well'. This 'tell-it-like-it-is' common-sense approach, though supposedly rooted in the so-called 'real world', conveniently ignores group synergy, individual timing and readiness, community dynamics and systemic patterns of resistance. Management developers and coaches who make comparisons with sports tend to fall into this category, as do solution-focussed approaches that presume that, if behavioural incentives are provided, conducive social conditions will naturally arise. Thinking like this causes my inner bullshit detector to spin ever faster!

At the last analysis, man is not a rational being, social behaviour is not logical, strong leadership is not a universal panacea and what you see is not what you get – but you would never realise this from most business literature.

i) Militaristic Influences upon Consultation

Two basic scenarios tend to repeat in tales of organisational change. One tells the story of a highly dramatic turnaround in a large multinational company, where we readers are encouraged to admire the clear-thinking, determined and charismatic leadership of the man at the top, who seemingly single-handedly mobilises immense numbers of previously unresponsive and unmotivated subordinates to action. Taking a stand, this inspired leader adopts a position which cuts a swathe through bureaucracy, removes dead wood and makes heroic and difficult decisions that set standards for success. This macho approach complete with a 'Boy's Own Hero' who accomplishes his mission against all odds, a hero who survives in a climate where 'taking a beating' and 'beating the competition' in return is the norm, supports a militaristic view where 'winning at all costs' and 'power' play the major part.

51

A second common scenario is one which anchors itself in corporate leadership, tells of a dramatic turnabout in a large enterprise which is achieved through the willing co-operation of employees who are won over at all strata of the organisation. In this version readers are encouraged to admire the visionary leadership of a heroic corporate executive team who accomplish success with a minimum of self-doubt and little employee resistance or organisational disruption to achieve nothing less than total organisational transformation. Your bullshit detector should now be spinning at the speed of light.

As for how the above perception of 'organisational change' has come about we need look no further than the history of organisational consulting and the cherished notions enshrined within its development. The earliest organisational consulting, functional in approach and known as 'Organisation and Method', was a 'nuts and bolts' approach hugely dominant up to the late 1940s and infused by a war-time mentality. It lingers still. This mechanistic approach, primarily concerned with the physical and social environment, offered specialised expertise in accountancy, finance and operations management. It survives in the legacy of 'time-and-motion' studies and notions of 'labour/industrial relations'. Modern organisation consulting, by contrast, is largely identified with the 'Human Relations' school and 'large system phenomena' birthed in the 1940s through the work of Maslow, Herzberg and Lewin who brought a focus upon group dynamics and sensitivity training (Saner 1999). 'Large system phenomena', as represented in the work of Likert and Eric Trist and largely focused upon Organisation Development and culture, also emerged at this time. This in turn gave birth to Total Quality Management cultural re-engineering (Nevis 1997). Most consultancies peddle these wares still.

Designed primarily to help clients become aware of their existing reality and behaviour, 'modern consultancy methods' – though relational in approach and attentive to subjective phenomena and learning – are still inclined to assume that there exist physical or social 'problems' which can be solved through the identification of blocks to effective performance. Such thinking supports the status quo by preserving illusions inherent within conventional common-sense reality. Gestalt offers something fundamentally different.

ii) Postmodern Influences within Gestalt Consultancy

Postmodernism influences – which care less for theoretical analysis and more for how things are actually working – according to Saner (1999) entered organisational consulting through several studies, notably Derrida's (1976) work which introduced de-constructionism and subtext analysis to organisational life; Maturana and Varela's (1975) work on systems which developed a theory of a self-producing or 'autopoiesis organisation' that was seen to organise itself; Foucault's (1982) study of prison systems and their control mechanisms; Robert Flood's (1990) application of complexity in his *Liberating Systems Theory*; and Kaufman's (1993) study of self-organising systems and ways of understanding complexity. Such field-influenced approaches as these, along with Gestalt, challenge the 'common sense' and 'culturally supported reality' taken for granted in the business school tradition of modern consulting. So how does a postmodern perspective pan out in practice?

The consultancy process in Gestalt is a deconstructive one which doesn't follow 'the plan' nor work towards a pre-arranged end product, nor intentionally set out to unblock behaviour, but presents to the client-system sufficient information, imaginative impressions, sensory and social data and creative vision to illuminate 'what is happening now'. Here participation is an absolute and the consumption or osmosis of a ready-made plan is off agenda. As 'existent' ways of behaviour are highlighted and re-constellated in the light of growing awareness, alternative options arise to challenge the status quo. In this way Gestalt locates itself squarely in the territory of postmodernity which rejects notions of progress founded on conventional knowledge and scientific research (Kvale 1992) in favour of an existential position which advocates social relativism, is critical of existing traditions and re-directs attention upon aspects which are neglected or ignored (Scott and Usher 1999). A facilitator in this tradition is not interested in grand theories but in 'what works for clients', 'why it works for them' and 'what they choose to consciously and unconsciously ignore'.

Although the borderline between 'modern' and 'postmodern' approaches to consultancy are somewhat fluid and difficult to draw, Nevis (1997) distinguishes between the 'problem solving' quality of modern consultancy, where problems are addressed by 'an expert', and the 'management of dilemmas' by postmodern Gestalt consultants who raise awareness to the ambiguity and complexities that envelop the consultant, their client and the larger field in which the organisation is embedded.

iii) Tenets of Gestalt Consultation

As a human organism I am always intimately connected and in constant interaction with my environment and totally depend on it. My existence is not only impossible but literally unthinkable except in relation to the wider field of influences that define me. Gestalt supports the notion of a 'relational theory of self' where what I call 'my self' is also part of 'the field' co-created from moment-to-moment interactions within 'the field'. In this context, the way I create myself through the choices I make cannot be separated from my co-creation with others and influence upon and from 'others'. This radical view entails seeing group members not as separate people who happen to interact in the group setting – for this, Harris (2005) reminds us, would be a systems approach – but as parts of the same field that co-creates and co-sustains the on-going group/community process. With this to mind, Gestalt attempts to look at 'the total situation' with a view to capturing the complex and ever-changing social dynamics and co-creations that characterise organisational life.

As Anne-Marie Chidiac reminds us, a Gestalt-influenced field theory approach integrates a rich range of influence:

> Unlike Gestalt's notion of field theory, systems theory does not look at the system from within, in terms of mapping the influences or contexts on an individual or sub-system. By field theory, I mean a gestalt-informed field theoretical concept which builds upon the work of Lewin (1951) and integrates fundamental Gestalt constructs as contact, and theory of self, as well as relational and phenomenological considerations.
>
> (Chidiac 2011, p.43)

As all too many fudge the distinction between a 'field' and a 'systems' approach, it is wise to delve a little further. Systems theory studies 'systems' from the outside with a view to elucidating principles that can be generalised and applied to 'all types of systems' whether in nature, society or science. Central to systems inquiry is the concept of 'system', a collection of parts connected together by a web of relationships – 'elements' in a standing relationship. It is a view honouring 'the parts' rather than 'the whole'.

The Cleveland Gestalt Institute seemingly favours a 'systems' rather than 'field' approach, one where consultancy is broken into 'units of work' with attendant components of 'input', 'throughput' and 'output'. 'Work' is defined as a process of development or change, either naturally arising or orchestrated, directed towards the resolution of an issue, completion of a task or learning experience – 'A successful unit of work creates energy that is sustained and purposeful' (Carter 2000, p.99). Here Gestalt interventions are equated with experiments consisting of four stages: 1) an assessment of 'what is' by heightening awareness of what appears to be happening; 2) choosing 'what to attend to' by defining the patterns and themes that exist; 3) 'acting on that choice' by illuminating the pattern and suggesting an experiment that tests out alternative ways of behaving; 4) closing out that particular activity by acknowledging 'what is new' and what has evolved from the experiment. Though the notion of consultancy interventions as experimentation appeals to me, 'inputs', 'throughputs' and 'outputs' feel too simplistic and the model as a whole feels too mechanistic for my blood. Within the above 'units of work' we find an implicit action learning cycle with the following attendant activities:

> **Concrete Experience** *(An Event):* Full involvement in new here-and-now experiences; experiment/pilot; simulation; case study; real experience; demonstration; field trips.
>
> **Active Experimentation Reflective Observation** *(What is to be done differently and What happened):* Testing implications of concepts; observation and reflection of learner's in new situations to make decisions experiences from many perspectives; laboratory experiences; discussion; small groups; on-the-job experience; buzz groups; internships; practice sessions; designated observer.

Planning for Implementation Abstract Conceptualisation *(How to be differently, What was learned and Future implications):* Defining what will be done; integration of abstract concepts; determining how will be applied generalisations into sound theories; action planning; 'what if' scenarios; sharing content; role playing.

(After Carter 2000)

This model, especially as it emanates from a Gestalt stable, makes me uneasy; there is insufficient organic and developmental flow for my blood, too many tasks and too few emergent influences at play, too much emphasis upon the socio-cultural level for me to warm to this representation which I rightly or wrongly see as systematising flow and leaning towards conventional rather than postmodern approaches to consultation. It contrasts with field approaches which stress 'what is unique' and look to 'the energetic whole' while emphasising phenomenology – which brings the way things present themselves to consciousness, the co-construction of meaning and reality into the equation. Here reality is phenomenological and co-created, not an object in itself. To my biased mind, 'systems theory' is mechanistic and 'field theory' organic.

Possibly I am doing the Cleveland Gestalt Institute's model a disservice; perhaps it merely communicates in a systems way but performs field theoretically! Maybe my critique is unfounded. But I can't from the outside see an appreciation of the field's ability to self-regulate and self-organise.

With regard to 'emergent self-organisation' and 'self-regulation, and teasing a distinction between 'group' and 'community', Anne-Marie Chidiac speaks of her own 'embodied phenomenological experience' of belonging to the place she grew up and the deeper connectedness that pulls her back to her Lebanese origins and family and friends, to observe:

> As I write this, I feel myself relax, an ease of being who I am – it is effortless! And this I believe, is one of the key differences between a community and a formed group or organisation; a community is organic, emergent, implicit in its membership, values and beliefs. A community does not need to be 'worked at' or have planned meetings, it just is! It emerges from the authentic need of its members for independent living, connectedness and belonging. A community does not need to be facilitated but self-organises to meet its own needs. This emerging self-organising process in communities is similar to Gestalt's conceptualisation of self.

> (Chidiac 2011, p.48)

A systems approach skips over 'phenomenological inner working' and consequently may speak of cultural change without cognisance of the deeper texture of 'community'. We often speak glibly of 'workplace learning communities' – but can a community in the above terms really exist in an organisation? Or does organisational structure and its defining tasks, let alone its commercial intent and proliferation of 'I–It' relationships, stunt organic development of the community she envisages? What say you? I've developed friendships in organisational settings and pulled together with others for strategic purposes, but I've never but fleetingly felt a sense of belonging in a community sense! But then I have a rather jaundiced view of organisations. Granted, I believe an internal field-based intelligence is at play in organisations, but what quality of intelligence is it? I suspect it is far from human. Although distilled from humankind, it appears to me everything we exile to the shadow lands: an intelligence bereft of conscience, mindfulness or social sensitivity – more reptilian than human.

At worst, I see organisations as primitive unfeeling entities often bordering on the psychopathic, serving their own mindless interests in which individuals often dumb themselves down to fit in! This individual dumbing down goes further than mere regression where we lose contact with personal responsibility, being more a surrender to primordial instincts of survival as in times of war – note the competitive and winning-at-all-cost drivers of many organisations. In this light, people may need to be brought back to awareness, released from a condition of organisational sleep walking and awakened from trance before we can gain their attention, and the organisation itself may require re-education – even though it isn't a body to be reasoned with.

I paint a rather black picture, but then I come from a mental-health background where institutionalisation and learnt helplessness were legion, where I saw the depersonalisation of nurses and patients at first hand in the asylum and hospital... I guess I worked in one to many degenerative organisations.

As to how a Gestalt practitioner sets about putting field principles into action to awaken individuals and re-educate an organisation: working to principles first formulated by Gestalt psychologists (Koffka 1935; Kohler 1947) who demonstrated the self-ordering nature of perception, where the 'figural' experiences that grab our attention are organised into 'meaningful wholes', a Gestalt consultant illuminates interests and needs by drawing attention to the formation of current 'gestalts' or 'meaningful wholes'. If the 'figure' they uncover is a meaningful one – lively and sharp and interesting – then attention is grabbed, group awareness shifts and 'change' occurs. Capturing and narrating a succession of 'perceptive figures' in this way a Gestalt facilitator illuminates, explores and utilises dynamics that give meaning to events.

I remember some years back in a consultancy inviting a team to share images that symbolised their organisation:

> There arose symbols of 'a large slow lumbering animal like an elephant'; 'a large woolly fluffy sheep'; 'a turtle in a round hard shell'; a participant who drew attention to an imagined 'large hole' in the centre of the group – drew from me the image of water, which was in turn seen by some as 'still and clear', and others as 'choppy', but noticeably without sharks or other dangerous creatures in its depths. Reflections upon earlier groups also illuminated, for some members, intuitive insights into what might be their life's purpose. There were also two periods of silence

56

when participants seemed particularly attentive and self-absorbed in a meditative fashion upon the quality of our being together. By the close of the workshop participants appeared more open to the unknown and unknowable, and more able to work at the level of metaphor.

(Barber 2006, p.177)

To add to the above, interestingly, team members following this imaginative speculation appeared more authentic and grounded in reality than they were before. Those 'gestalts' we co-created seemingly caught the imagination while illuminating the organisational climate and individual situation sufficiently to help the team appreciate their position. In stimulating the imagination, it loosened the organisational hold and released individual creativity, which in turn opened up novel and new adaptations.

When reading through the models and ideas of this text, bear in mind that you are merely acquainting yourself with facets of 'the field', surveying stimulants of awareness and reflections of 'wholes' rather than searching for solutions. To perceive 'wholes' it is necessary to look rather than stare, to release your focus on detail and scan. This phenomenological attitude of mind – common to Gestalt and qualitative research alike – is informed by three canons:

> *The Rule of Epoche:* Bracketing off initial biases and prejudices, judgements, expectations and assumptions so we might better appreciate primary experiential data and keep a clear mind and experience groups, communities and individual members in the unique unfolding moment as they are, rather than how we think or believe they are.

> *The Rule of Description:* Describing phenomena rather than trying to explain, focusing attention upon building a thick-description of 'what is'; remaining uncluttered and narrating immediate experience to get as full a sense of what is happening without jumping to premature conclusions about why something is happening or what it means.

> *The Rule of Horizontilisation:* Avoiding the valuing of some observations more than others, being alert and cognisant of everything without undue emphasis; endeavouring to see everything as potentially meaningful.

Phenomenological inquiry of this nature underpins all Gestalt approaches to organisational consultancy and does much to explain Ed Nevis's (1987) approach below with its comprehensive tracking of all available evidence, the consultant's own emotional state and how it is affected by the work and host organisation, its attempts to distinguish between the consultant's and the client's fantasies, plus what is indirect information and fact; namely everything that distinguishes mindful conscious from what is projected, imagined or unconscious:

- Attend to the client-system; observe and selectively share observations of what you see and hear; establish your presence in doing so

- Attend to your experiences inclusive of feelings, sensations and thoughts, and selectively share these to establish your presence in doing so

- Focus on energy in the client-system and watch for the emergence or the lack of issues for which there is energy; act to support mobilisation of energy so that something happens

- Facilitate clear, meaningful, heightened contacts between members of the client-system and between yourself and the client-system

- Help the client-system achieve heightened awareness of its process in completing units of work and enable those involved to learn how to complete units of works so as to achieve closure around problem areas and unfinished business.

(adapted from Nevis 1987)

True, we can't avoid our personal biases but, with practice, we can suspend our search for meaning and look beyond inner chatter. For example, I note I'm informed by a belief that many organisations are dysfunctional, bordering upon the pathological; this is my bias, but I bracket this off when entering a new consultancy, reappraising or updating it again later when I walk away with new data. If my original bias is not rattled and shaken by each new experience then I fear my contact was too shallow or my armouring too thick!

Searching mindfully for an impressionistic picture of the whole while alert to what is present or absent in any situation, a Gestalt practitioner never knows what will turn out as important later nor what the current picture will eventually transform into – all is mystery. This is the phenomenological discipline to which we are committed.

Reflections

* In relation to the sketch of consultancy approaches cited above, where would you locate yourself and your facilitation? *(I'm aware of my Gestalt inheritance and feeling drawn towards a postmodern perspective that questions all and everything. I'm also suspicious of simple answers and those who make an appeal to a common sense.)*

* How does a 'systems' differ from a 'field' approach to consulting – and where do you position yourself?

* If consulting is seen to have evolved from out of a mechanistic frame towards a relational one, where might consultancy and the management of change journey to next? *(Perhaps more fluid and holistic models are coming to the fore; answers and authority is certainly questioned more these days and an appreciation of complexity seems on the horizon.)*

3.2 Fermenting a Medium of Awareness – The Influence of Culture

There is a good deal of debate in organisational literature as to whether culture is something an organisation 'has', by virtue of absorption from the wider society, or something 'it is', a phenomenon that naturally emerges from the generation of shared unique symbols and meanings. Simply, can culture and social structure be distinguished? Culture, in the sense we are using the word here, relates to the shared beliefs and values that underpin the customs, practices and shared attitudes that characterise a community or group. Put simple, culture is 'how we do things here', and if you want to belong you must appreciate the same things we do or be educated to an appreciation our view of the world.

The value perspective expressed in this chapter challenges the viewpoint that individuals are passive recipients who merely inherit culture from the wider society. I view people as active life-long learners who are subject to continuous development (Bateson 1972; Jarvis 1985), mindful actors who have the capacity to transform both themselves and their environment. In this scenario, people and field conditions contribute to 'culture' through on-going dialogue. And 'change', well, unless we affect the cultural fabric of a community, 'the background' as it were, I consider it doubtful our facilitative influence will survive in a meaningful or long-term way. I am not alone in this view. Isabel Menzies Lyth points out that 'any significant change within a social system implies change in existing social relationships and social structure' (Menzies Lyth 1988, p.62). I therefore suggest that culture is the blueprint for structure and that, if you ignore culture, you end up merely re-arranging the furniture and leaving the infrastructure untouched.

'Doing Change' without 'Being Changed'

Stapley (1996) adds weight to the view that cultural change is central to group change when he cites a case where a consultant identified the need for greater corporacy throughout the Metropolitan Police, but without drawing attention to the cultural influences upon corporacy. Although the need was recognised, frequently referred to throughout the organisation and a new structure of group decision making was instigated – in the shape of executive meetings and new incentives – all was to no avail. Various groups were informed but, as cultural values were unaffected, little of consequence altered. Simply, real grass-roots change failed to occur because awareness got stuck at the cognitive level. Fail to impact at the deeper socio-cultural fabric of the client-system, the field, then the original blue print remains intact.

Values inform culture, culture informs structures, structures beget roles and culturally laden roles permeate groups to create an organisation's personality and everyday reality – everything interrelates with everything else. For example we saw in the above account how a community might undergo development without itself 'changing'; similarly 'growth' alone does not lead to change:

> Growth can take place with or without development (and vice versa). For example, a cemetery can grow without developing; so can a rubbish heap. A nation, corporation, or an individual can develop without growing.
>
> (Ackoff 1981, p.34)

Commercial organisations often ask facilitators to concern themselves with processes that lead to greater human effectiveness, but in their head-long chase towards functional efficiency they blind themselves to 'cultural change', 'personal growth' and 'development'. Seeing such influences as secondary rather than primary yardsticks of renewal – they fail!

So how and in which direction might a facilitator productively massage culture? The Royal Society of Art's review *Tomorrow's Company* (RSA 1995) – which owes much to the vision of Naisbett and Aburdene (1985) – suggests we need to facilitate a business culture where *personal development; coaching* and *mentorship; psychic and literal ownership of the workplace; democratic management* and *networking* plus *intuition* along with *creativity* are supported; that is, if we are to challenge the traditional 'it's all in the numbers' business-school mentality. Kline (1999) adds to this list 'male conditioned' macho influences to culture. It would be a very unwise 'agent of change' who chose to ignore these factors. As to internal qualities to foster in corporate and team-life: *communication, flexibility, recognition, cross-cultural fertilisation* and *new incentives* (Kanter 1985) have been cited as best serving cultural and social change in 'real terms'.

'Change', along with your impact as a facilitator, doesn't need to be planned; your mere arrival and title of 'facilitator', as well as who or what you are seen to represent, will generate ripples of influence before you even enter an organisation! Even a passive observer has effect.

Referring to the 'Hawthorne effect', a phenomenon where groups of workers showed increased productivity due to the attention poured upon them, Mayo (1933) concluded that non-economic rewards such as 'interest' and the 'affection and respect of colleagues' were most powerful social motivators, which when absent severely limited incentive. Remember, your 'social status' and alignment with respected others such as your organisational sponsors will mould the field long before your first facilitative act! In his observations of industry, Mayo also noted that members of a team did not set their own individual production quota, but rather followed their group's prevailing cultural norm. Etzioni's (1964) observation that, although workers were resistive to norms at the individual level, in a group setting their resistance melted away further confirms that 'culture' is a more important influence than the individual upon change. This in turn begs the question: what price individual coaching if the corporate climate can nullify newly acquired insights and possibly wash personal learning clean away?

Reflections

> Culture represents a construct, and the source of that construct is the human mind.
>
> (Stapley 1996, p.viii)

* In relation to the above passage, what qualities of 'the human mind' do you believe may permeate groups? *(I'm aware of how emotional energies often reach out to me on first meeting, and how groups are like mini-families who socialise and raise 'their children' in very different ways.)*

* In light of Mayo's (1933) and Etzioni's (1964) findings, how might you form a strategy for including and using to advantage 'group influence' in an event designed to ferment a culture where people are interested and respectful of each other? *(I guess peer-generated ground rules plus an appreciative or collaborative inquiry into 'what we desire of others and the workplace' might serve us here; self and peer assessment might also prove useful.)*

3.3 Cultural Resistances to Change – Unfreezing the Status Quo

Just as people resist change, so do group and organisational cultures. Below I have listed some of the resistances I've met with in the educational climates of psychotherapy training organisations. These behaviours, though superficially disguised as positive parenting and a preservation of standards, entrap creativity whilst defending against change. Some of these internecine patterns were originally associated with psychoanalytic training (Kernberg 1996), but my experience suggests they are as common a currency in humanistic and commercial environments. Indeed you might, if you are reading this text in an educational setting, consider how relevant they are to your own cultural setting. Though on first reading, you might want to laugh out loud at their absurdity – after all, no-one in their right mind would really wish to perpetuate these perverse messages. Or would they? Look carefully and you will likely meet them in some degree in most if not all training bodies:

> ***Systemically slowing trainees down:*** doubling the number of publications that trainees could reasonably absorb from one seminar to the next and insisting that they read core texts thus enforcing that critical analysis has to be postponed until original sources have been digested. *(Sometimes this arises as a consequence of trainers trying misguidedly to strengthen the academic worth of their training, as a consequence of over-zealous detail-chasing or because trainers are too passionate in their attempts to preserve known standards.)*

Reinforcing the basics: getting trainees to go over in detail what leading authors actually said and to summarise the same, thus dampening their excitement and desensitising them to the originality of the works. *(This can arise from an undue effort to instil the basics of practice and from over veneration and attention to the founders of a school or movement.)*

Over-tightening the academic noose: preserving 'a healthy respect for elders' by keeping a clear hierarchy of older and younger members of the training faculty – if juniors are caused to defer respectfully to senior views, the unquestioning acceptance of senior authority will be greatly strengthened. *(Attempts to preserve the continuing respect and control of students may result in the above, likewise indirect communication and a dependence on tradition adds to this picture.)*

Keeping seniors distant and outcomes mysterious: conveying the subtle message that what is being taught is really an art that must be mastered intuitively and by personal rites of passage – in this way trainees quickly learn that due to mysterious processes professional learning is beyond their control. *(A lack of unpacking and sharing of knowledge, plus a fear of being held accountable or being unable to satisfy the demands made upon trainers in blame cultures and over-formalised systems, as well as the separation out of trainers from supervisors all contribute to this dynamic.)*

Seeding uncertainty and compliance: referring all trainees' questions to the official brochure and avoiding information-gathering or information-sharing meetings. *(Opaque relationships, the lack of open communication systems and direct feedback, over-careful, formal and expedient systems can lead to the above, especially when tutors are too remote and distanced from the student body.)*

Treating trainees as children: relating all problems involving teachers and trainees, seminars and supervision to the irresponsibility and immaturity of trainees – undermine a trainee's legitimate rationale for dissatisfaction. *(Trainers, when they role-model good practice without a clarifying rationale and view student behaviour through a pathological lens, will naturally slide in this direction.)*

So how many of the above accompanied you through your professional training? More telling, how many do you inadvertently perpetuate in your role as a facilitator or trainer? Indeed, which do I unintentionally support in this text? Interestingly, many staff in areas where the above proliferated saw themselves as progressive and richly emancipated! What we are unaware of always returns to bite us on the butt in the end! Organisations favour the hierarchy; and espoused progressives, in an effort to stabilise their organisational position, can all too easily fossilise around such weaknesses.

As to how we may challenge such top-heavy characteristics, personally, I have found it useful to 'speak my truth', to 'say what I am seeing' and to 'share what I believe is happening'. I don't accuse or blame but say this in a dispassionate take-it-or-leave-it way, one encouraging of further exploration and reflection rather than push-back or defence. Your 'tone' is often much more important than your content. Simply pointing out the above dynamics while encouraging tutors or managers to put themselves in the student experience can be enough for questioning to begin and, if I'm invited to stick around longer, say to team build or culture change, I might suggest a bottom-up process like 'self and peer assessment' to rattle-and-shake and unfreeze the organisation's prevailing systems of control. This exercise, which humanises and enlightens professional appraisal, is reviewed below.

Self and Peer Assessment

As traditional modes of assessment do much to shape the social environment while preserving the political power of the culture-carrying elite, it is useful to consider alternatives. Self and peer assessment is a subversive exercise designed to encourage power sharing and to empower learners. It was promoted by the Human Potential Research Group at the University of Surrey from the 1970s to 1990s, where I applied it to professional update courses, personal growth workshops and master's programmes. This approach brings democracy, self-empowerment and active listening to the assessment equation.

So what does self and peer assessment entail? When a group of people wish to be assessed in a particular area, be it a skill, relational quality or subject area, they first negotiate a range of criteria, secondly self-assess themselves against this measurement and then arrange a face-to-face meeting with colleagues to enact peer assessment:

1 – **Self Evaluation** – The colleague opting for assessment provides a rationale for the belief they have achieved the learning and standard required – written work and other evidence may accompany this self-assessment. (While others listen in silence, they make their case: 'My evidence for having acquired learning in this area is found in the following testimonials and list of achievements…')

2 – **Clarification** – They field clarification questions from their colleagues. (A two-way question and answer session ensues – 'So how exactly did you set about designing your schedule of learning? When did you realise you had learnt this lesson? How do you know what you know?')

3 – **Challenge** – The colleague under assessment receives challenging statements 'in silence'. (For example, if a person were being assessed as a Gestalt practitioner we might say 'So what was particularly Gestalt in your case study and where did you feel the least Gestalt-like as a practitioner? What have you missed?')

4 – **Support** – The colleague under assessment receives supportive statements 'in silence'. (For example, 'I particularly enjoyed the sensitive way you described your client's reactions. I commend your effort. I value your ethical stance.')

5 – **Surfacing Learning** – The assessed share their personal experience of this self and peer assessment process while their peer assessors listen in silence. (For example, 'I was surprised to find your positives very hard to hear. I felt heavily challenged around my contracting process.')

6 – **Process Consultancy** – Combine with others to evaluate any highlights or difficulties of this evaluative process and how it might be improved in future. (A process review – 'So how might we improve this assessment process? What needs to change to make it more rigorous? What learning challenges have arisen here? Were we confronting of blind spots enough?')

In more formal academic settings, lead tutors are usually part and parcel of the process. Interestingly, listening in silence to challenging and supportive statements without chat-back or other deflection is often reported as a highly emotional and intimate process, one which builds a sense of community. Every group member goes through a similar process in turn. Depending upon circumstances and prior agreement, each of the above six stages might take as little as five or as much as thirty minutes and, when the process is complete, individuals (as peer assessors) take as long as is necessary to arrive at one of following recommendations:

- Success in accreditation

- Successful accreditation upon the receipt of further supportive material

- Re-submission of material with further self and peer assessment should the candidate still wish to proceed

- Withdrawal from the accreditation process.

This process is alive and well in the Independent Practitioner Network (IPN) under the tutorage of Denis Postle, a renowned humanist who birthed the IPN to counterbalance the depersonalising influence of traditional psychotherapy accreditation. I have used self and peer assessment often in a consultancy to promote behaviour conducive to team-building. I may begin this process by encouraging individuals to share 'their expectations of themselves and others as team members', encouraging them to distil from this information criterion for gauging team effectiveness. This can take a couple of hours or more to reach fruition, but does much to co-create a supportive team-building culture where 'self and peer assessment' becomes the icing on the cake.

To re-cap, in the form of personal-cum-professional assessment outlined here, participants create their own criteria, assessment remains open and autonomous, the individual being assessed is an active participant rather than a passive recipient, systemic power is owned and transparent to all and an intimate learning activity is engaged in where democracy and dialogue underpin the whole. So what might be a limitation of this process?

Reflections

* In terms of your own 'beginning behaviours' as a primary facilitator or lead consultant, how do you establish yourself in a new group? *(I think my more usual preparatory behaviours include sharing my understanding of why I'm there, surfacing needs and asking others to firm-up or to re-write the facilitative contract. I'm also aware that I frequently ask a group 'What do you think needs to happen now?' and 'Are you getting what you need?')*

* In terms of the organisations and training bodies you are acquainted with, how accurate a picture do the earlier discussed 'cultural resistances' associated with training organisations paint for you?

* In relation to self and peer assessment, when and where might you employ this approach and what do you consider to be its prime benefits and possible weaknesses?

3.4 Authority and Power – Formal Influence and Depersonalisation

To escape the company of human vulnerability and moment-to-moment responsibility, we sometimes embrace our ascribed roles or craft one for ourselves. Once in role, be this as parent, friend or boss, we do as expected so as to escape the chaos and confusion that attends moment-to-moment choice. 'Acting the part' rather than 'being ourselves', our life then takes on the characteristic of a performance and indeed, for a while, all is well. But as 'the role' grows stronger, our connection with 'the self' grows weaker – the machine is developed as the human spirit fades. It is wise to hold the roles ascribed us very lightly indeed.

Surrendering themselves to roles, 'human beings' detach from their more authentic selves and run the danger of becoming 'human doings' or 'cogs in an organisational machine'. When we reduce ourselves, our work and our relationships to this level, what are we really choosing to support? And what exactly are we choosing to dishonour?

> If you only awaken your will and intellect, then your work can become your identity... Often a person's identity, that wild inner complexity of soul and colour of spirit, becomes shrunken into their work identity. They

become prisoners of their role. They limit and reduce their lives. They become seduced by the practice of self-absence. They move further and further away from their own lives. They are forced backwards into hidden areas on the ledges of their hearts. When you encounter them you meet only the role. You look for the person, but you never meet him.

(O'Donoghue 1997, pp.187–8)

Put people in situations of power, give them a role and detach them from their usual supports and conditioning to authority does the rest.

In the 1960s, Stanley Milgram (described in Barber and Dietrich 1985) illustrated this point all too well. Milgram recruited white college students to experiments where they were required – by a man in a white coat – to give increasingly severe levels of electric shock to non-compliant individuals as an inducement to learning. These students, standing behind a 'learning subject' wired up to a dial before them with an accompanying lever calibrated from 'Slight Shock' to 'Danger – Severe Shock!', were instructed to increase the level of shock with every incorrect answer. Though with no more than a nominal $5 and a white-coated figure standing alongside saying 'Treat a refusal to give an answer in the same way as an incorrect answer', even when their subjects claimed they'd a heart condition and pleaded for them to stop – they pushed the lever to the top-most level! The subjects in the Milgram experiments of the 1960s were not 'poor white trash' from the under-class but well brought up, middle-class college students; yet instructed by a stranger in a white coat in laboratory conditions, they were prepared to give lethal levels of electric shock to strangers! Before this experiment experts believed only a few psychopathic personalities would proceed to the highest levels; in fact the majority did so. The students doing the 'shocking' in this experiment didn't know their subjects were really actors pretending to be shocked, but nevertheless were prepared to inflict injury and to risk killing others because they acquiesced to a role, which they then allowed to re-shape their reality and morals. Are you beginning to understand my underlying thesis now that society can make you sick?

Institutions at all levels enshrine our dis-at-ease – the human condition minus informed choice, individual responsibility and heart. This depersonalised self, lost and immersed within instrumental 'I–It' relationships, is a good soldier and follows orders. Hitler initially chose mental nurses to police his death camps – desensitised mental-health professionals conditioned to following orders. Man is indeed born free but everywhere in chains.

As 'social animals' with 'social needs' who fear rejection, we must constantly remain alert to the seductive allure of roles, for we have a built-in potential to acquiesce to group pressure and social conformity. This said, the more questioning we are as individuals the less likely we are to conform, irrespective of the size of the majority and the degree of ambiguity (Shaw 1971). Aronson (1976) suggests that in unfamiliar situations we conform to the expectations of people we perceive as 'knowing the ropes' and that, in most circumstances, people look for imagined or actual 'authorities' or 'parent figures' to respect. In this context, a facilitator or coach has immense power as a 'parental culture carrier' to whom others look for behavioural cues. Indeed, we might say that all professionals are agents of social control and that the power accorded to a role 'resides not in *individuals* but in the human *relationships* within and between organisations' (Wilson and Chesterman 2003, p.23). Professionalism in this context comes at a very heavy cost (Barber 2006a).

Backed by their sponsors, those whom an organisation sees as signatories of senior management, facilitators acquire powerful political trappings. While at one level we work alongside our clients and are part of a peer-learning community, as nominated incumbents of 'the facilitative role' we have more socio-political power than they do – even within their own organisation. This said, a consultant or change agent will always need powerful sponsors and patronage within the client-system to be successful. When riding high we may feel akin to organisational parents, but more often than not we are merely babysitters!

Failing through Success – 'Training' as Territorial Marking?

Not so many years ago I was called upon to run a series of personal development and counselling skill workshops for a south-coast police force that wished to give its management structure a less rank-conscious and more 'humane face'. These workshops were originally intended to serve inspectors and above, but after a couple of months when I was beginning to be accepted as user-friendly, the intake profile was changed to include all ranks. The force had previously tried – without much success – to reduce 'distance' between the divisions, and the personal and relational emphasis of my experiential workshops was now co-opted in to serve this end. For the most part this was a success, with chief inspectors, sergeants, CID officers and civilian workers sharing their relative perspectives of life in the police force and learning side by side. Reputation of the experiential person-centred approach I adopted travelled beyond the boundary of training, and in no time at all – some six months into the experiment – it was reported that attitudinal distance between ranks was being reduced and better communication was percolating out onto the streets. Problem individuals, those who were being ostracised by their 'teams' because of their behaviours were by this time also being increasingly referred to the counselling skills programme. In this way, when all else had failed, they threw their recidivists at me! But everything must die sometime and when the Head of the Training Division changed – my courses were dropped. It appeared that the developing familiarity between ranks was now seen as threatening by the newly appointed Head of Training, and internal police trainers would now take over my teaching to prevent further rot! Interestingly, in the police, where senior managers served a tour of duty, change – if not progress – was a constant. But in order to establish themselves new managers tended to rubbish the fruits of the previous regime, wiping out earlier cultural initiatives in favour of one of their own making.

> *Indeed, if a new manager could not stamp his impression on the organisation, in this macho culture he wasn't deemed to be worth his salt! 'All change' rather than development and growth thus characterised the nature of the Police Service in this place at this period (Adapted from Barber 1999).*

In respect of the legitimising effects of social power and authority, Max Weber, who was interested in 'why individuals obeyed commands', defined organisational communities in terms of their authority relationships (in Pugh et al. 1984). Making a distinction between *'power'* – the ability to force people to obey regardless of their resistance – and *'authority'* – where directions were followed voluntarily (Weber 1947) – Weber identified power as legitimised in three main ways, via the weight of *charismatic, traditional* or *rational–legal* influence:

- In the *charismatic group/community*, the exercise of authority was seen as stemming from the personal power of a leader who produced followers or disciples; Lord Nuffield, of Morris Motors, and Hitler and the Nazi Party represent extreme examples of this sort of leader.

- In the *traditional group/community*, the rights and expectations of people were seen as historically established and, due to custom and practice, viewed as sacred; although leadership is strong, it is more a consequence of imbued status than a function of personality, as in the ranking systems of the armed forces.

- In the *rational–legal group/community*, bureaucracy, rationality and working to specific goals, wedded to maximum performance, hold sway; authority here is exercised through a system of legalised rules and procedures geared towards precision, speed, un-ambiguity, knowledge of files, continuity, discretion, unity, strict subordination and a reduction of friction and of material and personal costs.

(Weber quoted by Pugh et al. 1984)

All the above are common currency within the business community. But from which quarter do you draw your own facilitative authority?

Obviously, the role of consultant or facilitator is subject to very different expectations and pressures in the above organisations. In traditional and bureaucratic cultures I find that although 'coaching' is asked for, 'mentorship' is generally expected; and that charismatic organisations favour a more 'person-centred' than 'systemic' or field approach. Although cultural acceptance and executive patronage are essential to facilitative success, because many organisational cultures are perceived by employees as punitive and bureaucratic, if we are perceived as over-identified with 'senior management', our objectivity and ethical stance maybe compromised in our client's eyes. In a consultation or coaching role, we must therefore position ourselves very carefully if we are to be accepted by senior management and shop-floor workers alike.

First Impressions – to Enliven or Live Down the Fantasy:

I once offered my consultancy services to a customs and excise team, arriving on the day to an all-male group in an open-necked shirt, brown shoes and cord trousers. A few days later, when I chatted over coffee to a senior member of the organisation, I learnt to my surprise that my dress had caused me to be stereotyped as a 'social worker' or other 'do-gooder', and that my beard was associated with 'drug takers'! This accounted for why they especially set out to test me when we first met. Indeed, until I demonstrated I could take aggression and confront the same, I could not get the group started! It was not so much a checking of boundaries and my ability to hold them energetically, but rather a test to see if I was worth investing time and effort in. When they felt I was strong enough to support and contain them, they relaxed, and only then began to work. I find that testing through challenge and personal confrontation is often deeply embedded within all-male cultures such as the police, armed forces and the prison service where you have to prove yourself able to 'roll with the punches' before you can be taken seriously.

If we are to avoid being perceived as antagonistic or counter-cultural by the more influential members and major power-holders of an organisation, we must gel at the social level for a relationship to form. But if we fit too neatly into the prevailing culture or 'go native', what will we have to add? Indeed, even when we get things right, say when we position ourselves objectively, support individuals while challenging unhealthy systems and seem to be making progress, we still need to realise that in many organisational settings 'nothing fails like success', for once we are seen to succeed we turn into 'a contender', and powerful others who are well served by the culture 'just the way it is thank you' become alerted to us as a 'threat'; then it is often only a matter of time until we are sabotaged by discomforted others in established organisational roles.

When working with a team or group within an organisational setting, in order to surface current conditions I have on occasion found it useful to invite individuals to consider the following questions:

Creativity:

- *Am I at liberty to create something new?*
- *Do I have sufficient resources to achieve my objectives?*

Connection:

- *Do I feel a part of a something bigger or a lone wolf?*
- *Are my values supported here?*

Appreciation:

- *Am I encouraged to grow in this environment?*
- *Is what I invest here recognised?*

Safety:

- *Am I stagnating or can I see a clear path before me?*
- *Is my experience recognised and valued?*

Support:

- *Am I supported and do I readily support others?*
- *Is communication open and honest in this setting?*

Fulfilment:

- *How caring of others and cared for by others do I feel?*
- *Am I working for the common good? Are my needs recognised in this setting?*

Satisfaction:

- *Am I enriched by what I do?*
- *Is my desire to create and to achieve met here?*

In this way a collaborative inquiry into an individual and team's experience of their relationship to the organisation gets under way, we start to appreciate the social and individual costs-to-date of working in the current mode as well as the effects of power and authority upon the cultural fabric of the workplace.

John Higgins makes the point that to see authority as an objective quality is a dangerous falsehood, for:

> Authority is a particular expression of identity. When that identity is hidden, confused or unexamined then it is a loose cannon. When it is brought into the light then the opportunity to choose one's relationship to authority becomes possible: you may choose to continue as you have always done, but by choosing to stay the same you have already brought a quality of consciousness to bear that will leave its mark.
>
> (Higgins 2009, p.217)

But what if you are an authority holder yourself, one of the bosses – a culture carrier? How might you spring-clean your own relationship with authority? In order for us to survive the mantle of authority thrust upon us, Higgins suggests we build in the following supports:

- Have someone who loves you to turn to, who'll keep you grounded
- Treat authority as a chore
- Know the fantasies you hold and recognise your vanities and vulnerabilities

- Have expertise that is of direct relevance to the area you exercise authority within

- Know how to get people to tell you how things are rather than how they think you want them to be

- Know how to get people to realise and take responsibility for the needs and desires they are projecting onto you

- Know how to notice and metabolise difficult or consuming emotions that have been evoked in you that may have nothing to do with the objective situation

- Know how much you can put up with and recognise your limits

- Know how to deal with bastards and bitches

- Have a sense of how much you are willing to give in service of others

- Know what 'healthy' means to you and how to maintain it.

(Higgins 2009, p.216)

It feels good to end with a common-sense and 'tell it like it is' view of authority such as this, with 'Know how to deal with bastards and bitches' ringing in our ears – for whichever way it cuts, authority is uptight and personal!

Reflections

* In terms of 'charismatic', 'traditional' and 'rational–legal group/community' cultures, how are you impacted personally and professionally as a facilitator by the power-dynamic at play? *(I'm aware that I'm most rebellious and supportive of playful exploration in rational–legal and traditional cultures, which I perceive as diminishing of emotional energy and the human condition; in charismatic cultures, conversely, I find myself negotiating boundaries and policing rules. I guess as a facilitator I often reflect back to an organisation its missing or denied parts?)*

* Bring an organisation or group you work with or within to mind, now evaluate its cultural fabric via the seven criteria and questions cited below:

- Creativity – *How empowered do I feel to make changes?*

- Connection – *How bonded am I to this relationship?*

- Appreciation – *Am I recognised for who I am and what I do?*

- Safety – *How secure do I feel in my present role?*

- Support – *How flexible can I or others really be here?*

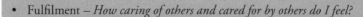

- Fulfilment – *How caring of others and cared for by others do I feel?*

- Satisfaction – *How fulfilled and celebratory do I feel?*

What results when you evaluate your own performance as a coach or consultant in the above terms?

* It has been suggested that in order be influential a facilitator or coach must keep three core conditions intact:

- Remain important in the eyes of clients

- Represent a consistent body of beliefs

- Be seen as presenting a strategy that is logical and convincing.

(Douglas 1985)

But is this really so? What case could you make for and against the above statement?

* Which of the self-support suggestions in Higgins' list have an especial relevance to you?

- Have someone who loves you to turn to, who'll keep you grounded

- Treat authority as a chore

- Know the fantasies you hold and recognise your vanities and vulnerabilities

- Have expertise that is of direct relevance to the area you exercise authority within

- Know how to get people to tell you how things are rather than how they think you want them to be

- Know how to get people to realise and take responsibility for the needs and desires they are projecting onto you

- Know how to notice and metabolise difficult or consuming emotions that have been evoked in you that may have nothing to do with the objective situation

- Know how much you can put up with and recognise your limits

- Know how to deal with bastards and bitches

- Have a sense of how much you are willing to give in service of others

- Know what 'healthy' means to you and how to maintain it.

(Higgins 2009, p.216)

3.5 Facilitative and Non-facilitative Leadership – Seeding Authentic Dialogue

While working with the Association of Therapeutic Communities in the 1980s preparing mental health professionals for the demands of large-group community facilitation, I was intrigued to discover during an experiment in which three groups shared the same brief but were subject to differing styles of leadership, how each approach generated a very different end product. With a relatively simple brief requesting them to build 'a model out of pins and straws', unbeknown to their teams the three nominated team leaders were briefed to enact an 'authoritarian', 'democratic' or 'laissez faire' style of leadership. Within each team an observer was appointed to record and to subsequently debrief upon the group dynamic. Later in plenary when the learning community came together the product itself was also evaluated in terms of it's a) aesthetic qualities, b) strength and stability, c) inventiveness and d) value. My many experiments with this exercise over the years suggest:

> **Authoritarian or hierarchical leadership** tends to produce an uninspired product, often in conventional cube or triangular form that is stable enough and doesn't fall over, but which individuals feel little emotional attachment or commitment to; in terms of the team dynamic, because the leader is perceived to be unapproachable and non-listening, members are seen to displace their frustrations with 'leadership' onto squabbles amongst themselves.

> **Democratic or collaborative leadership** produces a much appreciated product – often a model of something realistic and tangible, in which participants retain interest and identify as something they have played a part in creating; because the leader is seen as 'one of us' there appears to be a pulling together and sense of loyalty in the team.

> **Laissez faire or autonomous leadership** is seen to manifest a highly creative though somewhat unstable or humorous product, often highly imaginative but unfocussed, which is enjoyed at the time of creation but has little practical influence or lasting relevance; because the leader 'didn't appear to give a damn', group members also 'don't give a damn'.

It is interesting how the nominated leader was given power to stamp his 'reality' upon others, like a parent in a family, and while there was superficially 'overt conformity' an undercurrent of 'covert hostility' simultaneously arose – in all but the collaborative group.

Extrapolating out from the above to appreciate how the differing team cultures fared, I would suggest that *'authoritarian climates'* induce a defensive split between 'us and them' along with conformity and the displacement of anger onto peers

73

– in short a sort of schizoid–paranoid reaction. In contrast '*democratic climates*' appear to further interaction and synergy and to foster open dialogue and a shared sense of 'meaning'. Lastly, '*laissez faire*' climates solicit unbounded and undirected emotional release, a sort of catharsis of feeling but leave people feeling detached and ignored. Perhaps we have evidence here that democratic facilitation works after all! But can negotiated decision-making and collaborative leadership work in times of emergency, in survival situations where speed and action are of the essence – say at times of crisis management or in military settings? I would say yes, if a leader's presence and ability to nurture others positively have been established and what they represent is seen as worth serving.

Though charismatic leadership has generally received a poor press from modern writers, especially those of psychoanalytic persuasion, it would be remiss not to consider positive aspects of such personalised styles of leadership. After all, Winston Churchill got the job done in a dire situation and inspired and worked for the common good. Napoleon likewise achieved much. Both had more than their fair share of self-absorption, dare I suggest narcissism, but they also had presence – though not a therapeutic one by a long chalk! Nevertheless they were effective leaders. But Earnest Shackleton's approach is the one I'd like us to explore as an example of collaborative and democratic leadership applicable to our current task – facilitating change.

In Shackleton we do not find a Napoleon or a Churchill, or any other such self-serving or self-absorbed individual, but rather an altruistic and person-centred leader:

> He didn't care if he went without a shirt on his own back so long as the men he was leading had sufficient clothing. He was a wonderful man in that way; you thought the party mattered more than anything else.
> (L. Greenstreet, 1st Officer, *Endurance* – quoted from Morrell and Capparell 2001 in an unnumbered review by Barber 2001)

So here we have an example of leadership from a bygone age of someone who facilitates through example, a man who in his own words enjoyed the company of his fellow men: 'There are lots of good things in the world, but I'm not sure that comradeship is not the best of them all – to know you can do something big for another chap' (ibid.).

Shackleton, unlike his fellow Arctic explorer, Scott, was not a rigid Royal Navy man who, in the military mode, tried to orchestrate every movement of his men and who put discipline first, who still held inspections and had sailors attempting to swab the decks even as the water froze, but a merchant mariner who sought to serve 'the common good'. While Scott led externally from the fore and put the objective first, before his own life and the lives of others, Shackleton led from within the group and by example. For instance, in his 1909 dash to the Pole, Shackleton gave up 'the quest' in order to ensure the whole party returned alive. When dysentery overcame them on the way back he gave his own breakfast biscuit to another he saw as needier than himself. This kind of incident is reported time and time again: he constantly put 'service' to others before veneration of self and achievement. Simply, he was neither 'role' or 'rule' bound. A Victorian who admits to recognising a 'feminine' and rather modern caring aspect to himself: 'I am a curious mixture with something feminine in me as well as being a man… I have committed all kinds of crimes in thought if not always in action and don't worry much about it, yet I hate to see a child suffer, or to be false in any way' (ibid.).

Again, we are drawn back into a comparison with the more establishment, task-minded position of Scott. While Scott was dour and controlling, Shackleton was warm and humorous; while Scott was secretive and untrusting, Shackleton talked openly and frankly to his men; while Scott worked rigidly to plan, Shackleton adapted to the circumstances and the ever-changing territory. To Shackleton, although 'planning' was *everything*, 'the plan' itself was *nothing* – he was not blinded by the map.

Shackleton did not demand respect, he earned it. Again and again we see him taking a very modern facilitative stance, sharing his intentions and asking for the opinions of even the lowliest members of his crew, playing to their strengths and working to empower others. Sadly, there are still far too many Scotts in our contemporary business world and all too few Shackletons.

Shackleton grew up in an Irish Quaker family steeped in progressive reforming traditions such as abolitionism, prison reform, pacifism and women's suffrage. When he finally came to Sydenham, London, his position as 'the outsider' became the more acute: at school he was singled out as a 'Mikey' (Irish) and performed poorly. From this perspective he sampled at first hand the plight of the underdog; one wonders if this helped sculpt his extraordinary empathy with others – while fermenting a desire to achieve and to belong. His life was not without failures: a poor academic record; a failed attempt to become a politician; an aborted expedition to the Pole. Shackleton was also far from perfect: a jack-of-all-trades, a self-publicist, all of these things and more by turn – but never defeated and always learning from his mistakes. Most importantly, though he sought the limelight it is recorded that he hated being hailed as a hero. He sought to serve and belong rather than transcend his fellow men: 'He was essentially a fighter, afraid of nothing and of nobody, but, withal, he was human, overflowing with kindness and generosity, affectionate and loyal to all his friends' (Lewis C. Bernacchi, Physicist, *Discovery*, quoted ibid.).

Though Shackleton had 'the common touch', he knew how to catch the imagination with a showman-like flourish or two. For instance, when imploring others to jettison every ounce of unnecessary weight, he acted first by making the grand and dramatic gesture of throwing his gold cigarette case inscribed by Princess Alice – a treasured gift – into the snow. Showman maybe, but perhaps because of this, all the more entertaining to be with and all the more inspirational! Indeed, his men report his humorous songs, japes, celebration of birthdays – all under extreme conditions. Here was a man whose company you could enjoy in the worst of places.

Margot Morrell and Stephanie Capparell (2001), in their distillation of Shackleton's skills, suggest that to capture a little of his magic we must:

- Promote a sense of compassion and responsibility for others and never forget we have a far bigger impact on the lives of those under us than we can ever imagine

- Never insist upon reaching a goal at any cost without regard for our staff

- Breakdown traditional hierarchies and cliques by training workers to take on a range of roles from the menial to the challenging.

So here we have qualities of presence applicable to our role as facilitators, pointers reminiscent of person-centred therapy and Carl Rogers' (1957) core conditions of congruence and genuineness, unconditional positive regard and non-possessive warmth, empathy and un-conditional love.

Stepping back to appreciate the wider scenery of management development, I note that while the USA has emphasised 'personal motivation', the UK, especially from the 1950s onwards, has emphasised 'the team spirit', possibly as a consequence of our public-school ethos and the transfer into business of military analogies. In this context, Shackleton combines the best of both perspectives, illuminating a means whereby personal motivation is fermented through a leader's awareness and respect for individuals. If individuals do not feel seen, heard and valued, what good to them 'the team' and what values will associate with leadership? It is all too common to hear people say: 'We've moved to 'teamwork' – but our people still aren't working as a team!' For individual valuing is missing. Again, in the man's own words: 'The loyalty of your men is a sacred trust you carry. It is something which never must be betrayed, something you must live up to' (ibid.).

I guess Shackleton veers towards a democratic Servant Leadership style, Scott towards an authoritarian one. But even if Scott had been educated in Shackleton's way, I'm doubtful it would have worked for him. You 'become' a leader-cum-facilitator in a way which honours who and what you are, your own base material, for authenticity and congruency are vital. If you don't have compassion, you can't fake it with any success for very long. Remember, Gestalt cautions us to be fully who we are. This said, in general I believe it is wise, as well as ethical, for facilitators to veer towards a democratic style, especially informed by humanistic values – if they wish to take others along with them on a learning journey.

Having raised awareness to positive qualities of presence, I feel myself now drawn towards considering the negative culture into which we take the above positive qualities of being. For instance, Nixon has identified the following organisational features as frustrating fruitful dialogue, learning and authentic exchange:

- People blaming and complaining instead of taking personal responsibility

- A punishing, bullying climate which discourages risk taking and frankness

- A tendency to 'trash' and to criticise colleagues

- Too little appreciation or encouragement

- Competition, playing politics and difficulty in working collaboratively

- Difficulty in handling open conflict and a lack of respect for difference

- Widespread mistrust

- Isolation and lack of support

- Lack of honest two-way communication

- Unwillingness to acknowledge mistakes

- Over-control and a reluctance to involve others

- Manipulation rather than direct dealing

- A tendency to gross overworking

- Reluctance to take space to think or manage strategically

- Repression of energy, initiative and the talents of people.

(Nixon 1998, p.26)

These behaviours are the antithesis of the Learning Organisation and say much about the cultural fabric facilitators must address. Disturbingly, Nixon observes that beneath a thin veneer of humour, politeness and professionalism, such influences as these are the norm and represent a typical organisation!

As to where a facilitator, coach or consultant should focus to implant positive change, Nixon suggests we sow a culture supportive of: honesty and openness; encouragement and challenge; trust and confidentiality; appreciation and constructive criticism; real listening; balanced giving and receiving; excitement, fun and humour (ibid., p.28). Nixon is not humanist, yet such qualities as these characterise a humanistic approach, one where everyone is encouraged to take responsibility for outcomes, feelings are shared and disagreements are openly challenged. He suggests we take the following sequential strategic steps to co-create this climate:

1) *Review global trends:* exploring what is going on in the wider environment to affect the client-system

2) *Perform a rigorous review of the present:* examination of the current system and how well the team is responding to its present needs

3) *Focus vision towards a desired future:* systematic review and examination

of the whole organisation, the part teams and individuals play as well as how things would be if everything were going well

4) *Illuminate strategies:* exploring key strategic actions that the team needs to take

5) *Explore key issues:* identifying and working on key issues or obstacles within the team, and upon similar conditions beyond the team that likewise need attention

6) *Cultivate action and support:* planning and implementing the supports that need to be put in place… then returning to this whole process again until the organisation spirals its way towards health.

So here Nixon is nudging towards Gestalt and Humanism in a business school sort of way – and good on him, for I'm sure he reaches the more traditional end of the consulting market who would never ever entertain Gestalt or humanistic psychology.

Although I support an approach which humanises the working climate by encouraging individuals to give up pretence, admit mistakes, take responsibility and co-create a culture where they can learn to ask empowering questions and be heard (Simmons 1993), I can't help feeling that social re-education and re-engineering is but half the story – as it glosses over the deeper level of discomfort that must be faced for real-time change. I am not alone in this bias. Scott Peck reminds us that if we are to create a real sense of community we must first travel through a phase of *chaos* and *emptiness*. Simply, fears must be faced and the 'old' released if we are to actualise 'the new':

Phase 1 – *Pseudo-community:* characterised by low energy, a pretence that differences do not exist and a getting on with the task in a polite and amicable way which actively avoids the underlying issues

Phase 2 – *Chaos:* long-held frustrations are released, energy grows, people try to obliterate differences by persuading others to their point of view, but there is little space for people to be themselves and an awareness of group process is lost in the competitive struggle to come out on top

Phase 3 – *Emptiness:* two ways out of chaos now emerge: the group can either revert to a stage of pseudo-community or by emptying, that is giving up the belief that they know what is best, let go of control and begin to become authentic, move towards being open and respectful of difference so that trust and acceptance can begin to develop

Phase 4 – *Community:* characterised by a high degree of authenticity and a willingness to engage, conflict is resolved through open discussion, task and processes are managed simultaneously and difference is welcomed.

(Peck 1987 and 1993)

It strikes me that the above describes, in community terms, the passage from 'unconscious incompetence' to 'unconscious competence'. Returning to the 'fertile void' of *chaos* and *confusion*, in order to unfreeze our more rigid and relic behaviours is something we will return to again and again throughout this text, for chaos and emptiness are growing pains of the psyche.

Travelling Through Chaos and Confusion on a Two-day Workshop on Group Facilitation

This case study describes a two-day workshop in a large multi-national company which wished to enhance its facilitative base. The participants, 13 in number, were drawn from an international background and all except two had been in the company many years. Though the group considered themselves to be advanced facilitators, the impression I rapidly formed was that all but a few were more comfortable in the task domain, with a high degree of structure, than the cut and thrust of a more facilitative style. They appeared to my mind competent trainers rather than facilitators.

In an effort to prepare the group to a more emergent style of facilitation, one that could build communities rather than 'manage events', periodically throughout the first day I drew attention to the necessity for us to be 'led by the wisdom of our insecurity' and to 'welcome confusion', as these were akin to facilitative 'growing pains' and symptomatic of us moving into territory where new learning awaits. After all, I was contracted to run an 'advanced facilitator training' workshop where they may need to move beyond their comfort zone, where 'inquiry' and illumination were the order of the day rather than 'training to skills'. To my mind this was a superficially safe and over-polite group who wished to stay with 'the known' rather than conquer new territory.

Again, we return to the truism that in order for groups and teams to move out from a 'false sense of community' towards a more 'authentic' one, individuals must first travel through very necessary transitory phases of chaos and emptiness, where the 'old' is released in favour of a still-to-be-realised 'new' (Peck 1993).

In the first hour and a half – before coffee – I let things run as they were, watched the usual culture form and allowed the group to inform me. On this first day, before coffee, I believe we were primarily in what Scott Peck (ibid.) terms **'pseudo-community'***, a position characterised by low energy where people maintain a pretence that differences don't exist, are intent on 'getting on with the task in a polite and amicable way' and were 'avoiding the underlying issues'. Having watched this unfold for most of the morning – and believing that we would not travel very far as a group if we let it continue – following coffee I voiced observations as to how I was experiencing the group and challenged the role that laughter and the various in-jokes were serving for the group. Some felt shocked and others excited by my challenge to leave politeness behind in favour*

▶

of a more robust and challenging style. At this point, sides were taken: some agreed with me and others distanced themselves and formed antagonistic cliques.

*As we left our more 'conventional social world' behind I believe we began to experience what Peck terms '**Chaos**', a position where frustrations are released, energy grows, people try to obliterate differences by persuading others to their point of view and an awareness of group process is lost in the competitive struggle to come out on top. At this time, I strove to acknowledge difference, negotiated a more experiential and experimental structure by way of experiment, and helped to contain the group through the introduction of new Gestalt-informed ground rules which encouraged inquiry.*

*By the close of the first day I believe we were struggling within a phase of '**Emptiness**', where to escape chaos we would either have to revert back to a stage of pseudo-community or, by emptying and giving up the belief that we know best, release control and walk towards our fears! I think my non-defensive manner and invitation for people to face their fears helped move us towards a more authentic stance. After all, as I reminded them, they were now being expected by their company to facilitate team-building and to act as internal consultants, and if they wanted to be more process-centred and effective they would need to develop personally – and here was a chance to do just that. There were therefore sound reasons behind endeavouring to work in this 'new way'.*

Having slept on the experience, when we returned on the second day, miraculously, the group appeared to have integrated a great deal. For example, during check-in, people not only said 'for real' how they felt but shared their feelings openly in the group. They were also able to define complex principles relating to a Gestalt-informed facilitation style fluently! They had done their homework overnight and what they were rejecting yesterday they demonstrated competency in today! This was a group of bright people well able to adapt who had re-read the hand-outs of the day before and had spent time overnight integrating the ideas – but I didn't buy my own bullshit and realised they had acquiesced to my demands; that they had merely swopped an absent parent for the one now present: me!

*But this said, before coffee on the second day we were well into Scott Peck's notion of '**Community**', a position characterised by a high degree of authenticity, an ability to engage in conflict resolution where task and processes are managed simultaneously – but it didn't quite ring true. Though a little later during a facilitative exercise where individuals received and answered spontaneous questions while seated in the centre of the group, I saw the group functioning very effectively as a 'real self-facilitating community' and my role evolved into one of a process consultant, something was missing. We spent most of the afternoon sharing our learning and forming and contracting peer supervision to help us continue our Gestalt development post workshop. In plenary, the group celebrated the gains it.*

> *had made and individuals voiced a commitment to continue this more 'process-centred' way of working as a compliment to their existent skill-base – but I believed it not.*
>
> *Scott Peck says it takes months or years to move a community through the above phases – yet we did it to some degree in two days! Granted, it was a small group of thirteen, but it says much about what is potentially possible in an intensive facilitated climate where authenticity has flowered and the purpose is understood. Yet will it last? Alas no, for transitions such as this are merely adaptive rather than owned.*
>
> *When we are prepared to make 'emptiness' and 'chaos' close friends and accept Gestalt's invitation to stay in contact with what is happening, to speak our truth authentically and to inquire into the emerging need of a group – much is possible; but dependent groups will give you what you want time after time! Consequently, the learning stays within the workshop rather than percolates to the workplace or into people's hearts.*
>
> *Sometime later I spoke to one of the more senior workshop participants. A third of the group had really grown since the workshop, but the organisation didn't want advanced facilitators so much as advanced trainers, so the best of the bunch moved on.*

In an effort to build a more open and authentic team culture, I will at times enact a 'dialogical group sculpture'. For this I invite individuals to state their opinion on an arising issue, positioning differing points of view around the room. I then invite remaining participants to gather behind the individual whose views they favour. Rapidly, three or more positions can form. I then invite each sub-group to speak their differences openly, truthfully and in turn. While this unfolds I encourage others to listen, align themselves mentally and swop their current dialogical position if they feel swayed otherwise. At any time during this controlled dialogue individuals may be asked to move to where they feel they truly belong, or to form a new position if necessary. In the course of this exercise conflict is heard, differences are recognised, covert agendas come to light and each individual contributes to the arising arguments and emerging sculptural representation. In this way conflict and team culture are identified, opportunity arises for authentic communication and conflict resolution if necessary may be begun. Remember, action and movement impress themselves upon the psyche much more than words and ideas.

* Where do you position yourself on the spectrum of authoritarian, democratic and laissez-faire styles of leadership – and to what end? *(I aim to be democratic yet am often perceived at the beginning of my facilitation as laissez faire, when I stand back and let the group field form of its own volition. When challenging negative behaviours, especially in a large group setting, I feel I become and am perceived to be authoritative bordering upon authoritarian in style.)*

* How true a picture do you consider Nixon's (1998) description of a typical company culture, one where people blame and complain instead of taking personal responsibility, to be of the companies and teams you work within?

* In terms of 'pseudo-community', 'chaos' and 'emptiness', and 'real community', how do you react when these phenomena emerge in the groups you facilitate? *(I'm aware that pseudo-community is the norm in many cultures, where people seem to be 'doing what is necessary' to get through the working day – 'performing' rather than 'being'. When I scratch the surface, say in a team-building day, chaos and emptiness quickly ensue – and I take this as a sign that frozen behavioural defences are beginning to melt. In all these stages I stay curious and questioning of the unfolding process, and endeavour to support the person while challenging the group response.)*

* So how are you perceived as a leader – on your best days and on your worst days?

* What qualities of personality, in terms of your charisma, strengthen you as a facilitator and subtract from you as a facilitator?

3.6   Facilitative Styles of Leadership – Fermenting Human-friendly Cultures

Whenever the members of a group or team feel the need to define 'community', I take it as a sure sign they have lost it! Community cannot be planned or legislated; it develops organically and, at a predestined time, dies. Communities thrive when their energy is organic and growing and wither when 'community' is over-prescribed or imposed as an expectation of how a 'team' or organisation 'should' be.

Too many accounts of leadership in corporate and business climates seem to derive from the Henry Ford mode where authoritarian rather than facilitative interventions are the norm and communal change is believed to be best achieved by strong and charismatic executive managers at the top. Recently this archaic message has been challenged as more relational styles of leadership have come to the fore. One such approach, Alpha Leadership (Deering et al. 2003), acknowledges the need to promote individual and systemic health through 'right relationships'; it suggests we avoid conditions which promote 'the cult of the leader' in favour of attitudes which develop 'a culture of leadership'. As to how we might set about incubating 'Alpha Leaders', it is recommended we begin by putting into action three principles: *anticipating*, *aligning* and *acting*:

- **Anticipating:** Within a climate of constant change, 'anticipation' is seen as keeping leaders ahead. In contrast to fire-fighting, as anticipators, leaders envision the future from present evidence in order to create working hypothesises. Here flexibility is a must, 'the plan is nothing' even though 'planning is everything', for 'change' is the only constant. In decision making, hard evidence comes second to what is in emergence, for if we wait for hard evidence we will always be too late. Leaders in this context make in-course corrections towards ever-changing goals. They become entrepreneurs with fast reflexes, for they stay in dialogue with an ever-changing field rather than work to outdated maps that miss the present. In this scenario, in Gestalt fashion, agility and pattern recognition come before 'the plan' and knowledge comes second to imagination and recognition of what is unfolding now.

  The dials on our economic dashboard have started spinning wildly, blinking and twittering as we head into new territory. It's possible the gauges are all broken, but it is much more likely that the world is turning upside down.
  (Kevin Kelly quoted in Deering et al. 2002, p.11)

- **Aligning:** Good leaders inspire, poor leaders coerce and the very best leaders lead through example while supporting people to achieve. Such leaders as these aren't task-fixated but alive to process. They stay relationally alert and empathetic, endeavour to understand 'what people want', 'where they want to go' and 'how best they would like to get there', and are prepared to act as mentors and coaches as necessary. In this context, leaders of excellence are suggested to sow authentic and open communication and to influence culture in the manner of organisational horse whisperers! Simply, they know that relationships are key and that, if they get relationships right, tasks will take care of themselves.

  In the quantum world, relationships are not just interesting... they're all there is to reality.
  (Margaret Wheatley quoted in Deering et al. 2002, p.75)

- **Acting:** Although much effort is frequently expended on creating mission statements and trying to motivate an individual's buy-in to the organisational dream, such attempts can exacerbate the problem. Disappointed to have been fed a false dream and feeling led astray when the expected results don't materialise, employees lose hope and give up. 'Buy-in' can never replace being clear and direct. Open and tolerant of dissent, effective non-bossy leaders seek information from others rather than ramming it down their throats. They realise that, to act efficiently, cultures must be clear, adaptable and be able to work through conflict. In this regard they actively support mechanisms that encourage responsiveness and the surfacing of discontent, for they know that dissent must be heard and faced if an organisation or team is to maintain constancy of purpose and high performance. As failure results when leaders can't take people with them, leaders in this mode co-create measurable goals, loose enough to be appropriate for the foreseeable future yet understandable to the workforce, for in essence they serve.

Knowledge is only a rumour until it's in the muscle.

(Papua New Guinean proverb)

There is much 'Gestalt' in Alpha Leadership for me: a surrender to the field so you might be led by the unknown; 'anticipation' founded upon intuitive attention to the present and what is unfolding now; 'aligning', which requires an appreciation of 'the field' and an empathetic appreciation of others; 'acting', which in the Alpha Leadership context supports an 'authentic lived dialogue' plus open communication and co-creation.

Personally, I like to mix and match my leadership styles and find that a combination of Alpha Leadership with Servant Leadership (described below) catches much of what I believe a facilitative style of Gestalt leadership entails. Alpha Leadership speaks to me of the inner world of a facilitative leader; Servant Leadership of how it appears externally in practice. Essentially, Servant Leadership (Spears 2002) represents a person-centred educative approach which honours humanistic and Gestalt principles of:

Listening – getting in touch with the inner voice to understand what the body, spirit and mind are communicating (***holistic?***)

Empathy – strives to understand the world of others (***empathetic?***)

Healing – searches for wholeness (***attends to the total field?***)

Awareness – makes a commitment to foster awareness (***as in Gestalt?***)

Persuasion – seeks to convince others rather than to coerce compliance through positional authority (***democratic and dialogical?***)

Conceptualisation – nurtures the ability to dream great dreams (***encourages vision?***)

Foresight – uses intuition to perceive possible outcomes and to inform the present with lessons from the past (***intuitive?***)

Stewardship – holds something in trust for others (***entertains the transpersonal?***)

Commitment to Growth – works to foster growth and to develop the potential of all (***humanistic and educational?***)

Community Building – generates a supportive team and community culture (***group-centred?***).

Facilitators and coaches will hopefully, at the very least, work in the manner of Servant Leaders who serve the community and Alpha Leaders attuned to the wider client-system. Gestalt, in this light doesn't feel so much counter-cultural as an extension of current leadership ideals.

When I'm called upon to mine deeper into the nature of what individuals bring to their work-based communities, in the vein of an Alpha and Servant Leader, I find it beneficial to invite participants to mull over the following 'expectations', 'blocks' and 'options' that inform their behaviour in the host culture:

Expectations:

* What do I expect from others and this team/group community in general? *(Values and attitudes I require from those around me to perform well; ethics and conditions I desire in collegial relationships; how I believe the group/community might best serve me)*

* What future outcome do I long or strive for here? *(My guiding dreams and personal desires; the creations I hope to manifest; what I am holding out for)*

* What expertise and skill do I bring to use in this team/group community? *(My strengths and abilities; what I have and want to give personally and professionally; the unique role and function I might serve in this group/ community; how I can best serve the group/community)*

Blocks:

* What have I given up on in this team/group community? *(Lessons learnt from earlier events; hurts I still carry with me; times I felt abused, let down or hindered from giving of my best; crises of trust; issues that need to be resolved)*

* What challenges me the most and feeds my fears? *(Archaic patterns I hold onto here, old enemies I meet and fears that return to haunt me; what is the worst that might happen?)*

* What issues do I refuse to work on here? *(My barriers to exploration; what I deem appropriate and acceptable; fears of rejection; the level of risk I will take)*

Options:

* How might the team/group change in order to enhance its effectiveness? *(What needs to happen for this group/community better to support those*

within it?; resources the group/community needs to better its performance; growth points; problems that need to be addressed)

* How might I change myself and my behaviour to enhance this team/group's effectiveness? *(Recognising how my desired impact contrasts with the one I am having; raising awareness to where I might develop personally and professionally)*

* How might I best add value to myself and this team/group community? *(Desiring and daring to make a difference; positioning myself further within or further out from the group; striving for excellence or leaving to fulfil myself elsewhere)*

Taking a team through the above is a potent catalyst for raising 'group awareness'. Sometimes this exercise has structurally underpinned the whole of a three-day event, leading on to illuminative and appreciative inquiry into what organisational and relational conditions best support people giving of their best. Sometimes I also introduce notions of Alpha and Servant Leadership as a counterbalance to existent modes, stressing that while a 'team' may be described as a group of people who gather to 'do things together', that 'doing' is of far less importance than the quality of *'togetherness'* available, and reversing our leadership focus to consider 'followership' skills!

Having shared their expectations of the organisation and experiences of its blocks, and considered the options before them, participants, now with an inkling of what frustrates 'togetherness' and 'followership', may be invited to step into the role of co-consultants through consideration of the key points of organisational dysfunction below, plus ways we might possibly redress the same:

- **Non-constructive interpersonal functions:**

   Relational conflicts*: personal agendas get in the way of working together – Possible remedies:* illuminate what team members expect of others and educate members to the value of difference within team-work

   Lack of trust*: team members appear unable to commit to the team and each other – Possible remedies:* attempt to build individual and group trust and if this fails suggest they consider reforming the team

   Conflicting personal needs*: individuals work at cross-purposes – Possible remedies:* raise awareness to hidden agendas and invite people to share what they really want from the team

   No real will to develop or change*: team knows what is needed but are resistant to engage with the necessary action to do it – Possible remedies:* illuminate blockages while drawing attention to consequences of inaction

- *Non-constructive leadership functions:*

    Confused purposes, aims and goals: people don't really know what is expected or can't make sense of what is expected of them – *Possible remedies:* clarify the rationale for the team's existence and illuminate its key purposes along with its expected and desired outcomes

    Unclear roles: team members are uncertain what their job really entails or the legitimate actions and rights that attend their role – *Possible remedies:* clarify with team members what is wanted and needed from each other and what leadership expects of them

    Poor or absent decision-making: leadership is experienced as inconsistent or absent – *Possible remedies:* educate the leader to the need for them to serve their team and to consider ways they might keep its vitality and vision alive

    Lack of vision: leader fails to convey to the team its mission and value – *Possible remedies:* clarify the leader's role and expectations of members plus the team's wider purpose

    Lack of feedback: performance remains unmeasured and individuals feel uninformed and lost – *Possible remedies:* create systems of regular feedback and on-going team debriefing

- *Non-constructive organisational functions:*

    An anti-team-working culture: the organisation is not really committed to the value of teams and undermines team-working – *Possible remedies:* raise to awareness the mismatch between organisation's values and team-work with a view to informing the policy makers and creating alternatives

    Inappropriate rewards: people are rewarded for the wrong or confusing reasons – *Possible remedies:* implement a valuing of and rewards for team-working and team-outcomes rather than just individual effort

    Inadequate resources: team has the wrong tools and systems of support for the job expected of it – *Possible remedies:* identify team needs and ways to obtain resources and/or consider creative options and viable alternatives

    Inadequate policies and poor procedures: team is frustrated by current organisational systems rules – *Possible remedies:* collect evidence and identify routes to the policy makers beyond the team

    (Adapted from Harkema and Browaeys 2003)

Bringing my clients on board, as it were, by inviting them to become internal consultants nearly always provides rich pickings. Again and again I have found that people will often rise to the lowest expectation placed on them – and I expect a lot! So I guess I'm doing to you, as readers, what I do with my clients: orientate them to my approach, identify their needs (though this is a guesstimate with you), support them through chaos as traditional models of doing things are challenged (from afar dear reader), brainstorm them with information and content and invite them to walk alongside me until they leave their mind behind and begin to relate authentically with what is here and now. I always benefit from my clients' counsel, for they know far more about what they need and their workplace than I ever will.

The Therapeutic Community – Group Centred Culture Building:

The term 'Therapeutic Community' (TC) was first used by Tom Main (1946) to describe a 'social milieu' whole-field approach to mental illness that evolved at the Northfield's Military Hospital during the last war. This model, which treats the community group rather than the individuals within it, held individuals responsible to the community while inviting them to experiment with more satisfying patterns of relating and communal decision making.

At the same time as Main was developing his vision via family therapy at the Cassel Hospital, his colleague Maxwell Jones (1952) began experimenting with large group analysis with sociopaths at the Henderson Hospital (Rapoport 1960). The author believes it is no accident that this community approach to mental health was born in a time of war, in the military where alienation was rife, and during a period when society was itself spiritually dis-at-eased.

While the militarism and functionalism of the thirties welded the individual to the nation's 'war machine', the TC of the late forties sought to set them free:

> The therapeutic community involves the total community in a culture of enquiry into the nature of social processes within, and how these truly succeed or fail in caring for the specific individuals in it…
>
> (Main 1980, p.53)

From the 1940s through to the 1970s the TC was viewed as a counter-cultural force, but by the 1980s it began to impact more widely upon conventional practice and to shed its status as a 'movement' for the mantle of an accepted 'method' – at which time it also gained recognition as an instrument for training (Gauthier 1980; Hawkins 1980).

For me, the best aspects of 'servant' and 'field-centred leadership' plus side-by-side working are elucidated in Therapeutic Community practice. Many change consultants including Roger Harrison (1995) and Scott Peck (1993) are heavily indebted to its ideas and steeped in its traditions. As a community-cum-systemic approach to community transformation, it eventually drew humanists and analysts alike to its thinking, helping to sire encounter groups of the '60s, T-Groups of the '70s (Cooper and Mangham 1971), focus groups and collaborative inquiry of the '80s (Reason and Rowen 1981) while underpinning concepts of 'community development' (Lewin 1946) and 'the learning company' (Pedler et al. 1997); so much for its credentials.

Patients in isolation in Tuberculosis (TB) hospitals had long been recognised to self-support and to develop a special bond, which itself had therapeutic effect. Army psychiatrists wishing to capitalise upon the camaraderie of army life created conditions similar to the TB hospital with shell-shocked solders and found a comparable positive morale-boosting result. What especially seemed of benefit was the heightened sense of community that developed when individuals lived and worked as peers and contributed to the common good. Self-esteem and a keener sense of belonging and purpose were some of the advantageous outcomes seen to result from this experiment of 'community as doctor' and it didn't take long for the Tavistock Institute to research this phenomenon (Rapoport 1960).

In tracing the emergence of the Therapeutic Community, we begin to appreciate the cultural traditions that fermented during and shortly after the Second World War to cement individual, group and systems thinking together (Burke 1987). Essentially, the Therapeutic Community set out to provide an environment where social interaction and personal development could flower, within surroundings where individuals might experience movement towards group goals and democratic decision making. But although originally intellectually identified with systems theory, in practice its expression was pure field theory (Rapoport 1960; Barber 2005)!

In this open systems approach, where doctors and mental health professionals and facilitators worked to a brief where 'the community made the decisions', focus was on real issues and tasks; everyone was encouraged to participate in decision making; there was a willingness to profit by error and through experimentation; and community life was related to the rest of society. In this climate, a senior manager's rights and authority are exchanged for the more authentic role of an enabler in a 'real' rather than 'enrolled' community, one who is responsible not to hierarchical superiors but to what the community allows or demands (Main 1946). Simply, 'the community field' *is* the manager. For example, at the Henderson Hospital run as a Therapeutic Community, clients, staff, senior managers and psychiatrists came together in early morning and late evening community groups where they caught up with resident's progress, joined them in cleaning and gardening and cooking groups, facilitated small therapy groups, helped prepare meals, ran workshops and sat alongside them on management and community groups, selected staff and relaxed together. The residents here were recidivists, ex-drug addicts and alcoholics, diagnosed psychopaths whose personality disorders had caused them to be thrown out of other institutions. Many were ex-prisoners, yet a 15 per cent success rate was achieved, based on return to the community without re-offence over five years, with these so-called 'no hopers' others had long before given up on. Simply, the anti-social were re-socialised. So how was this achieved?

Robert Rapoport (1960), in his field theoretical seminal study of the Henderson Hospital entitled *Community as Doctor*, illuminated the following characteristics of the Therapeutic Community's working culture, namely, an attention to the:

- Morale-building effect of efficient communication
- Total social organisation in which the individual stands
- Relational dynamic, vital force and systemic energy of the community
- Developing culture, awareness and sensitivity to the community's own value system
- Quality of warmth and acceptance in general view and the emotional climate created
- Learning available through the engagement of institutional roles and democratisation.

When I began to apply the above to nursing education in the 1980s (Barber 1999), I found the following accrued:

1) Looking at 'the total social organisation' drew attention to the social context and cultural influence of the system we were interacting within

2) Raising awareness to the 'relational dynamic' and 'the institution's vital force' stimulated an exploration of the external pressures along with examination of the energetic milieu we were busy perpetuating

3) 'Democratisation' encouraged me to shed power, invited students to take greater responsibility and fostered power-sharing and experimentation

4) Attending to the 'developing culture' while fostering 'sensitivity to the community's own value system' raised awareness of the overt and covert rules we operated by, as well as the 'isms' we unconsciously sanctioned and acted out

5) Examination of the 'emotional climate' and the 'warmth' in view drew attention to how we individually and collectively handled intimacy and developed our sense of 'community'

6) Focusing upon the desirability for 'efficient communication' caused us to experiment with different ways of relating.

Implement such principles and no doubt similar results will follow for you. What the cultural shape-shifting approach of Therapeutic Community practice seems particularly good at creating is a group-centred intervention capable of moving a community from its 'present state' to a 'transitional state'. By unfreezing and reversing hierarchical systems of control it renders a community fluid and self-regenerating, while offering a social container for the holding and resolution of confusion that initially results. Interestingly, an account a few years ago in the Sunday papers (Preston 2005) described a so-called revolutionary new approach to education where there are no classrooms and teachers – only seminars and advisors. School children learnt life skills and chose what they wanted to learn, helped prepare their own meals, took an active part in managing the school system, interviewed and selected their own teachers – in short they did the more usual Therapeutic Community things. This innovatory approach to education won a donation of £40 million from Bill Gates, the computer billionaire, to set up 70 more schools run on similar lines. Amazing what you can achieve when you remove the politics of oppression while opening up experimentation and dialogue.

Reflections

Consider the following values associated with Therapeutic Community practice:

- Keeping the workforce small enough so that everyone can be involved with everyone else

- Holding regular meetings of the whole community

- Adhering to the philosophy that individual difficulty can be resolved best by face-to-face discussion

- Analysing the social events of the unit

- Attempting to improve the flow of communications

- Endeavouring to flatten the authority pyramid

- Providing protected situations where individuals might try out new ways of coping

- Constantly examining roles and behaviours in employees and managers.

* How applicable do you consider the above to be as ground rules for community building, training and consulting events, or yet again as indicators of organisational health? *(I guess I see the above as more appropriate for a consultancy team than the total client-system, as it would need to be a pretty adventurous client to let me implement the above; but this said, I would need to work towards such values as these if I were to run an action learning event or to seed a research-minded community.)*

* You are employed by a company with a workforce of 200 to investigate what people believe the company does well and what they believe the company needs to do better, and to build a culture of inquiry within the working community.

- Consider how you might incorporate Servant Leadership plus Therapeutic Community principles as supports to help you structure your facilitation for this event?

▶

91

* The following are viewed as characteristics of Servant Leadership:

• Provides new measures of human effectiveness which includes a means of becoming fully human

• Is holistic and takes into account meaning and purpose

• Is biased for people and seeks to serve as an example for others

• Community orientated

• Emphasises wellbeing over material riches

• Inclusive and involves everyone

• Generates connections and healing and 'goes against cultural wounds of separateness and winning through competing over others'.

(Schuster 2002, p.333)

So:

• What is the leader here attempting to heal and where are they taking us?

• What are you attempting to heal in your own leadership/facilitation?

• What or whom is the servant leader in partnership with? *(I believe the client is the group, the community ethos rather than the executive team, for such a leader is more values- than task-driven, though what results is likely to be more sustainable than results-driven leadership.)*

• Who or what are you personally in partnership with as a facilitator?

3.7 Educating the Social Field – Facilitative Styles and Interventional Choices

Having reviewed Therapeutic Community as a large-group intervention, we will now examine another re-educative approach to cultural change, one that attempts to teach 'individual excellence' in communication and cascade this throughout the organisation via peer counselling, namely John Heron's (2001) 'Six Category Intervention Analysis'. 'Intervention', within this perspective, is defined as a verbal or non-verbal behaviour offered in service to a client. As to how this model arose, after an exhaustive review Heron concluded there were six categories of intervention which fuelled two styles of facilitation – 'authoritative' and 'facilitative' (Heron 1989). In the authoritative style a facilitator is largely task-centred and primarily gives advice (prescribes), instructs and interprets (informs), challenges and gives direct feedback (confronts); while in the facilitative mode they are more person-centred and work to release emotional tension (cathartic), promote self-directed problem solving (catalytic) and seek to approve and affirm the client's worth (supportive).

In character, the 'authoritative style' speaks largely from a position of power, is task-driven and has a tendency to be facilitator-centred in the style of mentorship and prescriptive coaching. By contrast the 'facilitative style' is client-centred and attends primarily to emergent process. Both styles must be harnessed together if we are to address something approaching holistic facilitation.

Although I am loathe to educate a client-system to a reductionist vision of six interventions, I nonetheless note this model's usefulness as a springboard for discussing intervention styles, profiling interventions and charting 'facilitative intention' – especially when training novice facilitators. With the latter in mind, having introduced the model in workshops, I encourage a more subtle dialogue around how interventions alone, without being embedded in a supportive interpersonal process, counts for little. This said, hopefully you will nevertheless find the depiction below informative at the very least:

- *'Informative interventions'* must be timed appropriately and be offered to others only when they are in the right mental frame to hear you; when informing we must guard against dogma and information overload, which feels oppressive.

- *'Prescriptive interventions'* require that we use an appropriate tone of voice, more 'recommending' than 'commanding', lest we generate resistance or dependency rather than raise awareness to existing boundaries and 'rules of engagement'.

- *'Confronting Interventions'* are usually the most difficult to get right, for we walk a fine line between 'pussy footing' around an issue or challenging others to the degree they feel sledge-hammered; we need to remember we are seeking to confront to the degree a client becomes self-confronting, not trying to win or do battle; but as confrontation has a negative press we may feel uncomfortable ourselves and the emotional overlay we bring can make our message sound far more severe than we intend it to be; this said, in the interests of raising awareness to hidden agendas and blind spots, we must persevere to perfect an effective degree of healthy challenge.

- *'Cathartic Interventions'* invite an expression of feelings, be this laughter or distress, whatever emotional energy is held in check; but we should not evoke emotions so much as encourage a client to express authentically their feeling right now, with the aim of releasing disabling pent-up energy.

- *'Catalytic Interventions'* at best encourage an individual or group to reflect upon options and move towards self-generated solutions; here, we invite people and teams to problem-solve, locate and put to use their own store of skill and wisdom – client-centred coaching especially uses interventions from this band.

- **'Supportive Interventions'** should not judge, rescue or portray care in a seductive way that takes clients over, but rather encourage confidence and a sense of achievement and celebration; sharing your respect for a client or acknowledging and celebrating their strengths falls under this banner.

Bear in mind that the above model says much about a facilitator's intention but little or nothing about their authentic presence and interest – qualities they need to embody for interventions to be truly effective. Although such 'interventions' appear distinct on paper, I find they tend to shade into each other in practice. For instance 'support' should underpin every intervention. Verbally a facilitator might offer 'support' but be 'cathartic' in presence while 'challenging' in tone of voice. All this needs to come together or intention and reception will differ. Congruence is thus an important factor. A Gestalt facilitator especially knows there is action in waiting and waiting in action, so refrains from intervention until the field becomes clear enough to guide them. Timing therefore plays a major part.

We are also reminded that interventions should be tailored to the unique environment you are co-creating with your client (Holmes 2002; Maister et al. 2000). This said, many facilitators nevertheless play safe by starting off 'authoritative' with the intention of becoming increasingly facilitative as the client and facilitator–group relationship matures. While all this makes good horse sense and has a developmental feel to it, I must admit to being facilitative from the beginning and to being led by 'the field', then the above developmental plan. Whatever way we end up working, in the interests of transparency it pays as a general principle to make it known if you are seeking clarification, challenging or supporting what is currently manifesting. If we fail in this even our most facilitative of interventions will likely come over as mysterious and be open to misinterpretation.

Although I have many reservations about Heron's (1989) model, I find it useful as a springboard to more subtle considerations. I also find his checklist of what happens when interventions fail a useful self-monitoring tool and a sobering read. For instance, the *perverted interventions* he identifies should never enter a facilitator's pallet:

- **Perverted prescription** – the deliberate use of force or threat or compulsion to force a person to act against their own needs and interests (*facilitator as saboteur*)

- **Perverted information** – the deliberate use of misrepresentation and lies or slander to harm another (*facilitator as politician*)

- **Perverted confrontation** – deliberate and punitive psychological attack on a person intended to wound and incapacitate them emotionally (*facilitator as torturer*)

- *Perverted catharsis* – deliberately producing cathartic collapse and disintegration through subjecting a person to extreme mental and physical stress with a view to inducing suggestibility (*facilitator as brainwasher*)

- *Perverted catalysis* – deliberate and malicious seduction which leads a person into his or her own undoing by eliciting self-indulgent and self-destructive tendencies (*facilitator as seducer*)

- *Perverted support* – affirming, supporting or encouraging weak, distorted and corrupted behaviour in a person (*facilitator as destroyer*).

Perverted interventions are common to interrogation designed to destabilise or brainwash and represent the darkest recess of the facilitative shadow. Given that perverted interventions are the antithesis of facilitative health, the so-called *degenerative interventions* cited below are less extreme and stem more from a lack of awareness, personal neediness or absence of facilitative skill:

- *Prescriptive Degeneration* – *Benevolent takeover*: creating dependency by giving loads of advice to an insecure client who really needs encouragement to self-support;
  Moralistic oppression: imposing 'shoulds', 'oughts' and 'musts' on a client who may appreciate your reasoning but nevertheless feels impelled to reject the way you say (*facilitator as 'controller'*).

- *Informative Degeneration* – *Seductive over-teach*: a facilitator provides excessive information to the degree a client is seduced into passivity and diverted from self-directed learning;
  Oppressive over-teach: a facilitator goes on for far too long, gives out too much information and is insensitive to their client's need to contribute (*facilitator as 'specialist'*).

- *Confronting Degeneration* – *Sledgehammer*: the facilitator raises issues aggressively displacing his or her anxiety into a punitive attack rather than illuminating a non-helpful attitude or behaviour;
  Smiling demolition: a facilitator says hurtful things in a friendly or jocular way which is indirect and confusing (*facilitator as 'smiler with a knife'*).

- *Cathartic Degeneration* – *Encouraging dramatisation*: the facilitator mistakenly supports dramatisation rather than catharsis so encouraging the client to 'act out', in destructive ways, the drama which created the original hurt, thus re-enacting rather than releasing it;
  Nut cracking: a facilitator goes too deep too soon taking the client's defences by storm and surfacing deeply buried distress the client is not yet able to control, thus causing them to defend more intensely (*facilitator as 'dramatist'*).

- *Catalytic Degeneration* – *Implicit takeover*: a facilitator obsessively imposes meaning and order onto a client's experience in a way which serves their own rather than the client's needs;

Scraping the bowl: the facilitator with discreet compulsion goes far beyond the point of 'productive enabling' causing a client to unearth ever more exhaustive detail about their issues (*facilitator as 'ferret'*).

- **Supportive Degeneration** – *Moral patronage*: a facilitator handles the anxiety associated with caring and sharing by climbing into the pulpit to congratulate the client on their self-improvement, in consequence causing them to feel subtly put down;
  Qualified support: the facilitator gives support but at the same time discreetly reminds the client of their inadequacy and neediness (*facilitator as 'compulsive nurturer'*).

So which of the above degenerations are you most likely to enact on your worst, most debilitated day? That is to say, what shadowy influences do you hold in check?

You might find it instructive to return to the above lists of perverted and degenerative interventions after a particular facilitative event goes askew for you: you might find a piece of your shadow leaking through! But enough of you – how might this model be used to help build peer-learning-cum-peer-supervising communities?

Knowledge and skill in the application of Six Category Intervention Analysis has been transmitted to organisations through the medium of Co-Counselling (Heron 1998), a system of peer support designed to educate to interpersonal skill and emotional competence. This approach attempts to empower individuals through the release of creativity, assertion, love, self-acceptance and self-valuing, which it sees as buried under the emotional hurts people acquire over the years. So much for the rationale. As to how Co-counselling pans out in practice, at its simplest it is practised in pairs with one person working (the client) and one facilitating (the counsellor); they then reverse roles. The client stipulates 'the contract' they will work to, which generally takes one of the following forms:

- *Free attention*: where the counsellor gives sustained, supportive attention while the client manages their own working process – primarily a witnessing approach

- *Normal*: where a counsellor, alert to what the client misses, makes interventions that facilitate a client's contact with their issue – a supportive approach encouraging self-direction

- *Intensive*: the counsellor makes as many interventions as necessary to enable the client to deepen and sustain their process, ensures that the client holds direction, interrupts patterns and liberates discharge by drawing attention to areas being avoided – a more directive and challenging approach.

At all times, the individual in the client position has power to change the direction of their session and freedom to accept or disregard interventions made by 'the counsellor'. The counsellor is contracted to give supportive attention to the client at all times and to intervene in accordance with the client-generated contract. Sometimes in over-structured climates highly resistive to a Gestalt approach, I train participants through a series of workshops to Six Category Intervention Analysis and the rudiments of co-counselling, then encourage individuals to form on-going partnerships for the purposes of practising peer support.

So how does all this strike you as a model of peer-coaching? A self-sustaining approach where those you coach in an organisation can come together between your one-to-one sessions? What if you train those you coach to something approaching this model, then they train others: what might the effect be eventually upon the work community? Get the idea?

After all this discussion of 'intentionality' in service of facilitation, one could easily forget the role of timing, readiness and silence; so it's time to correct the balance. Angus Mcleod, in his review of coaching, notes the prime instruments of silence, questions and challenge – of which he holds silence to be the most effective (Mcleod 2003). He makes the point that no matter what a facilitator or coach says or does, however big the discovery or psychological breakthrough they enable, whatever they say is largely insignificant, for the real work takes place within the client's own thinking and feeling where the facilitator is little more than a silent witness. In this respect, the skill and value you portray rests not so much in the 'content' of your interventions as in their 'context', in your timing, presence and your art of knowing when to step aside to honour your client's process.

Reflections

* Examine this facilitative scale which I have adapted (after Heron) below:

+ 10   9   8   7   6   5   4   3   2   1   0 -
Informative   (Informing and attributing meaning)   Non-Informative

+ 10   9   8   7   6   5   4   3   2   1   0 -
Prescriptive   (Raising awareness to the task and objectives)   Non-Prescriptive

+ 10   9   8   7   6   5   4   3   2   1   0 -
Confronting   (Challenging hidden agendas and motives)   Non-Confronting

+ 10   9   8   7   6   5   4   3   2   1   0 -
Cathartic   (Addressing feelings and dealing with emotional energy)   Non-Cathartic

+ 10   9   8   7   6   5   4   3   2   1   0 -
Catalytic   (Raising awareness to values, boundaries and rules)   Non-Catalytic

+ 10   9   8   7   6   5   4   3   2   1   0 -
Supporting   (Sharing and meeting and expressing our true self)   Non-Supporting

▶

Consider what form your coaching-cum-facilitation takes and see if you can profile it on this scale. Where are you least active and most active as a coach? *(I'm aware that when coaching I'm fairly non-informative (4), non-prescriptive (3), non-confronting (4) and non-cathartic (2), but somewhat more catalytic (8) and supportive (6). I perceive this facilitative profile as consistent with my 'emergent' coaching style, i.e.*

+ 10   9   8   7   6   5   **4**   3   2   1   0 -
Informative   (Informing and attributing meaning)   Non-Informative

+ 10   9   8   7   6   5   4   **3**   2   1   0 -
Prescriptive   (Raising awareness to the task and objectives)   Non-Prescriptive

+ 10   9   8   7   6   5   **4**   3   2   1   0 -
Confronting   (Challenging hidden agendas and motives)   Non-Confronting

+ 10   9   8   7   6   5   4   3   **2**   1   0 -
Cathartic   (Addressing feelings and dealing with emotional energy)   Non-Cathartic

+ 10   9   **8**   7   6   5   4   3   2   1   0 -
Catalytic   (Raising awareness to values, boundaries and rules)   Non-Catalytic

+ 10   9   8   7   **6**   5   4   3   2   1   0 -
Supporting   (Sharing and meeting and expressing our true self)   Non-Supporting

In large groups, conversely – see below – I find myself more informative (6) prescriptive (5) confronting (8) and a little more cathartic (4). I guess the larger the group, the more I feel required to provide structure, police the rules, to invest and mould group energy, i.e.

+ 10   9   8   7   **6**   5   4   3   2   1   0 -
Informative   (Informing and attributing meaning)   Non-Informative

+ 10   9   8   7   6   **5**   4   3   2   1   0 -
Prescriptive   (Raising awareness to the task and objectives)   Non-Prescriptive

+ 10   9   **8**   7   6   5   4   3   2   1   0 -
Confronting   (Challenging hidden agendas and motives)   Non-Confronting

+ 10   9   8   7   6   5   **4**   3   2   1   0 -
Cathartic   (Addressing feelings and dealing with emotional energy)   Non-Cathartic

+ 10   9   **8**   7   6   5   4   3   2   1   0 -
Catalytic   (Raising awareness to values, boundaries and rules)   Non-Catalytic

+ 10   9   8   7   **6**   5   4   3   2   1   0 -
Supporting   (Sharing and meeting and expressing our true self)   Non-Supporting

Interestingly, when I consider the difference between my facilitative profile as a psychotherapist and as a coach, I find that in the therapist role I'm much more attentive to cathartic (8) and supportive (8) interventions than when I'm in the coaching role, possibly due to the emotional exploration this involves. Coaching conversely draws more informative and catalytic interventions from me.)

* In terms of the informal roles you might inadvertently pour yourself into as a facilitator, which, if any, resonate with or may otherwise inform your own facilitative shadow – all you hold in-check to be the practitioner you are? Dare you pull one of the following out of the hat?

Saboteur; politician; torturer; brainwasher; seducer; destroyer; controller'; specialist; smiler with a knife; dramatist; ferret; compulsively nurturer' – but maybe none of these fit because you don't have a shadow! Careful, my bullshit detector is starting to spin around again!

Under which category would you choose to place 'silence' as an intervention? *(I think I regard silence as a pause in a group's energetic breathing in and breathing out, a natural energetic lull between events, though it can also motivated by hostility or exhaustion. I often ask participants what are they 'feeling' or how they are 'using silence' if it persists. This said, as an intervention I have kept silent to break unproductive verbiage or word games, to keep a group with its current unease or yet challenge participants to take the initiative themselves.)*

3.8 The Facilitator as Social Researcher –
Facilitation as Co-operative Inquiry

In embryonic groups in an attempt to move individuals from a fixation with *what they can get* towards a more open altruistic culture focused on *what they can give*, I have found it helpful first to review, then actively to explore in practice, the following principles derived from Therapeutic Community practice:

- Work to flatten the authority pyramid and open up to examination any authoritarian or hierarchical responses when these occur

- Risk sharing thoughts and feelings so as to raise awareness to the hidden agenda of social interaction

- Engage in on-going analysis of the social events that unfold and explore the effect of these on yourself and others

- Test the philosophy that problems are mostly in relation to others and capable of resolution through face-to-face discussion

- Put to examination all roles and behaviours with a view to illuminating an understanding of the community's progress to date.

These principles shared at the start of a workshop can help generate a culture of social inquiry which simultaneously helps deconstruct fledgling dependency and challenge the 'power-dynamics' inherent to conventional tutorage. While in other settings individuals might be praised for conforming, I expect them to explore and chew thoroughly before they swallow what's on offer. I might invite individuals to consider their usual 'beginning patterns' and catch any stereotypical reactions they slide towards. We may begin to explore how it feels to enter this new group, scrutinise the expectations we brought with us or examine what takes our awareness at this time. No round of names or 'creeping death' as someone once called it, no introductions: we just unfold as the field dictates, shorn of its usual social artifice. Beginning in this way I find helps to 'set the scene' and to lay down concerns that might otherwise appear as resistances; it also provides opportunity for participants to test me and to assess my facilitative bias while exploring first-hand the interpersonal territory on offer. In short, it stimulates group ownership and a deeper level of contracting while providing criteria against which I, as facilitator, might be held accountable to the group.

As for the exploratory self-questioning Gestalt facilitators such as I carry into their work, these centre primarily on the authentic contact they and others portray:

Am I being true to myself and my beliefs?

Am I saying 'we' when I really mean 'I'?

Am I saying where I stand on an issue and owning my true position?

Am I talking about the past when a real live issue is with us in the present?

Am I 'talking about' and using abstractions rather than sharing my truth?

Am I saying 'No' when I mean 'No' or avoiding a more authentic connection?

Am I lecturing to others about 'what ought to be' rather than dealing with what is?

Am I sending mixed messages and disguising my irritations with a smile on my face?

Am I stopping when I am finished talking or going on to impress or to control others?

Am I pretending to look for information when what I really want is to make a statement?

Am I broadcasting to the group rather than talking directly to those I really want to reach?

Am I really seeing and hearing what's happening or is my mind thinking about the future or past or trying to imagine what someone else is thinking?

Keeping ourselves in good contact and authentically grounded is our primary duty – against which all else pales into insignificance. Against this cultural backdrop, our facilitative inquiry unfolds.

Cycles of inquiry are a constant in life. The life of a single cycle may be over in minutes or extend over an hour, while other cycles take a lifetime to complete. Inquiry cycles, the bedrock of action research (Lewin 1946) also permeate experiential learning (Kolb and Fry 1975; Fry and Kolb 1979; Heron 1981 and 1989) and have informed this text, both via the Gestalt 'contact–withdrawal cycle' and within the 'orientation-to-resolution cycle – which is unpacked further below to capture the intrinsic social inquiry this relational model enshrines:

1) **Orientating and Clarifying** – *a phase of Orientation where participants attune to their intuition and gauge their trust and emotional commitment to forming a relationship* – Here a coach and client, or facilitator and group, begin to orientate to each other's world view and values, build trust and assess if they have enough common ground to form a workable relationship and supportive bond – or if this feels impossible, cease their dealings with each other. (*Seeking assistance on the basis of a 'felt need', but one poorly understood, is often what brings our clients to us in the first place; it is the first step to taking a constructive step towards personal growth. The phase of 'Orientation' is essential to full participation later in the process.*)

2) **Identifying and Contracting** – *a phase of Identification where participants identify the way ahead and form a mutually satisfactory contract* – Here participants continue to pool interests with a view to identifying a mutually satisfying direction for exploration; hypotheses are raised at this stage for later evaluation and decisions may be made regarding how records will be kept to capture the outcomes of learning or inquiry. (*While defining how to proceed we simultaneously require the full integration of our client's 'stream of life experiences' within the process, for only when a client feels permitted to express what they truly think and feel will we be able to get to a deeper level of issue identification and pool together the inner potential necessary for collaborative inquiry and relational integrity.*)

3) **Exploring and Engaging** – *a phase of Exploration where participants attune to their senses to collect evidence and to their feelings to determine what is happening and what their experience means to them* – Here individuals begin to learn experientially through practical application as they apply themselves, and their earlier-envisioned methods and plans of the above identification phase, to a living engagement;

confronted by reality as they engage in mutual encounter, individuals in the light of experience may now put on hold their earlier judgements and hypotheses as they revise their opinion in the light of active engagement. (*When a client has bonded with a coach or consultant and can recognise and begin to understand the interpersonal relationships involved, a full use of the services available can then take place. Successfully orientated and with a co-created agenda before them, clients can now become more self-directing and realistic about the skills and services on offer, as fears of exploitation give way to co-exploration of the presenting issues.*)

4) **Resolving and Debriefing** – *a phase of Resolution where participants intuitively evaluate what they have experienced together, reflect on what has been learnt and discovered and intellectually structure, communicate and put into models and strategies all that has been raised to awareness* – Here participants debrief and reflect upon the insight they have generated, surface wisdom and knowledge born from earlier encounters, explore how their own experience resonates with others, review and debrief on their prospective findings, reject unsubstantiated hypotheses and consider future themes for investigation. (*Logically, the phase of resolution occurs when the presenting problem is resolved and sufficient insight and skill has been imparted to the client or client-system for self-support should the original problem return. This stage of resolution implies the gradual freeing from identification with the coach or consultant and the strengthening of the ability of a client to stand more or less alone. For this to happen, clients need help to move beyond psychological parenting, help in co-creating a need-fulfilling relationship and an ability to recognise and respond to developmental cues – however trivial – so as to expand their skill base to meet future challenges.*)

The above phases catch something of the process of co-operative inquiry inherent in Gestalt's client–facilitator relationship. Being alert to the position of a client or team within their own learning cycle helps a facilitator speculate where we might most productively journey to next. In this context, 'cycles' provide structure and opportunity and help us map routes from confusion to clarity. But beware: your cycles need to travel at sufficient depth to do justice to the complexity of what is experienced.

A facilitator, in a community inquiry, needs to differentiate between what is obvious and what a group keeps tacit, disowned and unrecognised, with a view to integrating these into conscious awareness. Facilitative acts, in this regard, are directed towards re-educating and developing people through the mending of splits in awareness and function; if emotive and shadowy themes are allowed to run and to infuse the undertone of a group, in my experience they eventually break out to disrupt even the best-laid group agendas. Change is not difficult for those who lack resistance and have nothing to lose, so travel lightly as a facilitator and be prepared to surrender to the rhythms of change and to be changed in return.

Summary

In this chapter, we have looked at many things. So many facets have been illuminated as to confuse us, a process which parallels the complexity and diverse nature of the socio-cultural level we are examining. At root, Gestalt confronts a good deal of our existence within the social domain. It advises us to 'lose our heads and come to our senses'. Accept and acknowledge society by all means, 'give unto Caesar the things which are Caesar's', but also strive to be the most natural and best version of yourself.

Many of our difficulties, Gestalt suggests, are due to misperception and a dependence upon second-hand knowledge. It cautions us to resist compliance, reminds us to state our needs clearly rather than suffering in silence and invites us to cultivate relationships which are alive to paradox, respectful of difference and true to self. As a facilitator in service of cultural change, I am ever reminded of the Chinese proverb:

> To get through the hardest journey we need take only one step at a time, but we must keep on stepping.

Reflections

* Zinker (1994/98) suggests the following principles support Gestalt's unique mode of exploration:

- Balanced relationships – acknowledge that human beings are both dependent and autonomous

- Nothing stands alone – see everything and everyone interrelating to everything and everyone else

- Me, you and we – aim to use interventions which are systemic and complimentary to the whole

- Complete what's incomplete – integrate disowned elements and complete incomplete patterns

- Here and now – base your interventions on process observation of what is actually happening

- Self-actualisation through self-regulation – support a client's balance and forward movement

- Holism – recognise that the whole influences all individual parts and is larger than their sum

- The importance of sharing power – observe and seek to understand current power dynamics

▶

- Developmental integrity – illuminate the simple beauty of each development and resolution

- Honour what is here now – accept your clients and appreciate their existing competences

- We are also a part of the whole – so track your own moods, desires, drives and conflicts

- Equality in experiential development – openly question yourself as well as your client

- There are exceptions to every rule – appreciate what is developmentally appropriate

- Change through awareness – support change founded on conscious and active choice

- The collective voice – attend to 'the unique voice' as well as 'the pattern of voices'

- Professional humility – respect the integrity of the person and the system before you

- Paradoxical change – the more you support 'what is', the more change will occur

- Process over content – how we express is more important than what is discussed

- Integration and aesthetic – encourage integral movement and graceful expression

- Learning through doing – encourage engagement and active experimentation

- Good form – support 'what is', 'what works' and 'what is good enough'

- Clear boundaries – work for good boundary definition and management.

So which of the above would you like to ferment or to strengthen further within your own work? *(Personally, I'd like to work further upon dovetailing my appreciation of 'me, you and we' to my facilitation, as I catch times when I can be overly abrupt with an individual in the interests of managing group boundaries or dismiss individual issues in favour of community concerns. I guess I'm less skilled in appreciating the 'we-ness' of groups and my position as 'part of the field' rather than as 'facilitator' – as I may take a little too much responsibility for what unfolds.)*

* In relation to the following action-inquiry phases:

Doing and Experiencing	*Discriminating and reflecting*
Attending to the field	Attending to specifics
Engaging with experience	Meditating upon experience
Flowing with the field	Creating models from experience
Expressing the self in motion	Reflecting on the self as witness
Relating to others	Relating to past experience

Where are you most comfortable – personally and professionally? *(Within group settings I tend to be better at energising and encouraging engagement than at slowing things down and promoting contemplation. This hypothesis is also supported when I refer back to the Gestalt cycle, where I see myself as good at raising attention to Sensation, Awareness, the Mobilisation of energy and Excitement and Action, but less proficient in furthering Contact and Withdrawal. Surprisingly, this reverses for me when I coach individuals. So why is this?)*

Reflections upon Chapter 3

You are appointed to explore and prepare the culture of a company approaching an impending merger. From your reading of this chapter how might you:

- Describe for the client your approach to organisational consultancy and locate your offering within the consulting traditions that inform you?

- Alert the client-system to the possible resistances it is likely to face with merger?

- Plan a facilitative event where you are required to prepare leaders for the challenges ahead and to alert them to positive and negative reactions to 'change'?

- Facilitate an inquiry into employee's expectations and needs for support at this time?

Later in the consultancy you are invited to help a group of senior managers to inquire into and reflect upon positive and negative aspects of the working culture they are co-creating, along with assessment of their own facilitation style:

- How might you set about facilitating a climate conducive to authentic communication within the subject group?

- What ground rules might you suggest to support your facilitative inquiry and the learning on offer?

- How might you enable participants to profile their own and each other's facilitation style?

As this consultancy progresses, you are asked to help seed the beginnings of a self-learning culture, one which is able to inquire into its current behaviours and, if need be, change in light of feedback:

- Which models of this chapter might you use to help frame your facilitation and its rationale?

- What style of facilitation might you employ and wish to seed in the managerial and leadership culture of this organisation?

I am conscious of the weave of the many roles that might inform a consultancy stance, namely the consultant as:

- A social researcher who is collecting and tabulating data

- An artist who is highly appreciative and expressive of the sensory world around them

- An educational agent who is aware of carrying an organisational responsibility

- A social psychologist who employs strategic thinking to solve the presenting problem

- A psychotherapist alert to symbolism and symbolic interaction

- A humanist who is interested in people and seeks to humanise systems

- An experiential teacher who encourages individuals to search out their own wisdom.

So:

- Which of the above role engagements do you portray?

- Which do you consider appropriate and un-appropriate to the client-systems you facilitate?

As our masks drop and our composure weakens and our vulnerability and human suffering is allowed to surface we glimpse below a deeper dignity beneath our social conditioning, plus an opportunity to truly respect each other as fellow beings.

Chapter four

Raising Awareness
to Emotional and Biographical
Influences

Facilitating 'air-time' and giving everyone a turn increases the emotional intelligence of groups. When people are accorded community space and realise they do not need to compete to be heard and will not be interrupted, they are freed to think faster, to be more expressive, creative, and to say less.

4.1   The Nature of Feelings – Emotions as Messengers

At the emotional and biographical level of engagement we explore the nature of our emotional world and the earlier patterns that drive us. We will look at positive and negative emotional states and how facilitators may chart and release disabling emotional blocks, while illuminating and addressing mental defence mechanisms in individuals and groups. In this chapter we also consider psychodrama and the effect of a facilitator's presence and mull over the emotional scripts that compel us. You will also be introduced to psychoanalytic and psychodynamic approaches to consulting which especially honour this strand of our reality.

Our emotions serve as energetic messengers, provide motivation and meaning, and dissolve the intellect. They are not products of reflection or contemplation, but are born of the moment; they do not accommodate distance, they are now. Deny feelings and you deny the energetic font of life, yet all too often we are taught to distance ourselves from our feelings. For instance we say we are 'uncomfortable' when angry; 'guilty' when we feel ashamed; 'respectful' when we feel loving; 'bored' when we feel rejected. In an effort to un-block complacency and to help my clients travel deeper into the core of their being, I will ask the following:

- Are you aware of any feelings you are blocking off or denying right now?

- Which feelings are you most often likely to shield from others?

- If these feelings were released what do you imagine might happen?

- Are you aware of any indirect or disguised ways that your feelings leak out to influence you?

- How might you enrich your emotional expression and invigorate your life?

In this way I treat emotions as energies to be used – not symptoms to be cured. Though emotions give meaning to events, energetically cement us to our experiences and socially and psychologically bond us to others, Gestalt practitioners don't take them so seriously as to identify with the messenger rather than the message:

> A student came to his teacher:
>
> 'Master, I have an ungovernable temper. How can I cure it?'
>
> 'Let me see it' said the Master.
>
> 'It arises unexpectedly' said the student.
>
> 'Then', concluded the Master, 'as you were not born with it, and your parents did not give it to you, it is not your own true nature. For if it were, you could show it to me anytime.'
>
> (Zen koan)

It is suggested in this chapter that emotions are expressed in two ways: externally in our reaction to environmental changes (to what is 'figure' for us at the time);

internally via the more permanent structure of 'character' (informed by the 'ground' of historically laid patterns of the biographical field in which we are embedded). This latter influence relating to 'prevailing patterns' and the 'presenting past' will be a central focus in our discussion of transference.

Though our emotional expression continues to develop and evolve, our enduring expressions and interpretations of 'feeling' owe much to the earliest years of life. As for the 'meanings' we accord our emotions, these have been suggested to emanate from an internal decision-making process that weighs up the congruency or incongruency of our current goals – which Brownell (2004) reminds us broadly relates to the Gestalt concepts of 'figure' – and a secondary process which concerns our appreciation of the blame, credit, coping potential and future consequences involved (Lazarus and Lazarus 1994) – the 'ground'. In this way our emotional life is seen as enacting a dialogue between the emergent 'present' and an informing and context-shaping 'past'.

As for how emotions emerge, Lewis (1992) suggests that by the first year of life all our primary emotions of joy, fear, sadness, surprise and disgust have emerged, but it is not until the middle of our second year that secondary emotions of embarrassment, empathy and envy are expressed, or that pride, shame or guilt emerge in our evaluations of the world. As to why emotional development is delayed:

> Most children below eighteen months, for instance, cannot recognize themselves in a mirror, an ability that signals self-identification and a cognitive-developmental capacity allowing a person to think of him or herself independent from an immediate environmental context (Keenan, Wheeler, Ewers, 2003). This ability is the basis for self-conscious emotions, and it can be traced to development of capacity, growth in the right, pre-frontal cortex, which is increasingly seen as the executive, the artist integrating life experience.
>
> (Brownell 2004, p.4)

Whether primary or secondary emotions figure in the groups you meet might in part depend on the 'emotional maturity' of your group – but possibly more importantly upon the quality of your own facilitative parenting! So what sort of symbolic parent are you?

From a Gestalt perspective, emotions are seen to move us from sensation to awareness and onwards into action. With this in mind we concentrate on loosening the blocks of the 'body–mind' so that an individual might better appreciate the nature and messages their emotional relay. Catharsis and control are lesser concerns here than experimentation and experiential learning:

> Emotion, considered as the organism's direct evaluative experience of the organism/environment field, is not mediated by thoughts and verbal judgements, but is immediate. As such, it is a crucial regulator of action, for it not only furnishes the basis of awareness of what is important but

it also energizes appropriate action, or, if this is not at once available, it energizes and directs the search for it.

(Perls et al. 1994, p.128)

John Enright (1980) adds another ingredient to the emotional equation: comparison. He notes that we are constantly comparing our present experiences to more pleasant or less pleasant experiences of our past – transference, plus other people's more or less pleasant experiences and to our fantasies of the experience we feel we deserve – 'projection'. We will examine 'transference' and 'projection' in greater detail later. Enright goes so far as to observe that:

the quality of experience in life depends less on what happens to you, than on what you compare it with. I often comment to clients… that if they want to feel consistently bad, just make sure they regularly compare 'what is' with something better; if they want to feel good, compare 'what is' with something worse.

(Enright 1980 quoted in Philippson 2002)

Having illuminated a little of what informs an emotional state, what can we do with this information? One thing I try *not* to do with 'feelings' is to 'judge' or 'categorise' them. Philippson (2002) notes that in contrast to the discharge model of Freud (Freud and Breuer 1895/2000), bioenergetics and co-counselling, Gestalt avoids evaluating some emotions as 'positive' and others as 'negative' in favour of exploring what they 'mean' and their relation to certain kinds of contact and action:

Joy: My response to my environmental contact is of attraction, wanting to deepen contact. My energy rises and flows to the boundary and out to meet the environment.

Sadness: Once again, my wish is to make contact with a part of the environment that attracts me, but here contact is not possible. The person I love has died, the opportunity is not available. My energy rises, flows to the boundary and then outward in expression of grief or sadness; inward in communing with the memory or fantasy of the denied contact. Physiologically, unusable adrenalin gets released in my tears.

Fear: Now the form of contact that is available to me is (or appears) dangerous to me. I energise, but that energy is to be used in my escape from the dangerous contact possibility.

Anger: Again, the form of contact is one I don't like, but I perceive the situation as different to the one where my primary emotional response is fear. Either I have a sense of commitment to the environment: a person I want to keep contact with, a mountain I want to climb; or I am in a position where I assess that I can neither run nor hide, so I need to find a resolution with the dangerous environment. In a way, my energy moves in a similar way to that of joy, outward to the environment and beyond; but the aim is in some sense to overpower the energy of the other and thus to neutralise the disliked contact: 'I will not let you do that even if you want to'.

This can be simplified (and slightly falsified) by saying:

Joy moves toward an attractive environment.

Sadness moves away from an attractive environment.

Anger moves toward an unattractive environment.

Fear moves away from an unattractive environment.

(Philippson 2002)

As facilitators, it might be useful for us to survey the nature of the more robust and common emotions that bombard us and to reflect on the wider meaning and inherent messages feelings convey. Reflecting upon the emotions of joy, fear, sadness, anger, embarrassment, shame and guilt, the more common emotional currency of life and indeed facilitation, I have come to regard their messages over the years in the following ways:

* *Joy* implies a celebration and actualisation of self, a big 'yes' to life. It involves a feeling of being at one, experiencing 'my' as a natural part of the universe and sensing my harmony with everything else. Indian mystics tell us there is only one reason why we aren't experiencing joyful bliss right now: it's because we're thinking or focussing upon something we don't have! Take away the wanting and you liberate bliss, for we have everything we need to experience 'joy' right here and right now! Whether we buy this idea or not, it nevertheless provides rich food for thought. Watch babies and young animals and they appear to brim over with joy. At root joy is not '*for anything*' – it is rather '*for the hell of it*', for when you start to analyse it you lose it! If you are interested in all that surrounds you, accepting and loving of all that is – you are naturally joyful. For instance Buddhists teach that the first step towards enlightenment and joy is to free ourselves from desire, desire for things to be different, for desire gets in the way of us living our life as it is unfolding – now. A mind that creates its reality around memories, fears and grief, as these relate to unfulfilled and fulfilled desires, is seen as never free enough to experience joy. But knowing that the mind is the creator of our joys and sorrows is not enough – for we have also to let go of this thought and all other intellectualisations to experience joy! Beyond images and concepts, in the total cessation of desire, joy is suggested to be our natural state. Exploring joy with my clients, I've been known to ask:

- 'What do you have to let go of to let joy in?'

- 'What might you do to establish joy as a constant in your life?'

- 'What words raise a sense of joy within you?'

112

* *Fear*, in contrast to 'joy', presents a resounding 'no'. It emerges when we step beyond our supports to meet with 'unwanted' excitement. Emotionally the anxiety-laden message fear brings is crystal clear, we have spread ourselves too thin and we have arrived at a point where we need more support. Fear is a subjective energy that rests in our expectations; in the space before a 'happening'; in a limbo zone where the worst is expected but yet to come. Fear is all the more fearful because of this ghost-like quality. Threats to our social identity and bodily survival stimulate fear. Fear is also a primary cause of heart attacks; and when is the commonest time for heat-attacks? Why, 9 am on Monday morning! So what does this tell us about the territory that 'fear' and its accompanying stress occupy? Some people get accustomed to 'fearful anxiety' as a constant in life and become quite upset when it isn't there to motivate them. Fear gives them a purpose, something to avoid, to fight or to plan against. In this way they become addicted to and dependent upon their fears. After all, doesn't an enemy 'on the outside' allow us a temporary escape from the less addressable 'enemy within'? And what is the nature of this inner enemy, our inability to detach ourselves from the part of us that fears? Jeffers (1991) makes the following points: fear will never go away as long as you continue to grow *(fear is a natural consequence of facing change);* the only way to get rid of fear about doing something is to go out and do it *(you cannot go round fear – only through it);* the only way to feel better about yourself is to do what you are afraid of *(face the fear);* not only am I going to experience fear whenever I am on unfamiliar territory but so is everyone else *(essentially, fear is part of the human condition);* and pushing through fear is less frightening than living with the underlying fear that comes from a feeling of helplessness *(working through fear is better than giving in to it).* Personally, I have discovered that my fears hover between *'where I am now'* and *'where I want to be';* they are projections of a fearful future I create to fill the gap between now and an imagined fearful future. They can also come in the form of secondary shock when I ruminate upon *'what might have been'!* In this context they are something I project into a 'fictional future' or upon an 'illusory past'. In this context, fear appears to be associated with imagined and emotionalised 'what ifs', for when I am engaged with a real crisis I am oblivious to fear as I have no time to indulge in or to haunt myself with 'imaginary fearfulness'. When I catch fear stealing into the moment, I attend to my senses, concentrate on my breathing, attune more mindfully to what I am seeing and hearing physically. Speaking about my fears dilutes them further. Attuning to my sensations and the sensory world also seems to support and to ground me. So positioned, I listen very carefully to fear's message. Sometimes it says 'Stop!' At other times it says 'Stay aware', 'Proceed cautiously' or 'Stay within your support systems'. Fear doesn't prevent me from progressing – it rather alerts me to my need for more support. When examining fear I sometimes ask:

- 'Are you ever haunted by internal fears of losing self-control or feeling powerless?'

113

- 'Are you haunted by social fears of offending others, being criticised and rejected?'

- 'How might you support yourself during more fearful times?'

* **Sadness** involves a profound loss of energy and interest in what surrounds us, it indicates a need for rest and reintegration, and calls us to redirect our energies and to reorientate to our true purpose. When we meet with depression it is often because we are deeply tired in our inner-most core, often as a result of doing too much – mentally, physically, emotionally, imaginatively – for far too long. Sometimes a change of environment or new emotional alignment helps us to refocus and energise. Admitting we are sad and depressed, resting and listening to the message of sadness while realising something fundamental needs to shift puts us well on the way to resolving it. Developmentally, Kleinian analysts (Hinshelwood 1989) suggest that the depressive position evolves in infancy with the realisation that '*good*' and '*bad*' are aspects of the same thing. The theory goes something like this. The breast is good when it feeds you, but bad when it is withdrawn. In this context, the good mother we depend on, love and need is recognised as the very same one we experience as being bad – and this shakes our infant world. Realising that they can love and hate the same object, in this case the mother, the infant attributes their mother's change from good to bad to themselves – and in consequence experiences guilt and despair at their own apparent destruction of the loved object. This latter state is suggested to be a description of the '*depressive position*'. In later life, this self-blaming attitude and apportion of inappropriate responsibility to the self may persist, with the consequence that depression and sadness becomes a characteristic of life and living. In groups, some people handle 'good' and 'bad' by scape-goating – attributing badness to others, then punishing these 'elected others' rather than themselves. Obviously a great deal of idealisation and fantasy – not to mention denial is necessary to maintain this *split*. Paradoxically, it sometimes becomes so exhausting to maintain this defensive split that those afflicted are brought back with a bump to – depression, the very thing they were originally fighting to deny in the first place. I notice I get depressed when I feel *that time is running out*, when I believe there is *too much to do* and that *I lack the skills and energy to achieve* whatever I am placing before me. I feel my depression lessen when I cease to criticise myself, when I accept the curriculum life has currently set me and when I realise that my experience of the journey, with all its bumps and hardships, is much more important than where I am trying so very hard to arrive. When working with sad or depressed clients, I sometimes ask the questions:

- 'If your sadness had a voice what might it say?'

- 'If depression were an alarm clock – who or what would it be attempting to awake?'

- 'If your sadness served a positive purpose – what might this be?'

* **Anger** is an emotional statement we select to express hurt, to protect our boundaries and to defend what we value – but can become destructive if driven by fear. Personally, I have learnt to love and to respect my anger. When it 'comes calling', I know an emotional part is standing alongside to support me; it empowers me. But I have found that anger runs in parallel with self-importance: it is a symptom of our becoming over-identified with ourselves or over-concerned with our identity, ego and the actions of others. So how does anger actually arise? First we exaggerate something's faults, ferment our antagonism and generate hostile feelings and direct these energies towards it, perceive it as threatening and harmful, then seek to harm the fearful entity we have created before it can harm us. And when all these are in place, eureka, we create anger in our lives. But anger is not all negative, for as a positive force it alerts us to our boundaries and is seen in Gestalt as an enabler. To dis-identify with the object of your anger, try diluting your fixation upon the target of your anger, practice distancing yourself and contemplate the wider message that anger brings. Personally, I find that my own anger says *'listen to me'*, *'see me'*, *'hear and attend to me'*. When I listen to and value myself, its energy dissipates and goes away. My anger's message to others is often *'respect my boundaries and tolerate my differences'*. When I am tired it says forcibly *'I have nothing more to give'*. Everything my anger says to others applies just as readily to myself. It is a symptom that I am expecting and demanding far too much of myself. When anger arises in those I facilitate I occasionally ask:

- 'Am I threatening you in any way?'

- 'What criteria are you using to feel threatened and angry right now?'

- 'What message does your anger want to communicate to me and the group?'

* **Embarrassment** to me represents acute self-consciousness, one that arises when I push far beyond my usual boundaries; it is a symptom for me that I am on an edge of personal learning and feeling socially exposed. When it arises in relation to a past memory, it is often a sign of the socially generated *me* feeling uncomfortable with actions of the more personalised *I*, for example: 'How could *I* have behaved in such a way as to let myself down, how remiss of *Me*'. Here we tread a path very close to shame. In this sense, embarrassment is symptomatic of a gap emerging between our *'ideal self'* and our currently *'known self'*, the self which we strive to become and the one we actually experience ourselves to be. From this perspective, embarrassment instructs us to come back down to earth, to give up our pretensions and to accept the whole of ourselves – vulnerabilities and all. It seems to suggest that, like Icarus, we have flown too near the sun and must now fall to earth. Embarrassment warns us that we are in danger of over-inflating our self-importance and are in danger of taking ourselves far too seriously. When

working with clients who are experiencing embarrassment, I often invite them to consider:

- 'When and where did you first learn to feel embarrassed?'
- 'What is your assessment of yourself at this time?'
- 'How do you think I see you?'

*** Empathy** – the ability to imaginatively project yourself into the position of others and daring to see the world through unfamiliar eyes – demonstrates an active identification with 'mankind as my kind'. Empathy has been defined as the attempt by one person to comprehend in a non-judgmental fashion the positive and negative emotional experiences of another. It requires us to project ourselves into another's shoes and to appreciate our essential oneness with others; it demonstrates an understanding that the suffering of another person is something to be alleviated. Without empathy relationships lose their purpose and meaning. Indeed, relationships which are without empathy have a tendency to be manipulative and self-gratifying. Venerate some people and make them much more important than others and you limit your empathy. Confined in this way, empathy ceases to be unconditional, respectful and loving, and becomes merely political. Compassion for yourself is a pre-requisite of true empathy. In equanimity, beings are equally precious, and territorial and boundary conflicts are overcome. The core principle we need to embody as a facilitator or coach, more than any other, if we are to walk with empathy is the notion: '*I am of mankind and the world's kind*'. In recognising that we are part of a larger community and have more in common than out of common with all we meet, we are more apt to meet ourselves, empathetically, in all that surrounds us. When exploring empathy with clients I sometimes perform emotional archaeology by asking:

- 'When in your life have you felt least empathetic towards others?'
- 'What conditions enhance your experience of empathy and help it to flow?'
- 'What conditions rob you of your empathy?'

*** Guilt** I consider to be less *a feeling* than *a political position*, a consequence of deflected anger and criticism being turned upon the self – it represents a situation in which we experience ourselves as estranged from our fellows. In this context we don't so much 'feel guilty' as accept 'guilt' as a social punishment. And how do associated feelings of self-rejection and shame come about? Fritz Perls (Perls et al. 1994) had an interesting take on guilt: he suggested that 'I should not have done it' should always be translated into 'You should not have done it', and that instead of allowing a client to say 'I feel so guilty that I didn't do this', we should encourage them to say instead 'I feel resentful that you didn't do this'. For guilt feelings he suggests are never genuine. Scratch the surface of guilt and you are likely to find a potent store of unexpressed anger. Shame and guilt – twin

116

rivets of our social chains! Take off the mask of the *me* and you find the *ego*; take off the mask of the ego and you find an *I*; take off the mask of the I and you find your *essence* – whatever you began with when your journey first began. Freeing the mask behind the mask undoes guilt. When examining 'guilt' with my clients I have been known to inquire:

- 'So is there anything I'm doing right now that might be causing you to feel guilty?'

- 'Below this remembrance of a sense of guilt, what other emotions lurk?'

- 'So what role does guilt serve for you?'

* **Shame** and guilt – entwined emotional souls of the social territory we inhabit. If we divide our thoughts from our feelings, our authentic and imagined selves from a socially contracted self, and put more attention and life into our social veneer than our true selves, when the mask slips – as masks always will – denuded, without our psychic clothes we naturally enough feel found-out and exposed. In this light, as a positive, shame alerts us to the approach of situations that provide little social support. In shame, our 'inner parent' rejects our 'inner child', that is to say our 'over-socialised-self' acts as judge and jury over our impulsive 'natural-self'. Because 'shame' is discomforting, we tend to repress it, but by pushing it out of mind we paradoxically empower it further, for hidden from awareness it festers unchecked and when it eventually breaks free from its camouflage it shocks us all the more. Shame is further exacerbated when we use it as a form of premature self-punishment, a sort of *doing to ourselves* before *others do it to us*. But unlike punishment – which can absolve us when we are seen to be atoning for our sins or paying back a debt back to society – shame lingers on and remains disproportionately humiliating and self-flagellating, for it evokes not only fears of rejection, punishment and isolation, but most of all a fear of social extinction and the withdrawal of love. What is more, not only do we feel rejected by those whose approval we court – we also reject ourselves. When addressing shame I will sometimes inquire:

- 'What thoughts and memories go through your mind when you are feeling shame?'

- 'How might you stay with shame, be fully informed by it but not be beaten down by it?'

- 'If you exaggerate this feeling – what happens next?'

The above approach to emotional phenomena is unashamedly Gestalt: it is here-and-now, exploratory, experiential, portrays genuine interest and curiosity in the phenomenon presented and tries to cast light on other aspects of the field in which a specific emotion is entrenched. It treats emotions as phenomena to be explored and understood – nothing more, nothing less.

4.2 Emotional Patterns in Personal and Community Life – Groups as Historical Entities

A contrasting approach to surfacing 'hidden emotions', one I feel worthy of examination as a counterpoint to Gestalt, is psychoanalysis, which conducts an investigation into the inferences, patterns, symbols and associations that relate to activities of mind. In order to glimpse 'the unconscious', analysts steal upon it, for non-rational processes are best seen in a slip or other un-intended act – the so called Freudian slip. In light of this, we can appreciate the reasons for the analytic couch, namely: to instil a relaxed, undefended ambiance; to allow the the analyst to remain out of direct vision, necessary if they are not to interfere with a client's unfolding processes; to produce a non-social, unstructured relationship which best invites 'projection' and 'transference'. Transference is a concept of primary importance to coaches and facilitators of groups and an apt descriptor of the blind spots we and our clients are subject to.

An individual's store of unconscious emotional learning and propensity to move towards old patterns of joy, sadness, anger or fear is often described within counselling literature as 'transference', which describes our proclivity to re-enact in the present emotional conflicts 'transferred in' from the past. At its simplest, transference describes an emotional misperception of one person for another, but this is further complicated as this originates outside our conscious awareness. In this context, enrolled as group facilitators we might find ourselves loved, hated, idealised or sexualised, depended upon or attacked, not because of 'who we are' but rather because of 'who we represent' from our client's past.

Though many authors use transference and projection interchangeably, I separate them out in this work in the following way:

> *Transference* = semi-conscious/unconscious emotional patterns of the past that are re-stimulated in the present, so that an individual is caused to re-live unresolved historical conflicts

> *Projection* = the disowning and separation of portions of one's self which are then projected outwards upon others and treated as if a part of them rather than a disallowed part of oneself

Simply, in 'transference' people re-live their history, while in 'projection' they imaginatively meet reflections of themselves and their imagination mirrored back to them. Though I accept that the above influences may shade into one another, especially at the border where emotional and projective phenomena overlap, in the interests of clarity I distinguish between them in this text. As for counter-transference – when a recipient of transference responds in keeping with how they are being enrolled – this to my mind stands nearer projection as it refers to the evocation of an 'imagined role'. I see this as a sort of reactive fantasy that is less attuned to the past than the current needs and desires of the individual possessed. We will return to counter-transference later in this chapter.

Freud (1936) first discovered transference when he observed that 'his patients' – male and female alike – kept falling in love with him. Indeed, mastering transference was a key skill he taught his clients. We shall see in this chapter how facilitators can be undone by transference, as well as how in many organisational settings 'followers' attach themselves to authoritative 'father figures', whom they then place beyond question – or have to kill-off to regain their power. In this way, transference may be seen – by turns – to be both a lubricant and a block to managerial and 'team' relationships.

To my mind there are also distinctive differences between male- and female-related transferences. For instance, while paternal transference may produce unquestioning obedience in power relationships, maternal transference I suspect elicits a replay of far deeper and primitive material. There is an emotional logic here. Historically, as our relationship to our mother was 'more' dependent, unconditional, survival-centred and regressive, thus female transference tends to strike deeper and at an earlier phase of development. The veneration and castigation of historical figures such as Elizabeth the First, Joan of Arc, Queen Victoria and more recently Margaret Thatcher springs to my mind here. While male transference often symbolises an externalised 'political' force, mother transferences are generally interwoven to our 'inner emotional life'. In this way maternal figures – and indeed female facilitators – I suggest, can re-stimulate much more intense love–hate relationships and unrealistic expectations than their male counterparts.

It is interesting to consider how differently various traditions view transference. Psychoanalytically orientated group facilitators and consultants (i.e. Skynner 1989; Harrison 1995) tend to view transference as relic behaviour and avoidance, something a person or group recreates in order to deny current emotional pain. In order to solicit and actively work with transference, analytic facilitators and consultants portray an opaque presence, restrain from dialogue and endeavour to reflect back everything a client projects upon them. Through this process they encourage their clients to imaginatively re-live – and hopefully to understand that their presenting emotional patterns originate with themselves and in the past, not in the facilitator. This surfacing, engaging, re-owning and learning from transference, as anyone who has experienced facilitation or consultancy in the Tavistock style will tell you, can be a long and drawn-out process, taking months and sometimes years to resolve.

Facilitators with more of a behavioural and cognitive edge (Pedler et al. 1997), although they rarely refer to transference by name, see this phenomenon as disordered reasoning and address it through re-education. From this route, transference is approached as a block to learning and clients are encouraged to transform themselves through right thinking and rational behaviour.

Gestalt and existential facilitators (Nevis 1996; Zinker 1998), conversely, attend to the here-and-now impact of transference and focus on how it shows itself in current relationships. A facilitator in this mode works collaboratively, exploring transference alongside their client within an on-going relationship with a view to raising awareness and understanding. Here transference is seen not so much as 'negative avoidance' but rather as a person's repeated attempts to bring to a successful conclusion earlier learning that was frustrated or left incomplete. In this context, transference is seen as an attempt to digest and assimilate unfinished 'emotional' business.

As to how transference develops in current relationships, Carl Rogers (1967) has suggested that transference feelings develop when a client perceives that another understands him or her far better than the client understand him- or herself. This has obvious parallels with parent–child dynamics and adds credence to the suggestion of transference's earliest of origins – the mother–baby bond. This attachment of transference feelings to infancy is further supported by systems theorists (Bowen 1978) who view it as a response to anxiety about undue closeness and/or separation from one's parent or family of origin. In this light, any facilitator who portrays themselves as all knowing, parental, authoritarian, over-empathetic

120

or guru-like is likely to court a regressive parent–child relationship, or yet a rebellious reaction against this, in clients and groups.

Most of us can remember first-hand experiences of transference, perhaps in a student–teacher relationship or then again on an occasion of a job interview when we felt suddenly child-like and met with feelings more akin to our schooldays. Remember, each and every relationship is subject to transference:

> People do not come empty-handed from their past. They have various means of manipulating their environments. But they tend to lack self-support – an essential quality for survival: their manipulations minimize their self-support; and these manipulations are endless. For example, people break promises, play stupid, forget, lie, and continually ask questions. These manipulative behaviours annoy, embarrass, and exploit others.
>
> (Brammer et al. 1989, p.204)

In the midst of transference individuals suffer what Brammer et al. (1989) describe as 'a being deficiency', a loss of contact and connection with their current self. Because of this, transference is the antithesis of adaptation. Since group facilitators and consultants must develop a close relationship with a client or group to generate mutual trust and acceptance, especially in consultations of the longer term, transference is a common companion of our professional lives.

Transference also plays its part in keeping 'organisational theory' stuck in the past. For example, Eric Trist (1981) and his colleagues at the Tavistock Institute many years ago demonstrated the value of regarding work-based communities as 'open socio-technical systems'; 'open' because they are concerned with receiving inputs from the environment and exporting products; 'socio-technical' because they need to control men and task relationships. Yet although such thinking has been commonplace for some thirty years, the time-honoured view of the organisation as a closed technical system, which need only pay lip service to the quality of its relationships and scant regard to its host community, remains transferentially rooted in the community psyche of the workplace. Simply, culture enshrines transference – as we can see in the case study below.

Organisational Transference – Institutionalised Emotional Blocks to Change

In the 1980s, the nursing profession became concerned with the attrition rate of its nurses and called in Price Waterhouse to conduct a survey to inquire into why so many nurses left the service. At this time nursing management was still by-and-large run on Florence Nightingale's 'military' lines, in an authoritarian way where medics were venerated and nurses – somewhat like handmaidens – served doctors and the medical cause. This divide was not unlike the old 'officers and

▶

men' mentality of the army and had a similar class dynamic, in that nurses were predominately working class and not university trained whereas doctors were predominately drawn from the university-educated middle class. There were few tensions between medics and nurses at this time for, as in the army, each knew their place and the ranking system made debate inappropriate and unnecessary. In this sense, the resulting transference positively supported the prevailing system and its norms.

Some years before Price Waterhouse came on the scene, in the late 1950s, in what has since become a classic piece of consultancy in the Tavistock tradition, Isabel Menzies Lyth (Menzies Lyth 1960) conducted an investigation into the low morale and dissatisfaction of nursing staff within the old Charring Cross Hospital. Though Menzies Lyth's work was seminal and much talked about by consultants and analysts, the psychoanalytic language of her report did not go down well in the client domain. The consultant had succeeded in illuminating excellent insights, the report was the toast of analytic consultancy circles, but the client-system by-and-large ignored the information. In medical terms, the operation was a success and the surgeon performed brilliantly – yet the patient died.

In the Menzies Lyth study we see exemplified all the negative features ascribed to a 'survival-centred' working climate: namely blind uniformity; the denial of individual differences; the detachment and denial of feelings; the reduction of anxiety by adherence to ritual and routine; checks and counter-checks; the pushing upwards of decision making; in sum, a total avoidance and denial of the need to adapt or change. Throughout her report Menzies Lyth describes the impact of transference, especially institutionalised transference, which served to eliminate the burden of decision making by the use of ritual and task-fixated performance. Simply, the hospital environment by-and-large acted as a total institution fuelled by a 'blame culture'. The anxiety surrounding decision making in a setting such as this was acute. In order to spare staff such anxiety, Menzies Lyth observed that the nursing service attempted to minimise the number and variety of decisions that must be made by imposition of ritual, which de-humanised the nurse while denuding her of personal and professional responsibility:

> For example, the student nurse is instructed to perform her task-list in a way reminiscent of performing a ritual. Precise instructions are given about the way each task must be performed, the order of the tasks, and the time for their performance, although such precise instructions are not objectively necessary, or even wholly desirable.

> If several efficient methods of performing a task exist, e.g. for bed-making or lifting a patient, one is selected and exclusively used. Much time and effort are expended in standardizing nursing procedures incases where there are a number of effective alternatives. Both teachers and practical-work supervisors impress on the student nurse from the

beginning of her training the importance of carrying out the 'ritual'. They reinforce this by fostering an attitude to work that regards every task as almost a matter of life or death, to be treated with appropriate seriousness. This applies even to those tasks that could be effectively performed by an unskilled lay person.

(Menzies Lyth 1960, pp.11–12)

Obviously, with the student nurse being infantilised and actively discouraged in this way from using her own discretion and professional initiative, or otherwise planning her work realistically in relation to the objective situation, she was induced to regress by the influence of systemically and institutionally induced transference. And the findings of Price Waterhouse some 30 years later when investigating why so many nurses left nursing? Well, similarly to Menzies Lyth, they found that the main reason nurses fled nursing was because they were unduly stressed, emotionally compromised and at root infantilised, and they felt uncared for.

And the intervention the nursing profession and government of the day implemented in response to this finding, what was this but to bring in Project 2000, a multi-million pound incentive aimed at producing graduate-level entrants to the profession. Graduate entry, they reasoned, would raise the profession's status and make a more attractive career path which would bring the necessary man- and woman-power in. And what was the effect of this upon the nursing service and within the health service in the long term? It divided the nursing service between those trained in the old way and those with newly acquired graduate status; challenged the traditional power base of the profession's relationship with the medical profession; gave nursing a far greater managerial profile and re-focused the national preparation of nurses upon theory rather than practice, with the consequence that nurses forfeited many of their bedside practitioner skills.

And surprise, surprise, guess what many new entrants fresh from progressive college education did when exposed to the conservative clinical management of the hospital ward that was little changed – attitudinally – since the war years: they transferred out of nursing-based college courses to more enlightened professions with better pay, working conditions and relationships. In short, the nursing profession ended up as a recruiting agency for other professions! But is it really a surprise that bright, academically prepared youngsters withdrew from the clinical setting with its unquestioning traditions, poor pay, long hours of service and fixation on measuring and cleaning bodily waste?

And the current price we are paying for all this in the UK? Well, because entrants to nursing have to attain graduate entry, fewer are currently coming forward to join the health service, attrition levels remain at a level that causes national concern and the profession still remains short-staffed, to the degree that unqualified carers predominate in clinical settings and standards of care continue to fall.

In the fifties, the nursing profession recruited from the job-hungry north of England, Scotland, Ireland and Wales; in the sixties it looked to the West Indies,

> *Mauritius and Malaysia; in the seventies targets were reached; in the eighties down-sizing began as qualified nurses became clinical managers; in the nineties recruitment again focused overseas in the Philippines (The Mail, 16 December 1998). It seems from this that the best of consultancy-led solutions can cause their own very special problems – especially when the ecology of the organisation is forgotten.*
>
> *Changing the focus of nurse preparation from the bedside to the classroom and from hands-on practice to theoretical models has also had more sinister effects. Expert nurses now tend to manage rather than provide care, unqualified care assistants now do the jobs qualified nurses use to do and, consequently, the patient is less well served and standards fall. All because – at one level – transference dynamics of the ward were unaddressed (Barber 1998) and remained in place to sabotage modern day recruits, who are unprepared to tolerate the militaristic dictates that nursing management had carried over from its past. There are no real winners in this consulting-for-change story.*

In the above account, many levels of transference co-exist: we see relic emotional patterns enshrined in the culture of the nursing profession, Victorian military values being transferred into hospital life, systems of psychological survival being ingrained in nursing procedures and observe that Menzies Lyth herself – looking through analytic eyes – carried analytic language into the consultancy. So what can we learn from all this? Personal and organisational history constructs the emotional field we live within, culture keeps this transference-informed reality alive and we must update the emotional blueprint of an organisation or team if we are to sow seeds of change.

As facilitators, what are we to do with transference? Yalom (1975) observes there are two major approaches to resolving transference in groups: we should mobilise *'consensus validation'* by soliciting observations and feedback of others, or *'work transparently'*. Then again, why bother to address or resolve transference at all? Basically, when transference grips us, current stress can't get out and the nourishment on offer can't get in. So has transference no positive function? Well, I note that the maintenance of a professional façade is an expensive process (Edelwich and Brodsky 1980), as resistance and the holding-in of emotional energies is far more exhausting then their release; perhaps transference fulfils a cathartic purpose here.

Reflections

* How do you imagine unconscious emotional patterns may be co-created and transmitted throughout an organisation's culture? Is it that organisations develop disturbed or defensive personalities which are then expressed through

their culture, or does the disturbance of those within permeate out to an organisation's the social systems?

(Personally, I think most people live out their lives in a cultural daze where they let socialised patterns do their thinking for them. This peaks in organisations, I believe, where we can let 'systems' and 'routine' guide us rather than an on-going here-and-now situational appraisal! No wonder that institutions can run us and that we may surrender our independence in favour of the comfort of a guiding, parent-like cultural force. I guess some people are over-socialised in their families and tailor-made to become organisational folk! Certainly my job appears, at least as a facilitator, to wake people up from their organisational sleep! All non-mindful and unquestioning cultures I see as damaged and damaging, addictive and controlling by turns. Though organisations often quote rational reasons for their behaviours, I find it a truism that feelings and fantasies, often paranoid survival or ego-boosting ones, represent their real drivers.)

* What positive functions might transference serve?

(As transference represents earlier emotional problems we have not yet learnt to solve, I guess it could be seen as a recurring 'learning opportunity'; something that won't go away until we have laid it to rest. In this regard, it is worth considering what emotional prior learning, both good and bad, we transfer into our own practice as coaches and group facilitators.)

What prior emotional leaning – cum transference – informs your facilitative role?

4.3   Emotional Recreation –
The Energetic Atmospheres of Groups

Psychodynamic energy, it is suggested, increases when a person's desire to carry out a specific task meets with frustration. As un-discharged energy associated with 'uncompleted tasks' causes tensions to remain active and remembered long after 'completed tasks' have been forgotten, unfinished business is a prime motivator. In this regard, transference may be seen as a driver for the psychological completion of 'unfinished business' and Gestaltists and analysts appear to sing from the same hymn sheet at this juncture. So what does this imply about groups and the human condition? Essentially it supports the psychodynamic treatise that:

• Individual behaviour is fundamentally group psychology – as the behaviour of one person influences and is in turn influenced by all others

• The rational workings of a group are profoundly affected by the irrational feelings and motives of its members – and its potential cannot be actualised until these are recognised and dealt with

- Administrative and management problems are essentially interpersonal problems expressed in organisational terms

- A group develops and evolves once it gains greater contact with its current reality.

Although I'm Gestalt in orientation, I have no quarrel with the above principles. But I have reservations with psychodynamic practice where a facilitator 'adopts a role'. For example, Bion (1968), who worked in a classic analytic mode within the Tavistock Clinic, encouraged transference in his experiments with groups by speaking symbolically and metaphorically – which served to unsettle participants and to stimulate fantasy to fill 'the information gap'; he further abetted this process by staying remote, opaque and non-participative – akin to a critical parent. Because he put forward no agenda, supplied no rules, clarified no tasks, refused to be drawn into individual conversation and spoke to 'the group as a whole' rather than to individuals, his groups remained in a state of heightened expectancy which eventually expressed itself in three transference reactions: 'dependency', 'pairing' and 'fight and flight':

* Dependency: Here a group meets as if it is there in order to be 'sustained by a leader on whom it depends for nourishment, material and spiritual, and protection' (Bion 1968, p.147). Here members seemingly regress, behave as if they are inadequate and immature, knowing nothing and contributing nothing. At the same time they act as if the leader is all powerful, omnipotent and omniscient, a figure to whom they look for magical solutions to all problems. This pattern flourishes when the leader encourages a leadership cult and acts into becoming the expected and emotionally desired parental figure. Eventually, when the leader is proved human rather than divine, the group turns upon them with hostility fuelled by disappointment. Strangely enough, when the earlier idealised leader is rejected, the group will often appoint the sickest and least capable member to lead. When this new, inadequate leader in turn fails, as fail they must, the previous leader is re-appointed:

> This oscillation between believing that the leader is at one time 'good' and at another time 'bad', or 'mad' and then a 'genius', results in a highly emotional and explosive situation that may not be able to be contained within the group.
>
> (de Board 1978, p.148)

Such a situation may then result in petitions being made to a higher authority, or yet again a schism or division. The object of both reactions, Bion suggested, is to avoid the intrusion of reality and the loss of the on-going excitement and drama.

* **Pairing**: Here the group acts as if it has met together in order to create a new and as-yet-unborn leader. This 'hoped for' act of creation Bion sees 'as essentially sexual, although the sex of the pair is unimportant' (de Board 1978, p.40). As to the purpose of this messianic group process, firmly focused upon the future it maintains the group as a closed system while shielding members from the reality of what is actually happening, the painful realisation of being so dysfunctional a group.

* **Fight and Flight**: Here the group unconsciously assumes it has met to fight something or to run away from something, which it will do indifferently as the whim takes it. A leader is more important in this group than the other two as he/ she is expected to co-ordinate action to defend against an external threat. But if a person accepts leadership, he is expected to act and lead the group to fight or flee from a common enemy and, if necessary, to create one:

> He is expected to recognise danger and enemies, and spur on his followers to courage and self-sacrifice. However, this leadership is based on paranoia; 'they' are endangering the group and 'they', wholly evil, have to be attacked and destroyed. Once the danger is passed, the leader is ignored and any statement made by him that does not involve fight or flight is also ignored.
>
> (de Board 1978, p.41)

Such a leader as this rapidly becomes the group's creature with little volition of his or her own. Again, with all energies directed towards a fantasised enemy, no real or productive work begins and projective aspects of reality are not confronted nor tested.

Bion reminds us that to create a truly productive working group, one which engages with 'objective reality' and the 'real' task, a facilitator must support individuals to move beyond the above 'basic assumptions'.

In terms of unconscious psychodynamic group processes, Bion (1968) suggests that dependency, flight or fight, and pairing serve as mechanisms for emotional release – but I wonder how much was stimulated by his facilitative style. After all, did he not set up the conditions for emotional energy to grow in this way? As the potential for energetic manifestation formed, group members become so filled with fear and excitation that they desperately sought a direction in which to focus their mounting anxiety – abetted by the absence of a nurturing leader – and as if by magic, dependency, fight or flight, and pairing appeared! Although it may be suggested that these mechanisms offered safe vehicles for emotional release, and that they served to divert from the reality of how ineffective and powerless individuals felt in a non-productive group of their own making, in his withholding facilitative role Bion nevertheless helped to co-create the neurotic, reality-shielding and stress avoidance behaviours he records. This is for me the major critique of a psychoanalytic way of working – it sets up a self-fulfilling prophecy, for it generates the self-same conditions it believes in. If you act as a negative, ambiguous parent others will naturally manifest the dynamics of stressed, needy children!

To be fair to Bion, others have confirmed his original conclusions (Bion 1968; Bennis and Shepard 1956; Tuckman 1965; Peck 1993). In fact, research into the functioning of T-Groups by Bennis (1987) has added a developmental dimension to his findings, where the following phases come into play:

Phase 1) Dependence – Flight: When a group begins, it often seeks to alleviate its anxiety through a search for group goals and the engagement of roles; there is also suspicion that the leader is holding something back

Phase 2) Counter-dependence – Fight: At this stage the group comes to feel the leader has failed them badly and try to bully or ignore him or her; yet there still remains a hope that this is a part of the master-plan that has been kept from them

Phase 3) Resolution – Catharsis: This is a most crucial and fragile phase, in which the group struggles to discuss openly and/or challenge the leader's role; if this is successful, autonomy develops

Phase 4) Enchantment – Flight: Resolution of the authority problem gives way to euphoria and a flight into pseudo-harmony

Phase 5) Disenchantment – Fight: The group now has a tendency to sub-divide into 'over-personals' and 'counter-personals', those who want intimacy and those who reject intimacy; absenteeism and boredom can emerge at this stage

Phase 6) Consensual Validation: Here, with the end of the group approaching, pressures arise for resolution of earlier issues and an evaluation or debriefing of the experience.

Having been alerted to the above dynamics of group life, perhaps you can recognise similar dynamics in past facilitations or consultations of your own? Again, we appear to be casting further light onto the nature of the chaos and confusion participants need to engage before emergent groups become 'working groups'.

Although I don't work in an analytically informed way, I appreciate its difference and have experienced much of a 'Gestalt' nature in group analytic settings, i.e. 'staying with what emerges', 'opening to process', a concern with 'unfinished business' and 'attention to the larger field'. But while analysts stand apart better to observe their clients, Gestalt practitioners work intimately from within the fabric of a relationship. Not only do they facilitate – but position themselves as genuine fully functioning group members.

Reflections

* In terms of the psychodynamic and analytic thinking presented above, how might you set about critiquing this school of thought and its approach to facilitation; then again, what most intrigues you about such thinking?

(I like its intention to look deeper into inner motivations, but feel it is not so much 'experimental' as imposing of a belief system upon events. This said, I see the openness and staying with what is unfolding, without being seduced into more usual social roles, as highly commendable.)

*In terms of the politics of facilitation, do you believe your groups see you as a:

- Remote and detached observer?
- Critical authority?
- Nurturing figure?
- Rescuer?
- Victim of the process?
- Peer?

(For myself, I've often found I've been associated with nurture and peer-hood, a critical figure on occasion, but rarely with the other roles listed here. So what about yourself?)

4.4   Psychodramatic Approaches to Emotional Exploration – Acting into Feelings

Impulsively driven behaviour that breaks free of our control is termed 'acting-out' in psychodynamic climates. Gestalt has an interesting variation of this, namely 'acting-in' – where we consciously choose to experientially engage, magnify and explore our hidden emotions. In this psychodramatic, way we attempt to cast light on the emotional parts of ourselves more often in shadow. For example, when I sense an emotional undertone in the ascendance, in contrast to bracketing it off or pushing it from awareness, I sometimes follow my emotional energy to see where it leads. Using 'acting-in' to inquire into the emotional undertone of my humour, I have discovered that below my superficial display subliminal irritations sometimes lurk. For instance, I have found my humour comes in four characteristic forms:

- *Tight humour – which covers annoyance and irritation, when I smile but really want to bite*

- **Releasing or cathartic humour** – *which is used to discharge discomfort or mounting physical and emotional tensions*

- **Re-framing and self-effacing humour** – *which helps me laugh at my seriousness and its related unreasonable expectations of myself and of others*

- **Warm humour** – *which bonds me to myself, to others, to life and everything around me.*

Taking time to act-in to our feelings before they build up enough steam to overwhelm us is an act of emotional and relational hygiene. Finding time to release pent-up emotions is a socially responsible, self-educative and self-caring act which helps build emotional intelligence; for a facilitator it is a necessity.

In treating our emotions as experiments and by mining into them through a process of 'acting-in', we come to know ourselves. For example, how are we to acquire self-control unless we practice releasing control? Through a process of acting-in to our feelings, catching the impulse to 'act-out' and listening to its message, we open a dialogue between conscious and unconscious aspects of mind. Catching our impulses in this way we convert impulsiveness to illumination. This process is an important one for, as with needy children, 'feelings' settle down once they are heard and appreciated, but lock them away and they fuel discontent, fulfilling the prophecy that every part of our personality we dislike becomes hostile to us. Psychodrama enables this integrative process.

Based on the theories and experiential methods of Jacob Moreno (1999), psychodrama has been applied in a wide range of mental health, business and educational settings. So how does it work? By closely approximating real-life situations in a structured environment, the participant is enabled to recreate and enact scenes which encourage insight and the rehearsal of new skills. Initially, the client (or protagonist in a group setting) focuses on a specific situation – the one to be enacted. Other members of the group act as auxiliaries and support the protagonist in his or her work by taking the parts/roles of significant others. Because 'action is key', psychodrama is suggested to empower in a way that exceeds verbal approaches to coaching and/or therapy.

The specific psychodramatic approach described here, a Gestalt-informed one suggested by George Bassett (2004), is crafted from the work of Constantin Stanislavski – the originator of 'the Method' school of acting who sought to bring more truthfulness to the theatre of his time by bringing the inner experience of the actor to the fore, so that what they 'inwardly felt and sensed' became 'outwardly manifest':

> Stanislavski believed that working the above way an actor could, in the Here, Now, Today (his own terminology), produce a series of emotions and states of being by natural organic processes. His aim here was to bring the actor to the point of fusion between the person of the actor and

the 'life' of the character. He termed this a state of 'I am Being'. 'Being' for him was theatrical truth. For Gestalt therapists, it is as it is – 'Being'. The shape and form of our being, our self being realised at the contact boundary of our lived experience.

(Bassett 2004)

Just as Stanislavski taught his actors to analyse and to experiment actively with their physical posture and movement, and look to the wider field of experience for an indication of what might happen next, so Bassett similarly helps his clients explore how emotions shape their world. Putting to test Stanislavski's hypotheses that once you find the appropriate action feelings will follow (Benedetti 1998), Bassett (2004) encourages clients to engage the following steps:

- Initially, after surfacing *'a description of a problematic emotional event'*, with the facilitator's support a client is invited to 'explore their life circumstances' plus the 'given circumstances' that have brought them to the present situation

- The 'super-task' is next analysed with regard to *'the major or dominant theme'* that directs a client's actions, forms the essential character of their life script and shapes their past and present emotional patterns and configurations

- Last, the action of the client's 'life-play' is broken down into components – inclusive of its *'major episodes, related facts and actions'* and how these illuminate further the scenario under discussion; here attention is also paid to the relevance of a client's actions to their desired 'life objectives'.

In an effort to illuminate the 'subtext' of a client's behaviour the facilitator examines everything that goes on in the mind during times of action, inclusive of:

- *'Inner monologues'* – the internal running commentary a client experiences as events unfold

- *'Mental images'* – fantasy and pictures that arise

- *'Emotional memory'* – spontaneously charged memories that percolate to mind with a view to clarifying authenticity and en route to 'truth'.

While Stanislavski provides a useful procedure to bring into focus what is 'figure' and put it to the fore of our client's awareness, a fellow thespian Bertolt Brecht provides a vehicle for the illumination of 'the ground' or context:

When we consider the Gestalt notion that meaning is derived both from a knowledge of 'the figure' and 'the ground', and that the relationship between the two goes some way to defining the whole, then in Brecht's methodology we have a strong representation of paying attention to the 'ground of experience' to inform meaning, whereas Stanislavski created empathy with characters through a focus upon the arising figure. Interestingly, Brecht required that the audience and the actors were engaged in a critical reflection and reading of what was being presented. Here the human being was the object of the enquiry, with emphasis being placed on the actors and play to arouse a robust cognitive engagement within the audience, and by inference – a capacity for action.

(Bassett 2004)

Citing the so-called 'Verfremdungseffekt' or 'Alienation effect', where the intention is to make the audience pay attention to something they might otherwise miss or take for granted by 'making it strange', Bassett observes the usefulness of getting someone to see and to engage critically with a previously accepted incident in a completely new light. Indeed, I have sometimes used to advantage the ruse of 'making an event strange' by inviting a client to repeat a well-rehearsed tale of woe with a lightness and sense of play! To like purpose, asking a client to take the part of their main protagonist or persecutor and to describe events through their eyes, I find, does much to break the spell of an entrenched emotional pattern.

Like facilitators, actors in the Brecht tradition are asked not so much to immerse themselves in the role or character but to 'stand outside' and offer a critique of the motivations of the character and their actions (Willett 1977). Through this process the audience/group is invited to cognitively examine the motives and to consider wider influences. In the theatre this may actually happen on stage when the character 'freezes' and the actor steps out of role to comment on what has just taken place. In the facilitation of groups I have used similar processes, for example:

- Asking a client to freeze and to solicit feedback and support from others when they are feeling particularly 'stuck' (*in this way I attempt to educate them to the notion that they are not alone, they need not soldier on but can ask and get support from the wider resource available in those around them*);

- Soliciting the reasoning capacities of a client when they appear to be drowning in a sea of emotions by asking them to change positions, to take my place and to speak from the position of a wise mentor or coach (*I never cease to be amazed as to how insightful many of my most needy clients become at such times!*)

- After a period of individual sharing asking other participants within a group what stood out for them, when they felt the most engaged, when they were most emotionally fired and what memories came back to them of similar events in their own lives (*hearing others emotional reactions can sometimes help a more emotionally frozen member to 'feel' their own position more readily*).

Another example of Brecht's practice, Bassett reminds us, is to emphasise the 'social gestus' or social gesture that best indicates to the audience the interpersonal relationships and power dynamics at play (the social gestalt). In this way, inviting a client to demonstrate the posture that best sums up his or her feelings can also help to unfreeze them by drawing attention to their body language while experimenting with sculptural ways to 'capture experience'. Group sculpting will be explored later in this text.

Reflections

* A client persistently arrives late for your sessions on a three-day workshop geared towards team building:

- How might you use a psychodramatic way to explore and invite feedback from others relating to 'lateness' without shaming and naming the participant?

- How might lateness be explored as a symbolic or covert message? *(I guess in a group I might draw attention to the group's tendency to arrive late, and pose in a reflective rather than punitive way such questions as 'How common is being late here?' and 'What factors contribute to this lateness?' I might invite a few individuals to leave the room and walk in after a few minutes as if they were late, ask them how they feel in their bodies, what they fantasised they might receive from others before they opened the door etc. I would then invite those in the room who were waiting for them to arrive to act-in to their feelings and verbalise – possibly with accompanying movements – what they were thinking and feeling when they finally arrived.)*

* How might a psychodramatic dynamic approach be employed to explore and express the undertone of a group?

* What if any are the drawbacks of psychodrama and in what settings might you limit its use? *(I think hysterical or histrionic climates might be least appropriate for this way of working, as it would possibly push such groups further into their dysfunctional zone.)*

4.5   Locating Emotional Phenomena –
Multiple Influences upon Group Facilitation

Imagine you are contracted to facilitate a day's team building for a government agency. You walk into the appointed room at the appointed time and are met with unfriendly, non-verbal individual expressions and general group restlessness. During your introductory opening to the day you notice certain members displaying indifference, seemingly demonstrating boredom with the whole venture – even before you begin! When things get under way, the group remains fragmented and you feel yourself being pushed ever further into an alienated position. If you were facilitating a group such as this, what would you imagine to be happening?

What might you do? And what interventions might you make? As the behaviour you are meeting does not directly relate to what is happening right now, it makes good horse sense to explore what might be being transferred in to this day from elsewhere. As for the questions you might raise to examine the dynamics at the transference level of the group, you could ask:

- What has happened in earlier training/team events you have shared together?

- What ground rules do you need to support you in this workshop, that is, if you are to move further and to gain more than you have achieved before?

- What expectations have you brought with you to this day?

- What professional and personal needs would you like to meet here today?

You might even ask for a brief check-in from each member, invite them to 'share how they are right now' and say something about 'what they need from this session'. Such interventions as these are designed to move gently between the socio-cultural and emotional-transference levels of the group; later, when sufficient structure and sharing has occurred, you may choose to explore more rigorously the underlying transference, raise the ante and ask more pointed and challenging questions, such as:

- If this group were a family, what children would it rear?

- Who act as the lawgivers or parents for this group?

- How does this group punish those who infringe its norms?

- How is authority and power managed here?

As this team-building day progresses, hopefully with participants gradually gaining in safety and trust, you notice certain stereotypic relationships are part and parcel of the group, with certain individuals receiving more than their fair share of punishment from their colleagues in the form of sarcastic humour. Later, as more of group life floats into awareness you may begin to suspect that individuals are splitting off their angers and hurts and projecting these on others, yourself included. Sometimes I find it useful to explore the family patterns of participants by asking:

- Do you find any fit between how you act in this professional family to your original family?

- How are relationships to seniors here different to the ones you have with your parents?

- What do you feel is expected of you here – and does this resemble anything else in your life?

- Where and when did you first learn to relate in the way you are doing here?

Illuminating the hidden emotional agenda and making conscious the familial roles that participants in groups are apt to enact can take the steam out of group transference while liberating much insight into why people and teams adopt the behaviours they do. Given that you have timed your interventions well and individuals feel supported to experiment actively and explore the group field, and have de-briefed sufficiently to move beyond the routines and perceptions they earlier employed, you might hold an open, non-agenda plenary session towards the close of the day. Here, participants can say something about their own biographies and how these inform their group behaviours. At this time you might ask:

- What has this day taught you about yourself, others and this community?

- How has this session confirmed your expectations or shaken the same?

- How might you react differently within a session like this next time?

In the above account we have an appreciation of the various 'levels' of transference and prior learning that could influence a day in a group's facilitated life. This imagined account also says something about how we might explore the 'communal mind' or biographically informed personality of a group or team. Remember, as individuals may be suggested to have conscious and unconscious components, overt and covert sub-personalities, so too groups, teams and organisations. But how much of a group's mind is generated by the individuals within it and how much is transferred in by the field will always be open to debate; likewise the nature of the 'intelligence' inferred by the Gestalt notion of an intelligent field!

In a facilitative context we may say certain components enter the group ready-made and fully formed – such as a facilitator's 'facilitative style' and the 'intrapersonal processes' (transferences and prior learning) individuals bring with them; that in contrast, a group's unfolding dynamics arise from the interplay of the 'inter-personal relationships' the facilitator and participants co-create, the 'group context', the 'unfolding culture' and 'facilitative influences'. Conversely, the results or changes that accrue as a result of facilitation are evidenced in its 'individual' and 'interpersonal effects' and the trace it leaves in its members, within the wider organisational field and the culture or communal psyche of its host institution.

In the above context, a facilitator has a great deal of influence over some variables of a group, such as: *the style of leadership* and *the facilitative interventions employed.* Some, they have a degree of influence over, such as: *the interpersonal relationships participants create, changes that accrue from experience, the group context* and *the after effects of the group.* Other influences facilitators have little or no influence over, for example: *transference and prior learning each individual brings to a group.*

Some influences represent a group's non-negotiable *'givens'*, some it's *'dynamics'* and others it's *'results'.*

But I wonder, are groups and places subject to transference? Certainly emotional atmospheres linger in many organisations; infuse structures and permeate its physical environment. I find my body impaled by certain emotional climates. So imagine this. On the appointed day, I drive to a venue feeling my usual unruffled self; having parked my car, I wander across the forecourt to the training centre – being gradually permeated by the emotional tone of the place. Having arrived early, I wander into the work room. Then it hits me! I may feel light-headed, a nausea stealing upon me like I've eaten what I can't digest, a descending sense of soporific dullness or rising sense of anxiousness. This energetic invasion is not like the eruption of emotion from within – I'm used to that – nor the play of imagination projected outwards – I know that too – but like sinking into water. When the folk I'm to facilitate arrive, they often 'feel' very much of the place, vibrating in resonance with what I received earlier.

Energy from the organisational field reaches out to us. We 'feel it', are duly informed, and sometimes controlled by it. But the organisation nevertheless remains an 'it'!

Reflections

* Bring to mind a group you have recently facilitated and reflect upon the following:

- What effects did participants report (individual effects)?

- What shape did the group climate you helped create take (unfolding culture)?

- What individual experiences and behaviours flowered in the group (intrapersonal processes)?

- What relational conflicts emerged (interpersonal relationships)?

- What was the intended purpose of the group (group context)?

- Were any changes to the host organisation's culture noted (interpersonal effects)?

- In terms of the above exercise, what new awareness might you carry into future groups?

4.6 Counter-transference –
Dancing in Tune to Transference

When your dreams come true it is likely counter-transference is at play. For example, when we meet a person who treats us with the respect we've always craved and we in return find ourselves feeling special, we are deep into the territory of counter-transference. Counter-transference emerges when you dance to another's emotional tune and is especially powerful when it resonates with unsatisfied needs of your own. In this context, we are more susceptible to counter-transference when we are needy and carrying unresolved issues from the past. Analysts have always known this to be so:

> The emotions of patients are always slightly contagious, and they are very contagious when the contents which the patient projects into the analyst are identical with the analyst's own unconscious contents. Then they both fall into the dark hole of unconsciousness and get into the condition of participation. This is the phenomenon which Freud described as the counter-transference. It consists of mutually projecting into each other and being fastened together by mutual unconsciousness... all orientation is lost.
>
> (Jung quoted in Perry 1976, p.136)

Both transference and counter-transference originate at the level of idealisation; being historical in origin they take you from the 'here and now' and drop you squarely in 'the there and then'. Beginners and needy facilitators, we have been cautioned, are especially prone to counter-transference. As to how we might set about working through counter-transference, it has been suggested we decontaminate ourselves by:

• Recognising a person's feelings for what they are, transference, so that we do not take what comes our way over-personally

• Talking over your responses with someone who is uninvolved with the situation, an objective and trusted outsider

• Contemplating an alternative strategy of relating with the person involved, one which is potentially satisfying and mutually beneficial

• Looking within ourselves for the possible source of our reactions and asking:

'Who does this person remind me of?'

'What impels me to behave in the way I do?'

'What emotional needs of my own am I seeking to satisfy in this relationship?'

Understanding and analysing our own developmental history helps to mute impulsive emotional patterns – though it will not eliminate them, for our emotional history is a 'given'. We must consult and integrate our emotional history and utilise the same to become facilitators of excellence. When we are comfortable with our 'emotional reality', we achieve a more mature alliance where realistic alternatives can flourish.

So what are we learning? Well, counter-transference includes reactions to a patient that are determined by your own life history and unconscious material; it can include unconscious hostile or erotic feelings toward a client that interfere with your professional objectivity and personal effectiveness; it takes two unaware people to flourish. For instance, a client or group dancing in tune with what you desire might appear changed and impacted, in a counter-transferential way, yet be fundamentally unchanged when beyond your influence and orbit – the so-called 'transferential cure'!

Contemporary understandings of counter-transference stress its co-created aspects; for instance, the client pressures a facilitator into playing a role congruent with their own unexpressed needs, and for whatever reason the facilitator responds! Sometimes a facilitator might act into counter-transference as an experiment, to help illuminate an individual or group's shadow in order to bring it to light. As long as counter-transference is not unconsciously acted-out, good can come of this – but it demands considerable skill.

The challenge to facilitators is not to be driven away emotionally through the evocation of our inner demons but to stay in dialogue with the same, no matter how intense the explosion of feeling or lacerating the attacks on our self-esteem and professionalism. To withstand such an onslaught we need to develop a rich store of personal insight, plus the professional dedication necessary to approach both ourselves and our works experimentally in an ever-deepening critical and research-minded way.

Plato suggests an interesting addition to transference, namely that we house an inner store of *a priori* intuitive knowledge of 'all that has been and is to come'. Here learning is basically seen to be a 'recovery or recollection of what we already know', but this latent wisdom, it is suggested, gets lost in the maze of what we are told we 'should know'. From this perspective, facilitation is an act of re-awakening, a drilling into intuition, and transference is seen to include innate wisdom.

So why do you bother facilitating, performing consultancy or coaching? What is in it for you? When and where did this need or desire arise? Go some way to understanding this and you will likely escape a headlong plunge into counter-transference.

Gestalt reminds us that emotions are energies, potentialities and results of our on-going dialogue with our energetic environment. It invites us to experiment with the notion that emotions are 'better met and lived through' than avoided. We explore creatures of the imagination in the same way, as you will hopefully come to appreciate in the following chapter.

Reflections

* Below are some common symptoms of counter-transference:

• Not listening or paying attention to a person's message

• Finding it difficult to shift positions and finding oneself tighten up

• Becoming sympathetic, empathetic and overtly emotional when faced by another's feelings

• Constantly reflecting or interpreting too soon what is happening

• Consistently missing or underestimating a client's depth of feeling

• Being unable to identify with and feeling emotionally remote from another

• Discovering a tendency to argue with a person or being defensive or otherwise vulnerable in their company

• Feeling that this is the best or worst person on earth

• Being preoccupied with an individual client or group between meetings

• Being consistently late to meetings

• Attempting to solicit strong emotions from another person by making dramatic statements

• Feeling a compulsion to be active and to deliver at all cost

• Dreaming about a person

• Being too busy to make time for another

• Working excessively hard with a client and then complaining of overwork.
(After Brammer et al. 1989)

* In light of the above, what counter-transference might you be especially susceptible to?

* Having been employed to help reduce stress and to help develop communication in a well-established executive team, you are surprised to meet with a good deal of reluctance from members to discuss the organisations earlier history:

• How might you help to unfreeze this group?

• What processes might be at play that seemingly conspire against open communication?

• Which group variables might you seek to address in order to help move this group on?

* As the group progresses you find yourself being elevated to something akin to an 'all-knowing leader'. This unsettles you because these are senior executives and you begin to feel as if you are being set up in some unaware way:

• What might be happening in terms of the group's process?

• What emotional patterns and/or defences might be being replayed in this group?

• How might your facilitation style have contributed to this unwarranted group dependence?

• How might your own counter-transference play a part here?

* In later sessions with the same group, they ask you to help them to enhance their 'emotional intelligence':

• Which of the interventions described in this chapter might you employ to raise their emotional awareness and expression?

• What models of this text might you use to help raise the general level of intellectual awareness?

• What criteria would you use to gauge facilitative success?

* As defined by Trist (1981), 'old management thinking' emphasised the technological imperative; people as extensions of machines and expendable spare parts; maximum task breakdown to simple narrow skills; external controls (supervisors, specialists, procedures); an autocratic style; competition and gamesmanship; the organisation's purpose only; alienation and low risk-taking. In these terms:

Consider the historical emotional patterns that have contributed to the old-paradigm world view which represents the culture consultancy

▶

and coaching often seek to change. *(I believe influences of the '40s and '50s, indeed a good dose of Victorian value and militaristic thinking, are perpetuated in the more traditional enclaves of business culture. So I wonder if 'culture' can ever be current, especially while the business community looks backwards for its guidance or feels drawn to an idealised image of the future – and the following of fads. Only by awakening people to where we are now can we forge an integrated way ahead. Guess I believe it's better to stay alert and open and to respond to moment-to-moment changes than to believe in a solution or look forward or back for strategic guidance. I don't know best, the client doesn't know best; yet together and via a developing relationship and dialogue with others in the client-system 'a way forward for now' might begin to emerge.)*

The person who uses only the vision of his eyes is conditioned purely by what he sees. But it's the intuition of the spirit that perceives reality. The wise have known for a long time that what we know through our eyes isn't equal to the intuition of our spirit. Yet most people rely only on what they see, and lose themselves in external things. Isn't this sad?

(Chuang Tzu)

Chapter five

Raising Awareness to Projective and
Imagined Influences

Diversity raises the intelligence of groups and conformity limits it. Uniformity is a form of confluence and a denial of difference.

.1 The Imaginative Energy of Ideas –
Myths that Drive Ideas of Change

At the projective and imaginative level we consider the imaginative power of ideas and the influence of imagination and 'projection' upon perception. In this chapter we review conscious and unconscious influences within the individual and group psyche and illuminate more shadowy features of 'group-think' and organisational functioning. Group sculpting; Transactional Analysis and archetypes will also be examined as components of our intervention strategy.

My exploration of projection, imaginative energy and other tacit influences of the psyche are complimented in this account by a further foray into psychoanalysis. I make no apology for the chunks of psychoanalytic thinking I am exposing you to in the text, as I believe the best of analytic practice is enshrined in Gestalt and that too few practitioners are privy to the psychoanalytic crucible that the originators Fritz and Laura Perls drew from as analysts. Even if you hold the old-fashioned idea that analysts are the opposition, no doubt you will still support the notion 'keep your friends close but your enemies closer still'! So I'm laying down an each-way bet here. Nevertheless, by keeping especially group analysis close, I hope to illuminate a richer and wider appreciation of phenomena found at the projective-imagined level – the analyst's prime territory and subject of interest. But what exactly is the analytic position? Let's pause a while to consider what is implied.

Regarding organisations, superficially, a psychodynamic rationale is not so very different to Gestalt. It observes that periods of organisational change put great strain on the ability of its members to contain their anxieties, cites the course of change as evoking and being shaped by heightened anxiety, and recognises that emotional toxins often result from a resistance to transform. Where it begins to depart from a Gestalt world view is in its emphasis on primitive aspects of the psyche, paranoid and schizoid elements it sees as anxiously and unconsciously acted out in times of stress. Bracketing off our Gestalt differences, I believe we have much to learn from analytic vision, not because it is 'right', but because it presents another facet or aspect of the field we as Gestalt practitioners are apt to forget.

For example, psychoanalysis remind us that even under relatively stable conditions organisations are obliged to cope with the psychological regression of their members, and cites two main factors as accountable for this. First, anxieties evoked through the performance of everyday tasks are seen to carry innate meanings that resonate with earlier experiences and to stimulate unconscious fantasies around competence and belonging – in times of change such intense anxieties are aroused that they have to be defended against. Second, the psychological challenges imposed by the need for collaboration with peers, superiors and subordinates echo configurations and relationships within our family of origin. In Gestalt terms, we are being reminded here that organisations have an ability to challenge imaginatively our deeper sense of belonging and re-stimulate unfinished familial conflicts of our past. Just as individuals develop mental defences to defend against anxiety, so too do organisations (Menzies Lyth 1960), which in turn effects their ability to function. Hopefully, an organisation can help its members contain and put to use the primitive fears and anxieties it evokes, otherwise toxic levels of splitting (the allocation of good and bad characteristics) and feelings of paranoia (brought on by identification with what is being projected) will result, polluting the work environment. When this happens, thoughtfulness and collaboration give way to blame-ridden, rigid and concrete thinking, with the consequence that an escalating downward spiral of fragmented and persecutory functioning may further embarrass an organisation's capability. We are cautioned here that 'the threat of change' can undermine the very features of organisational life most needed to allow successful change (Krantz 2001)!

Wilfred Bion (1968) documented that an anticipation of change disrupts established behaviour by destabilising traditional attitudes and established relationships, and that loss of familiarity and the threat of an uncertain future elicited profound anxiety. We should not underestimate the powerful weapon called 'change' we clasp as consultants, nor the potent symbolism we evoke as bearers of change. So how best to proceed? Well, analysts emphasise that organisational change of quality must include:

- Genuine investment in structures designed to contain and address anxiety associated with change

- Realistic assessment of the time required to effect significant change

- Appreciation of how much time must be devoted to bringing change about and the impact of this on productivity

- Acknowledgment of the anxiety evoked by change and recognition that people may be disadvantaged and hurt

- The provision of opportunities for people to acknowledge and work through complex feelings inclusive of depressive and angry reactions

- An awareness that learning from inevitable mistakes will necessitate mid-course adjustments

- Appreciation of the future to which change is directed which needs to be communally shared and understood

- Acknowledgement that change represents continuity as well as discontinuity and an appreciation of how it is linked to the past

- A carefully planned and thoughtfully executed rationale which acknowledges human as well as economic and technical factors contributing to successful outcomes.

(Krantz 2001)

In short, change should be grounded, realistic and understandable to those involved. Conversely, factors adding to organisational toxicity and exacerbating its negatives are identified as:

- Unrealistic expectations of change and short time frames

- Inconsistent leadership and changing and implausible images of a sought after future

- Clever epithets and superficial ideologies used to avoid the real struggle or to deflect from the painful difficulties associated with change

- Grandiose self-idealising leadership that is prone to believe in magic elixirs and simple solutions that promote technology associated with change which like mantras are recited to stop thought

- Denial of the impact of change upon the human condition plus an absence of structure to contain change processes as when the human cost is accorded lip service and change is managed covertly.

(Krantz 2001)

The Tavistock Institute, representative of the psychoanalytic tradition of organisational consultancy, has been active in this field for over fifty years, so we had best heed its insights. Though Gestalt has much in common with the above, thinking such as this critiques 'the learning organisation' (Pedler et al. 1997) and other humanistic notions where experiential learning and qualities of curiosity, forgiveness, trust and togetherness hold sway – along with all modes of change that refuse to acknowledge the unconscious and the primitive nature of humankind! Gestalt, no doubt, would be seen from a more rigid psychoanalytic perspective as one more utopian approach dismissive of destructive features of human nature, foolhardy at best and irresponsible at worst! So is Gestalt barking up the wrong tree? I think not, for we acknowledge the complexity and dis-at-ease embodied in the human condition, while field theory keeps us attuned to the complexity involved and causes us to suspect simple solutions – hence we remain alive to what is hidden and paradoxical.

Our analytic colleagues, I am sure, would not balk at an approach which builds in quality relational support as an emotional container and is appreciative of the organisation as a whole with its 'out of awareness' and irrational components – for this is essentially what they do themselves. Krantz suggests, in his seminal analysis of organisational change, that a model of change that holds the developmental tensions of schizoid–paranoid splitting 'at the centre of inquiry, as a creative force in itself' (2001, p.18) still remains to be created. I respectfully suggest that Gestalt fills this gap. What's more, we do not merely apply a pre-formulated notion (such as analytic thinking) but remain on the lookout for what is unique!

Analysts suggest everything we disown in order to conform socially is exiled from conscious awareness. In this way, it is suggested that we create an 'unconscious' or 'shadow' part of ourselves that performs like a psychic immune system to define what is *self* and *not self* (Zweig and Abrams 1991). Whatever is 'too much' goes this route, be this too much creativity, too much empathy, too much love, too much vulnerability or too much compassion. Some authors also see the shadow as storing lost depths of the soul (Assagioli 1976). If we are fully to develop and mature, they say, we must re-engage with the shadow to reintegrate these forgotten elements. Raising and expanding awareness is also a tenet of Gestalt.

Bly (1988) compares the shadow to an invisible bag in which we put everything our parents and teachers dislike. When a child is told to 'stop that' or 'don't do that', he says they assign that part of themselves to the black bag of the shadow. By the age of twelve, Bly suggests, our shadow is a mile long! And when we eventually look within the bag again, say in a personal development setting, its contents have by this time transmuted to become virtually unrecognisable to us. Worse still, these psychic creations now appear alien and threaten all we have 'socially' become, but they tend to leak back to inform our perception – especially through the mechanism of 'projection'.

In a more limited sense, 'projection' denotes a coping mechanism where we deal with unacceptable or uncomfortable feelings by splitting them off from ourselves and then *projecting* them outwards onto others. Having attributed our own unwanted characteristics to others, we then begin to work on ourselves by proxy, that is, by criticising everything the recipient of our projections does and says. In the throes of projection we appear to be communing with others, but our critique is essentially addressed to ourselves.

People often believe they are looking out on the world as if through a window when, in fact, what they do is more akin to gazing into a series of co-created mirrors upon which they project an imaginative mix of prior socio-cultural learning, 'unsubstantiated ideas' and disowned portions of themselves. If you accept this notion, 'perception' becomes a marriage between sensory information and creative imagination, and culture is as much a shaper of the world as our sensory organs. In this context, 'conventional reality' may be a learnt phenomenon maintained through consensual mass projection!

Mental defences, of which projection is one, were first defined by Freud (1936) as mechanisms serving to protect our 'ego' – or socially developed self – from other non-socialised elements within the psyche:

> The defence mechanisms are ways and means by which the un-integrated infant, and later the developing individual, wards off anything which threatens biological and psychological equilibrium. Such threats include dangers to survival; pain; frustration; conflict; the onslaught of overwhelming imagery, feeling or impulsive behaviour; the severe attacks and punitive forebodings of conscience.
>
> (Perry 1976, p.96)

Stalking our own blind spots and defensive reactions is a difficult art, but without becoming proficient in this art how will we ever see through our own bullshit? It is sobering to consider that the law of resonance implies that we only ever come into contact with that which we resonate (Dethlefsen and Dahlke 1990) – which, put crudely, means we act as shit magnets for our own projections.

In the related concept of 'projective identification', projection takes a magical turn. Here unrecognised and unwanted aspects of the self are projected onto others but this time the recipient experiences a pressure to feel and behave in a manner that echoes what is originally projected. In other words, a recipient feels possessed by projected material – so strong is the psychic energy involved. This process has been used to explain moments of uncharacteristic impulse or transient madness in therapists – or otherwise stable individuals – when they are caught 'like a rabbit in the headlights' by the emotional energy of a disturbed individual or group. Facilitators may especially be affected by projective identification when they become over-empathetic or otherwise blot-in more of their client's inner world than is good for them. Because this process, it is suggested, is unconscious, our first indication of projective invasion may take the form of us feeling unnaturally retaliatory or acting uncharacteristically towards the person or group doing the projecting; interestingly, the projector – because the process is unconscious – remains oblivious to the process. Subjectively, the recipient of projection in projective identification feels 'right enough' until they come contact with the person or group doing the projection. I recollect one particular mild-mannered woman in a workshop who had a knack of driving others to distraction, until she unearthed and began to own her own repressed store of anger and frustration. Because 'the projector' seems totally oblivious to the process, the recipient has to 'process' the projection in a way the projector can take it back – hopefully in a less toxic form. This is the meat of facilitation. Perry (1976) makes the point that how a recipient emotionally processes the projector's projection is more important than what they say. This is as true for humanistic practitioners as analytic ones.

Joan Wilmot (2005) records how her partner and herself were suddenly overcome in a training group with a sense of utter powerlessness. They had used all their tried-and-tested facilitative tools to no avail and nothing they seemed to do shifted either the group or their feelings of powerlessness. During the break they conferred together, and as powerlessness was not common to their facilitative experience they speculated as to whether they were picking up something of the group's distress. On return they shared with the group how they were feeling and asked in return how their clients felt at work. The group shared that they often felt useless and, until the facilitators had shared their recent insight, they had seen them as pretty incompetent also! Recognising, seeing through and over their own projections, as well as holding and reflecting back the projections of others while attempting to resolve what is projected upon them – I believe this is the single most important multi-task a facilitator must address to foster relational health. Simply, by and large, facilitators are in constant danger of getting from the group what they give as well as what they withhold.

When imaginative energy in the form of 'projection' informs communication, the following become commonplace:

- We finish people's sentences for them

- We act defensively even before being accused

- We use platitudes and verbal formulas such as 'He's the kind of person who...' or say 'I just know what she's going to do'

- We over-react as if at the mercy of an inner emotional script by getting angry when someone's opinion disagrees with our own

- We feel routinely misunderstood

- We see a threat in the faces of authority figures or feel that senior colleagues secretly dislike us, even when there is no evidence to substantiate this belief.

Any bells ringing yet? In projection, our beliefs and fears do our perceiving for us. Our worst fears also come true as our unbridled imagination causes us to believe our spouse is having an affair or that strangers are out to get us! Paranoid reactions are projective ones. Projections are often whipped up intentionally by advertising 'hype', in the films and sports we watch and by political parties. You are never in touch with the void or confusion when you evoke paranoia!

So how might a facilitator interrupt a projection's interruption to contact? Well, encouraging our clients to check-out and consider the evidence behind their assumptions; to reflect upon the origins of their beliefs; to question whether their opinion is founded on an observation, value or belief – all these help to dilute the flow of un-evidenced presumption. It is obvious that we must look beyond our own projections if we are to appreciate wholly another's experiential reality.

In groups, I often encourage people to experiment with personalising their observations by using the following form of words: 'I like my [whatever] which I see in you' and 'I dislike my [whatever] which I see in you'. Prefacing our observations in this way often opens up how self-referencing much of our feedback or supposed 'objective reporting' can be. Think for a moment of all those qualities you dislike and detest in others – now consider how they relate to you.

Reflections

* Perls (1972) suggests that to work through projection we need to employ the following four-stage exercise:

- Identify what we don't like in ourselves

- Share this with someone else using the statement: 'What I don't like about myself is…'

- Now imagine seeing this in someone else and notice what you feel and how you react

- Imagine again seeing what you don't like about yourself in someone else, but this time imagine that you feel and react differently: in other words, break your own pattern.

Enact this exercise and reflect on the results.

* So which part of yourself do you hold in check and what feelings do you routinely find yourself repressing?

* What inner messages do you generally leave unsaid and what about yourself do you usually choose not to share? *(In the facilitative role, as a matter of information, I will often share with others what concerns or perplexes me in my life and work currently, but I hold back from sharing those deeper vulnerabilities and emotional aspects of my life I am struggling with; I leave these to my counsellor or coach.)*

* What thoughts and feelings commonly haunt you? *(The more usual fears attentive to facilitation: no-one turning up, being overwhelmed by group needs, not being heard or valued; but these are now fleeting prior to a facilitative event rather than ghosts that haunt me throughout.)*

* If you were a character in a film what part do you imagine you would play?

All these unpack something of the nature of your imaginative and projective world.

.2   Projection Rules –
Management Gurus and their Literature

Advertising and marketing, pop music and car design, film and theatre all seek to capture our imagination; if you have read the more popular consultancy literature, no doubt your imagination has already been caught by what Huczynski (1993) terms 'hero managers', organisational consultants and facilitators held in high esteem by the business community, figures who market themselves as enshrining knowledge and power derived from life-changing personal beliefs that came to the fore as they were forced into challenges eliciting an heroic, superhuman response. But although such individuals describe their work in detail, there is often a large gap between 'what they deliver' and 'what they claim to deliver'. Indeed, it may be suggested that 'hero managers' and 'hero coaches' offer in their accounts little more than banalities, platitudes, idiosyncratic reflections and ad hoc justifications – and that your projection does the rest. Collins (1998) cites Green and Moscow's (1986) *Managing* and Harvey-Jones' (1988) *Making it Happen*, works with an inherent deep distrust of academia, as examples of this kind. At root, such works are by and large products of the imagination and say more about the projective world of the authors than empirical events.

In contrast to the above 'hero managers' – whom Huczynski (1993) equates with medicine men – are the so called 'gurus', those who due to 'sound research and analytical techniques' are elevated to be containers of great wisdom and knowledge. Charles Handy possibly qualifies here. Note that the term 'guru' tends to refer to religious leaders, 'divine beings' who promise magical influence and results. The base of guru authority rests upon the supposition they can 'see into the future' or have 'a superior understanding' to ourselves. In short, they evoke the image of an 'all-knowing parent'. Collins (1998) cites Peters and Waterman's (1982) work *In Search of Excellence* as an example of this kind. The personas of gurus appears to be created in a similar way to that of the leader in Bion's (1968) groups, creatures formed from basic assumptions who, when invested with 'projective energy', become larger than life. Rosabeth Moss Kanter (1985) in her work *The Change Masters* evocated the pioneering spirit of America by appealing to 'the romantic past':

> If America is to build on its past competitive strengths and to secure a better future for itself, innovation – and the risk and change that implies – is a necessity not because it alone ensures our survival (and ultimately, therefore, profit). To get more innovation, we need to re-infuse more American organisations with the entrepreneurial spirit responsible for America's success in the past.
>
> (Kanter 1985, p.23)

Such blatant charismatic invitation as this causes the heart to miss-a-beat and the imagination to leap to a place where anything can happen. Inspiring, yes – but sound? It's doubtful.

Interestingly, both Peters (1982) and Kanter (1985) were writing at a time when 'the recession' was beginning, during a period when doom was upon the horizon and foreign competition, especially from the Far East was causing major national concern – a situation ripe for the dynamics of 'fight and flight'. In this light, it appears that if consultancy ideas are to catch on they must be timely and resonate with the contemporary field. Take this example from Pascale and Athos (1986), writing at the time when Asia-Pacific and Japanese competition had begun to bite:

> Japan has come to dominate in one selected industry after another – eclipsing the British in motorcycles, surpassing the Germans and Americans in automobile production, wrestling leadership from the

Germans and Swiss in watches, cameras and optical instruments and overcoming the United States' historical domination in business...

(Pascale and Athos 1986, p.20)

Such cries as this are similar to the ones issued in Victorian times when the British working class – and thus society's supply of potential solders and fighting men – was seen as less physically robust than that of the 'deadly Hun', an argument that supported physical education in our schools. Group facilitators and coaches must guard against such charismatic trends which provoke unquestioning compliance and tempt us towards quick fixes rather than experimentation. It is always better to let uncertainty guide us than certainty, for the latter, like as not, is of projective origin.

In *Management Gurus: What Makes Them and How to Become One*, Huczynski has identified the following features of ideas that catch the imagination, prosper and have a tendency to grow in popularity over time, namely that they:

- Develop an audience and resonate with a large number of people

- Are pitched to address and to appeal to the fears of management

- Legitimise management activity and the role of managers

- Can be practically applied to the workplace by managers

- Have a stamp of authority and proof about them

- Are both easily communicable and memorable

- Give managers a sense of being in control

- Consist of a number of steps or principles

- Have a malleable vision of human nature

- Promise improvement and results

- Claim universal applicability

- Focus upon co-operation

- Have a leadership focus.

(Huczynski 1993)

Perhaps the most effective of interventions hits us imaginatively, stimulates us emotionally and only later enters cognitive awareness. In this notion of influence and change, ideas grasp our imagination, fire our emotions and are eventually supported by intellectual theory and ad hoc retrospective rationale.

In terms of how ideas and ideals beyond our awareness influence organisational culture, in his classic work *Gods of Management*, Handy (1991) classified the management style and power culture of organisations by aligning them with Greek

153

gods. As you read through the following, reflect upon which gods you, and indeed the organisations you work within, serve and worship:

Power Culture: **Zeus**, the ruler of the gods, echoes throughout this culture, in which a central figure who sits at the head of the organisation radiates rays of charismatic influence throughout. Here 'trust and empathy' are the basis for effectiveness with 'telepathy and personal conversation' forming the primary mode of communication; power is maintained by 'getting the right people in place'; little faith is put in communities or collaborative ventures and committees.

Role Culture: Bureaucratically constructed and working by 'logic and rationality'; guided by **Apollo**, the god of reason, with strength in 'functions and specialties' where control is maintained by 'procedures' and 'job descriptions', and instituted by creating procedures and rules. Settling of disputes in this climate is usually institutionalised through grievous procedures, communication is by 'memos and email' and co-ordinated power is exercised by a narrow band of senior managers.

Task Culture: Job- and project-related, the so-called 'matrix organisation' where emphasis is placed on 'getting the job done', to which end the organisation seeks to bring together the appropriate resources and the 'right people at the right level', to whom it then gives the space to get on with it. Here influence is exerted by 'expert power' rather than personal power or position. This culture is more adaptable than most, with people having greater control over their work. Within this context **Athena**, the warrior leader, rules.

Person Culture: Here 'the individual is the central point', with the system and structure serving the practitioner's needs. Here we find a collection of individuals who have mutually bonded together to pursue their individual interests and careers, to evoke a culture in which **Dionysus**, the deity of self-orientation, reigns.

(After Handy 1993)

As a deckhand on the Manchester Ship Canal, Athena guided my way as I consolidated my manhood alongside other working men. In my early mental health career, I worked in Zeus-inspired organisations under the influence of medical superintendents and senior consultant psychiatrists and learnt how to be an agent provocateur while successful and championing the plight of the underdog within, finding freedom within the existing form. As a principal lecturer in the Royal College of Nursing, I found myself in the territory of Apollo and raising shadow qualities of person-centeredness and authentic relating. As a facilitator working in academic climates, I found myself treading a journey shaped by Dionysus. I have rarely been of the faith and respectful of these gods, choosing more often than not to define myself through battle with them.

154

Some cultures are anti-spirit and anti-life; they deny the soul its intelligence, invent a psychology of social adjustment and portray nature as a dumb machine. Such thinking furthers the wasteland of postmodernity. Which of the gods described – Zeus, Apollo, Athena and Dionysus – drive you and your organisational relationships? And which do you worship through your life's work? Beware, sometimes the gods you serve turn into demons!

Reflections

* If change, in 'real terms', is seen as an organic, emergent and largely unconscious process, rather than the outcome of something we have consciously planned, what does this imply about the nature of facilitating change? *(Much change theory, to my mind, seems to have emanated from the business community and suffers from a stable of thought heavily biased towards human cause and effect. It seems to be implied here that 'change' can be 'managed' and subject to human reason and controlled by human 'will'; but if everything is interrelated, complex and influenced by forces largely unseen and unrecognised, a 'field of influence' as it were, it stands to reason that 'reason' itself is but one facet of the whole complex process. Indeed, management theories of change, I would suggest, are focussed primarily within the socio-cultural domain infused by imaginary thinking and projected meaning rather than physical evidence – which implies our 'beliefs' rather than our senses order how consultants and the business community perceive the nature of things.*

So what does this stance imply for facilitators and the facilitation of change? Well, as a part of the whole complex field, we are as much subject to unseen forces as those we facilitate, so it is well that we recognise the limitation of our vision and effect. We can offer theories and processes which support people through change, but to impose a false sense of rationale and order will only lead to disappointment later, when our cherished solutions and prized strategies fail. There are no lasting cures, no remedies, only current adaptations in a constantly re-constellating field. Anything else is imaginary. In this light, all facilitators can do is to help their clients awake to an appreciation of the complex field they co-exist within, to facilitate a safe exploratory space and help craft individual and corporate strategies that support adaptation and flexibility in a constantly changing now. How far from this view are the notions of those 'hero managers' and 'change gurus' cited above.)

* In light of the above discussion, it is useful to consider how planning may both support and frustrate change, and to reflect upon how much 'change' is virtual rather than actual. *(I guess some planning is useful in the earlier identification phase of a facilitative relation when we are co-creating hypotheses to consider but a too rigidly held plan might cause us to miss other, more relevant information. I guess I'm saying planning is useful but a firm plan will get in the way.)*

▶ * In light of your reading of Bion's work in the previous chapter and his notions of 'the basic assumption group', what do you believe may be happening during times of mass adoration and/or compliance? *(Could it be that what Bion identified at the micro level might well be happening at the macro level of the business community, a sort of mass dependency upon 'parent-like figures' by the business community, and a fight-and-flight effect during times of crisis on others promising magical solutions? A sort of denial of the complexity of things and the helplessness and powerlessness people/groups feel when events threaten to break from control.)*

* As to the popularity of charismatic authors and management leaders and the imaginary symbolism they evoke, what unfulfilled needs may be clamouring for satisfaction within the followers of gurus? For instance, what are you searching for when you read similar texts?

* How might organisations of the kind described in Handy's (1991) *Gods of Management* influence the reception of your facilitation? And what might these cultures be blind to?

* How does the psychoanalytic vision differ to that of Gestalt and how might this difference show itself in facilitation and notions of change?

5.3   Addressing the Shadow –
Projective Identification in Teams and Organisations

When groups of individuals work alongside and closely identify with each other, it is natural for them to evolve a similar set of rules, values and beliefs and a collective identity. Indeed, Bettelheim (1969) has observed that a communal super-ego is generated by the collective demands and plural influences of organisational control, which then evidences itself as an internal voice, one much more powerful than the individual's own conscience and just as inescapable:

> We can try to hide from a parent, even from God… but we can never hide from a control system of which we are quite consciously a part.
>
> (Bettelheim 1969, p.126)

By this means organisations come to make collective demands which infiltrate every part of us.

The development of and our identification with a 'collective consciousness' or community field severely limits our ability to reality-test – for we are asked to take much for granted if we want to belong. In this context, it is as if the individual and his reality are sucked into the outer personality structure of the group (Stapley 1996). This image of the organisation as a 'communal vampire' no doubt inspired

Whyte (1960) to write his classic work *The Organisation Man*, which portrays mechanisms by which individuals become bonded, take the vows of company life and commit themselves body and soul to the projective reality of a supposedly beneficent organisation.

Indeed, Whyte (1960) argues that because the Protestant ethic of thrift, hard work and the sacredness of property do not reap the success and wealth promised, it produces a deluded organisationally absorbed committee person who seeks permission from the corporation. This tendency of the organisation to take the person over, Whyte implores us, must be resisted at all costs, for in suppressing individual imagination and creativity it furthers mediocrity. For example, people may become skilled at getting along together but forget to question 'why they should get along'; consequentially, they merely adjust – rather than achieve. Indeed, it is his contention that man must fight the organisation, while simultaneously accepting the conflict that exists between himself and societal pressure to conform. In this context, facilitators become agent provocateurs on the side of psychic wellbeing.

Threaten the organisation's collective consciousness with change and you provoke anxiety within all involved, for the organisational personality cuts both ways, communally and personally:

> Every major organizational change will affect the culture. The culture is developed by the members of the organization producing forms of behaviour that are most advantageous to them under the conditions imposed by their holding environment. With this in mind, any change that affects the culture will be potentially chaotic. … All challenges to organizational culture will involve a loss – a loss experienced as not as badly as, but with similar results to, the loss of a relative.
>
> (Stapley 1996, p.183)

Even 'successful' and healthy change will often in the short term, before surfacing its long-term benefits, be seen and felt as destructive to an organisation's ecology; don't then expect thanks or immediate results!

At the projective level within the imagined world of a group or organisation are located its symbols, its coded language. It is a very rash and foolhardy facilitator who believes they understand a team or company's private language, its own unique meanings better than those who already co-exist within it, even though their clients may not be able to put their experience into words. In this regard, 'fools rush in where angels fear to tread'.

I am reminded here that Meltzer (1992) has alerted us to the personality type of those who often rise to eminence in organisations. I'm sure we all know the type and have met more than a few in our clientele over the years, people who 'just have to win', who are intrinsically competitive and desperately ruthless, who Meltzer suggests 'live in their internal worlds at the very end of their psychic digestive tract' – the claustrum, just inside the anus, where they are constantly in the grip of perpetual and acute psychotic anxieties about being expelled into robust contact with others in the external world, which they fear would precipitate a mental breakdown! Fragile personalities such as these are drawn to external sources of power where they can over-compensate for their deeper, all-too-real feelings of inadequacy. In this position, masked by leadership and set up as recipients of communal projection, they feel cushioned from deeper fears, but when their role is threatened they are caused to experience afresh their hitherto-repressed anxieties all over again. Such people as Meltzer's 'arsehole leaders', desperate to maintain their superior position, fight tooth-and-claw to maintain the status quo and treat all disagreement as symptomatic. With all the kow-towing and edification that comes the way of leadership, even the most grounded of us needs shadow consultancy or supervision to purge our demons and to keep us sane.

Stapley makes the point that a consultant has a responsibility for 'relating to the emotional and cognitive state of a group' (Stapley 1996, p.183), and suggests that facilitators when working at this level should view themselves as a relational container – similar to a parent, who temporarily sustains a holding environment while change is addressed and undertaken. For this to work, I believe facilitators need to retain a state of 'evenly suspended attention' similar in part to Rogers' (1962) concept of 'non-possessive warmth'. From this stance, a facilitator or consultant proffers insights to help the client-system escape unhelpful methods of thinking and behaving, while supporting individuals to go through the trauma of adapting to change.

i) Institutional Defence Systems

Isabel Menzies Lyth (1960), whose work we reviewed earlier, writing about projection and fantasy in the organisational life of the hospital in the 1950s, observed how the imagined world merged with individual interpretation to influence perception. Describing the impact of physical illness upon nurses and the magnification of stress through the need to deal with others' stress, Menzies Lyth saw that, even in short conversations with nurses, patients and relatives, their conscious concept of illness – and its treatment – portrayed a 'rich intermixture of objective knowledge, logical deduction, and fantasy' (Menzies Lyth 1960, p.7) and that individuals, unconsciously, tended to associate the distress of others with that experienced by figures in their 'phantasy-world'. Note here how Menzies Lyth spells 'phantasy' – with a 'p' to denote its unconscious nature. This situation, where an individual's own store of anxiety and unconscious 'phantasy' is compounded by others' anxieties is all too common in organisational life. For what we imagine becomes what we believe, co-create, and at the projective level eventually get:

> The nurse projects infantile phantasy-situations into current work-situations and experiences the objective situations as a mixture of objective reality and phantasy. She then experiences painfully and vividly in relation to current objective reality many of the feelings appropriate to the phantasies.
>
> (Menzies Lyth 1960, pp.7–8)

158

In the above mode, projecting 'phantasy' into objective reality, individuals in much of organisational life could be suggested to living a communal delusion.

Menzies Lyth's classic paper on psychic defences in organisational life (Menzies Lyth 1960), which arose out of a consultancy at the old Charring Cross Hospital by the Tavistock, highlighted social defences legion to many institutions. For example, below I describe a few of her more salient findings which I observed for myself as a patient in the 1980s, some 40 years later (Barber 1992/98):

- *Splitting of the nurse–patient relationship:* Tasks demand more attention than individuals; patients are treated all the same and personal distinctions and one-to-one relationships strongly discouraged. *Example:* Nurses were constantly on the lookout for physical jobs to do. A senior member of staff encountering juniors talking to clients exiled them to the sluice room to clean up or the laundry cupboard to stack linen. In this way task-vision ruled and ward-maintenance jobs prevailed.

- *Depersonalisation and denial of individual significance:* Clients are referred to by their label rather than name, uniformity of response and client management is encouraged. *Example:* My experience testified to the fact that patients were rarely referred to by name, but rather identified by diet, condition, or with reference to the consultant surgeon – I was 'Dr X's thorax in bed 4'!

- *Detachment and denial of feelings:* Shows of emotion are discouraged and juniors are disciplined rather than counselled. *Example*: Nurses tends to have two forms of presentation or communication style. To colleagues, the tone of voice portrayed was generally feeling-less and businesslike; to patients, it was jollying and patronising or chiding. When a patient died, nurses plunged themselves into ward tasks with increased energy and seemed desperate to keep themselves busy.

- *Responsibility diluted by checks and counter-checks:* Individual action is actively discouraged and everything has a tendency to be obsessively recorded; trust of others – and their skills – unless they are seniors is a rarity. *Example:* Even aspirin, a common enough drug in the home, was given out in a manner one would expect of a deadly poison; blood pressures recorded by juniors were nearly always counter-checked by senior staff and observations by patients themselves given little weight.

- *Delegation to superiors of professional and personal choice:* Disclaimed responsibilities are forced upwards to seniors and staff routinely performed well below their level of competence and skills. *Example:* Largely due to the aforementioned dynamics, seniors were forever overloaded with petty decisions; individuals appeared to need to be seen as a 'work heroes' and staff appeared dangerously close to burnout.

Do any of the above resonate with experiences of your own? They should: they are commonplace in one degree or another in all organisations!

ii) Facilitation as Dancing in the Shadow

In its development of a structure, a culture and a means of functioning, an organisation or team is influenced by multiple influences: its primary task, its network with suppliers, its market connections, its management style, the pressures it produces in its workers and the way it addresses or ignores its blind spots. The company shadow represents the calmative effect of its multiple blind spots. A successful company must therefore manage its shadow and the anxieties and fantasies of its workers as much as its manufacture and sale of products. But be warned, change the environment and you inadvertently affect the fantasies and myths individuals act out within the workplace, many of which may be antagonistic to communal living.

Projection and 'splitting' sculpt much of organisational life. For example, we can all too easily attach our irresponsible impulses to juniors and inner critic to seniors to create a projected reality in which our subordinates are viewed as irresponsible and seniors are seen as stern disciplinarians, thereby creating a 'psychic truth' where juniors are irresponsible and seniors are harsh disciplinarians. There is also an objective truth here also, since counter-transference and projective identification can cause individuals to enact the roles we ascribe to them – such is the nature of magic!

Working with Projective Mechanisms – A Psychodynamic Account of a Gestalt Event

* Dynamics during the Orientation Phase: In the orientation stage there was an initial resistance or holding back from social engagement, a reluctance to invest energy in the new 'family' about to form. Early family dynamics were enacted including dependency and other age-inappropriate behaviours. For instance, there was a flight from 'what was new' towards traditional 'tried and tested' behaviour; concrete and black and white views of the world were projected out and fought for; the social and conventional level was clung to as emotions began to bite; transference appeared to give way to projection as participants forsook sensory information and reasoning in favour of an imaginative interpretation of events. As a facilitator I was aware of feeling more and more as if I were being enrolled as a parent figure. With primitive energies of the group running high, it also felt as if a life and death struggle was going on as issues around birth and beginnings proliferated.

* Dynamics during the Identification Phase: In this phase projective energies began to subside and reasoning returned, as concentration upon the task focussed group attention. A gradual working through of resistance now occurred, as a 'letting go of the old' in favour of 'the new' began to be glimpsed. A critique of traditional vision and beliefs also surfaced as participants contemplated the very real possibility for 'change'. Earlier projections and defensive reactions were now recognised for what they were – imagined, rather than real actualities. Ground

---

160

rules, what people wanted from the group and strategies for fulfilling their needs, now began to be contemplated. At this stage I caught some positive transference coming my way as my earlier mantle of 'unknown and fearful parent' appeared to give way to that of a 'nurturing parent'.

***Dynamics during the Exploration Phase**: In this phase a testing out of group boundaries and rules was enacted as my power and authority was brought into question. When a sufficient number of people had taken risks and were seen to be accepted and listened to rather than punished, a culture of permission seemed to grow. As defences retreated, trust started to develop. Experimentation flourished as individuals gained in confidence. At this time personal learning strategies were suggested – then gradually enacted. By the fifth session, participants were sharing evidence of how learning in the group was filtering through to professional practice, and individuals were reporting back the gains and cost of their personal learning and experimentation's in the workplace. At this stage a wide range of influences were identified, systematically explored, and new models of experience created.*

*** Dynamics during the Resolution Phase**: In the resolution phase with the end of the group in sight, participants reviewed their history together. Fleeting moments of dependency surfaced, but this was quickly replaced by a celebration of what we had achieved. Themes of grief and loss also arose spontaneously as feelings around earlier endings were stimulated. People seemed less dependent now on a contractual or social level of engagement, and more able to tolerate greater emotional honesty. Indeed, the perception and interpretation of events was now considerably more philosophical and far less rigid then before. Though there was a fleeting reluctance to end and a little denial that things could not go on as they were, eventually celebration of what we had achieved together became the central theme, and individuals began to separate themselves from the group by reporting on what they would be doing next.*

I wonder how recognisable, if at all, the above developmental features are in the groups you facilitate.

Trevor Bentley (2001), a Gestalt consultant of many years standing, observes that most consultants facilitate the legitimate system but ignore the organisational shadow. This, he suggests, is a grave omission, as organisational harmony is best achieved through a situation of equilibrium where the legitimate system and shadow – or 'projective system' – are in balance. For example, the legitimate system holds the structure and boundaries that provide a sense of containment, while the 'shadow system' allows unmet individual needs – such as repressed negative emotion – to be expressed. In this model the legitimate and shadow systems need each other. When things are going well, say when issues are contacted and communication is open there is sufficient overlap between the two systems for each to support the other. Conversely, when the legitimate system eclipses the shadow, personal and emotional expression suffers; and when the opposite is the case, a lack of supportive structure predominates. Indeed, too strong a swing to legitimacy leads to rigidity and ossification, and too strong a swing to the shadow breeds anarchy and disintegration (ibid.).

In conclusion, it is recommended that a consultant should facilitate a sufficient degree of chaos in both systems for them to unfreeze, re-constellate and ebb and flow with renewed vitality.

Reflections

* In the light of the notion that 'we only perceive that which we have first learnt to conceive', consider the interrelationship of imagination and perception and how we might verify for ourselves when we are actually 'seeing' something as opposed to fantasising or thinking about it. *(Emptying our minds of thoughts and fancies is not easy, but it's nevertheless essential if we are to see clearly. I guess exercises cited earlier in the text might help me here – see Chapter2.)*

* How alike do you consider an organisation to be to an iceberg where two-thirds are hidden from view? What other metaphors come to mind? *(I'm conscious of some organisations that provoke in me the image of a machine where workers are mere cogs; others that bring to mind an over-loaded oil tanker at full steam out at sea and unable to stop in less than three miles; and one which reminds me of a theatrical production being delivered by a troop of actors.)*

* In terms of the findings listed from the Menzies Lyth study of nursing:

• How many of the institutionalised defences she lists are commonplace in your workplace, and how many do you inadvertently perpetuate?

• How would you go about rectifying the same as a consultant consulting for change?

• What effect do you suspect Menzies Lyth's psychodynamic language and thinking might have had upon her clients?

* How might you monitor and counterbalance the effects of your own imagination and the projections it fuels? *(I guess there may be some clues to this in the earlier sections relating to facilitating at the physical–sensory and social–cultural levels – counter-balancing influences as it were.)*

.4 Undoing Blocks to Experience – Encouraging Flow

Knowing your projections – what you are susceptible to project out and the forms of projections you invite by virtue of who and what you are; plus the stereotypes-cum-archetypes you portray; not to mention your tolerance of being labelled and your ability to live this down or allow the projector to take their projections back – these are real facilitative skills that sort out the sheep from the goats! So which are you? Baa baas?

Below I've grouped projections that facilitators may field at physical to transpersonal levels of their experiential engagement alongside the projections groups may in turn invite from them:

The group as mirror of the physical world (*domain of sensory/physiological input where the facilitator/leader is representative of a physical container or pack leader*):
Here the group may represent to the facilitator a primordial energy and re-stimulate primitive and instinctual reactions; at this level a facilitator needs to be physically anchored and grounded, centred within their own physicality, perceptively attuned and alert to physiological needs and the necessity of building physical support.

The group as mirror of society (*domain of cognitive learning and socialisation where the facilitator/leader is seen as representative of conventional authority and a task leader*):
Here the group may represent to the facilitator a social milieu demanding of task and conventional leadership, re-stimulating issues of inclusion and exclusion; at this level a facilitator needs to resist being enrolled as a leader rather than as a resource, clear regarding their social contract, the culture they carry and the role models and role sets they operate within.

The group as mirror of our past (*domain of past and historical influences where the facilitator/leader is seen as represent to a group a parent and/or authority figures of the past*):
Here the group may represent to the facilitator 'family' and invite a parental response, or yet re-stimulate earlier family reactions and history; at this level the facilitator needs to avoid being seduced into a transference role, becoming intimate or confluent, collusive or over-responsible for a group.

The group as mirror of the self (*domain of the ego and projective identification where the facilitator/leader is the recipient of imaginative meanings and projections*):
Here the group may represent to the facilitator their unconscious self or personal shadow and re-stimulate a need to enact or flee from their inner imaginative world; at this level the facilitator needs a clear sense of self and objective reality, to receive supervision or shadow consultancy so that they might withstand the projected energies that swirl around them.

The group as mirror of the cosmos *(domain of the collective unconscious/mysticism where the facilitator/leader may represent symbolic meanings and higher states in a guru-fashion):*
Here the group is representative to the facilitator of the unknown, the fertile void or the unfathomable mysterious universe, re-stimulating of a sense of insignificance when facing the cosmos; at this level a facilitator needs to be alert to symbolism and able to tolerate being idealised plus face confusion without being overwhelmed by a meeting with the unknowable.

Having been alerted to an appreciation of the source of our own projective reality, it may be expedient at this point to examine the mechanisms we use to keep our 'projective world' intact. For instance, I have listed below the more common mental defence mechanisms met in facilitation, along with ways we might set about resolving these projections when foisted upon us:

- ***Repression*** involves the exclusion of a painful or stress-inducing thought, feeling, memory or impulse from awareness. The more emotional energy you push out of conscious awareness, so the theory goes, the more fuel you provide for unconscious, emotionalised and distorted thinking – unfinished business? All unconscious behaviour stems from this root of repression. When repression is habitual and fully fledged, any amount of direct questioning fails as there is a deeply rooted refusal to face the facts or address issues. Conversely, if you confront what is being avoided, your persistence will only increase a subject or group's entrenchment and anxiety. A facilitator's job is to free-up the underlying threat that fuels repression. This may better be performed by massaging the culture rather than focusing in upon individuals. For instance, role modelling non-judgemental and 'relaxed attentiveness' can take the urgency out of events and defuse the build-up of 'shame' that may have originally led to repression. Resolve the sense of 'anxious excitation' that can prevail in repressive climates and material earlier denied may come back into view – then you have something to work with. Asking an individual or group what rules they would like to operate by, imparting humour or fostering acceptance, all counter the need for repression.

- ***Denial*** occurs when an individual or group discards or distorts reality in such a way that the original event becomes unrecognisable. It is commonly found at times of culture shock, such as when, as facilitators, we move too quickly towards an emotional agenda. Sometimes jocular, cocktail-party-like behaviour may cloak a group's denial. Mild good-humoured cynicism can also give rise to a 'league of gentleman' dynamic as when people attempt to avoid, dampen proceedings or stall for time. A facilitator might raise awareness to denial and gently draw attention to the purpose it is serving in a group. They might also negotiate rules where people are encouraged to be more direct by speaking in the first person: 'I think...', 'I feel...' etc.

164

- *Identification* relates to the wish to be like and/or assume the characteristics of another; often to the degree that a subject becomes estranged from his or her authentic self. Unconscious imitation of this nature is an integral part of socialisation and sexual programming and is well established within all of us. Identification may occur in groups where passive reciprocity has taken the place of problem resolution. Individuals so affected tend to become over-confirming, supporting and identified with an external object, be this an organisation, a boss, a supervisor or facilitator. An individual responding in this way feels by turns seductive and dependent – so causing us to be less questioning or exploratory than we would otherwise be. Group confluence, where everything the facilitator suggests is readily agreed with, is a classical feature of over-identification. When identification occurs in a group it is useful to raise awareness to the socialising influences of the setting, the prevailing and imagined norms, plus what happens when these norms are breached. Alternative strategies to the usual tried-and-tested routines may also be explored. Another way to interrupt collusion is by highlighting individual difference and drawing attention to what is unique; investing more challenge and gently raising to awareness hidden agendas can also help here.

- *Rationalisation* describes a process where intellectual reasoning is employed to hide the emotional impact or significance of an incident. An uncomfortable incident might in this way be reasoned away without exploration of the core issue. When a theoretical presentation is held onto at all costs and no space is allowed for other views or self-critique, it is likely a person or group is suffering the hubris of rationalisation. Here inquiry may be made into the emotional significance of an argument and attention drawn to the purpose 'reason' is serving. Counter-positions and critiques may also be invited. Gently surfacing awareness to the underlying discomfort motivating rationalisation can also prove useful.

- *Displacement* refers to the discharge of pent-up emotions onto events or persons that are less threatening than those which initiated the original reaction. Sometimes anger which originated as a response to a senior manager may be carried across to safer targets in a team or group, or yet displaced upon the facilitator. It is sometimes useful to ask people to check-in with the pressures or anxieties they are carrying, or to share the preoccupations they carry into a meeting. Getting people to voice what they are thinking about – right now – or to trace the origin of their present mood can also help.

- *Regression* describes a reversion to earlier, age-inappropriate behaviour in order to avoid responsibility or current demands; it may occur when an individual's emotional and intellectual resources are overwhelmed by what is perceived to be a crisis situation. A person's regression may be compounded by their perception of subordinate status, feelings of passivity and inadequacy, or by a sense of being at the mercy of a strange environment or caught in the throes of a child-like past. A facilitator needs to be on the lookout for any hierarchical, authoritarian or parental responses that have crept into their presentation and can work towards peer-hood in their relations to counterbalance this dynamic.

Three further mental defences, termed 'interruptions to contact' and beloved by Gestalt practitioners, are also worthy of discussion, namely confluence, narcissism and retroflection:

Confluence is a term literally used to describe two rivers flowing into one and thus, in a Gestalt context, it relates to our tendency to merge, indicating the erosion of boundaries between people when they lose self-identity. A person who is unable to manage conflict, or who feels he or she has no choice but to surrender to avoid rejection, may merge rather than withdraw. Perhaps in earlier relationships they experienced a disabling sense of hurt or abandonment and are fearful of facing the same again. Whatever the cause, confluence describes the merger of two into one. Whether enacted consciously or unconsciously, confluence boils down to the same thing: a denial of difference in an attempt to escape conflict. We see confluence at work, to varying degrees, in relationships high in co-dependency, collusion and dependence. But although seeking to resolve conflict, nobody comes out satisfied in a confluent relationship. Although in the short term a transient sense of escape may be felt, eventually both parties feel de-skilled and dissatisfied as authenticity and contact – the raw stuff of healthy relating – are banished. Feeling trapped and angry, losing more and more of themselves, each may then end up blaming the other in preference to facing the shame of their own all-consuming dependency. After all, can you truly love someone you feel dependent upon? And how permissive and free can you be when you are addicted to another? At the last, it must be acknowledged that a robust acknowledgment of difference is necessary for the generation of healthy, mutually fulfilling relationships. Certain relational scripts are especially inviting of confluence:

- *Please and Please* – In this situation, a couple exist in a seemingly stable relationship cemented by mutual dependence, where each is so terrified of being alone that they rigidly comply to an unspoken agreement that each will behave as the other demands; here both receive the emotional security they crave, but at the cost of stifling spontaneity and authentic expression. Every so often, the pent-up resentment of feeling dependent on the other breaks out in angry quarrels, but in the end politeness wins the day and dependent equilibrium returns.

- *Please and Try Hard* – In this amicable but somewhat dreary relationship, where risk and potential hurt is avoided along with ambition and stimulation, each partner tries ever so hard to conform to an abstract 'respectable norm' so as to avoid friction and to please the other.

- *Please and Hurry Up* – In this scenario each partner seems to believe that you have to earn the love and respect of others, and so ends up manically trying to keep the other happy by showing off how good they are.

(After Klein 1983)

Developmentally, confluence naturally occurs in early infancy, at the time before the baby separates its mother from itself. In these terms, it may be suggested to be a regressive act, perhaps evoked by an unconscious longing for the blissful oneness we experienced prior to the development of our individual ego – a time of revelry which harks back to a time before 'the fall from Eden', a time before we were cast out from that heavenly feeling of oneness we felt within the womb or at our mother's breast, long before we were alienated from the universe and caused to fend for ourselves. Raise awareness to and cultivate an appreciation of difference to disengage scripts inviting of confluence.

Narcissism relates to a largely unconscious intrapersonal process where the world mirrors the ego. Remember, in the original story Narcissus did not realise he was seeing himself within the pool – he in all sincerity believed he was falling in love with another. When we forget that we create our own reality, that we project outwards upon the world our thoughts and feelings and that we author our perceptions and feelings, we cultivate Narcissus within us. Narcissus represents the alienated ego that cannot love, an individual who is unable to invest interest and libido in life because they are too wrapped up in themselves. At one level to fall in love with the reflected image of oneself can only mean that one does not yet fully possess a realisation of oneself. Narcissus yearns to unite with himself because he is alienated from his own being; after all, we only yearn for what we feel we lack.

We learn through Narcissus that self-knowledge and self-valuing are prerequisites of genuine love and that to move beyond our projections and imaginings requires a descent into the unconscious – a sort of symbolic ego-death. For instance, in Greek mythology, the narcissus flower that Narcissus turned into following his death was sacred to Hades – because it opened the gates to the underworld, the realm of the gods. This suggests we must surrender our ego if we are to advance spiritually! Remember, when Persephone picked a narcissus, Hades arose and dragged her down to his unseen realm. False identification is the culprit of narcissistic thinking.

Sometimes, when an infant feels deeply hurt and worthless in their innermost core and their self-image-cum-ego-structure feels in danger of rupturing, they protect this wound with narcissism. Later, as the repressed hurt is felt to be too deep to acknowledge, further narcissism is layered on the site of this earlier damage. Eventually, narcissism may become generalised as a routine defence and integrated into the personality structure. In this light, narcissism can be appreciated as an armouring of a fragile ego by the implanting of grandiosity. Redressing and healing the narcissistic wound is a long and gentle affair that treads a path through shame. When we forget that we are looking in a mirror we fall into the trap of Narcissus. When all is said and done, life is a constant process of disillusionment, a process where illusion after illusion is stripped away from the self until we can see and hear the truth.

Retroflection relates to an unaware turning of emotion inwards upon the self, when emotions boomerang back to us. In retroflection, what we really wish to do to others, we do to ourselves. In these terms, masturbation may be suggested to be a retroflection of the desire to make love; self-damage a retroflection of wanting to harm others; self-criticism a retroflection of a critical impulse towards powerful others turned back on the self. Retroflection is said to occur when we hold back our emotional, verbal and behavioural expressions. It is best undone by exploring the associated beliefs and expectations we have clustered around what we believe might be the consequence of releasing what we are retroflecting. Suicide is often cited as an extreme form of retroflection, where strongly aggressive, potentially murderous feelings felt towards something or someone are frustrated, cannot be expressed and end up turning back on the self.

The above mechanisms skew facilitation and facilitative inquiry. Their continued presence denotes a considerable degree of psychological stress which might well lead us to hypothesise about the psychological health of a relationship or the underlying stress inherent within an individual or work community. But imagination can be used as a creative force also. For instance, I find guided fantasy a helpful integrator of complex experience. When a group feels weary or tired and appears to be losing contact, such as on a workshop following lunch, I will at times go with this energy, ask individuals to: 'Close your eyes… breathe in and feel full… breathe out and let go and feel relaxed'. Then starting from the feet and working up the body I first ask participants to: 'Relax and let go of your legs… relax and let go of your buttocks… relax and let go of your waist… relax and let go of your hands… relax and let go of your arms… relax and let go of your shoulders… relax and let go of your neck… relax and let go of your face and scalp' etc. Then, continuing to speak in a slow and relaxed way, I will encourage participants to count back the years, stopping every five years to consider what in their life returns from this time, what they are doing and what's important for them. I might start this process at the age of forty by suggesting: 'Imagine being forty again… What preoccupied you in your fortieth year?… Who is important to you at this time? … What dreams motivate you?' Than after a pause I will say, 'Let's count back the years a little further, 40… 39… 38… 37… 36… 35… What clothes did you wear when you were 35? … Who were your closest friends… How important was your career to you?' Stopping every five years, we soon arrive at five years old: 'So remember waking up in your bedroom at five years of age… look at the wallpaper… be aware of what's in your bedroom… Go to the bedroom window and look outside – what do you see? … Turn around – notice how high the door knobs are… find a mirror and gaze at yourself – what do you see? How are you dressed? … Walk downstairs… who do you find there? … Which people and pets are important to you? … Now imagine sitting as you are now opposite your five year old self… what advice might he or she give you?' Such journeys as this may focus upon earlier periods of life, an individual's career stages or professional history, and can surface memories and insights long dormant. I might even invite participants to become those who figure large in their reminiscences and to explore what it's like to look and think from their position. Renewed insight and integration is the purpose behind this experiment. Finally, I will ask participants: 'Breathe deeply and feel full… gradually return to the room… open your eyes in your own time… find a partner and share your insights and learning with them.' Though people often surface slowly as if awakening from a dream, in a few minutes I notice the energy and engagement of sharing in pairs often builds into a long-lasting crescendo. Tiredness is now a long way behind. I wait until this settles before drawing participants to the larger group and plenary discussion. So how does an approach like this strike you?

Reflections

* How would you deal with dynamics of repression, denial or regression within one-to-one coaching or adapt your facilitative style and presence to counter the effects of transference and projection?

• What qualities, if any, seem core to our address of the above dynamics? *(I think I endeavour always to support the person, even when challenging their behaviour, to retain my authenticity, to evidence my observations and to give feedback in a take-it-or-leave-it manner, to stay curious as to what is happening and inviting of my client (group or individual) to experiment with being different.)*

* When in your life have you experienced or felt drawn into confluence?

• When you reflect upon such times, what is familiar and what core conditions seem to fuel these occasions for you? *(I think I'm more prone to a confluent reaction when I'm feeling lost and unsure, undermined and confused, when I fear rejection or feel out of my depth and seemingly regress to a child-like place and am on the search – symbolically – for a nurturing parent to support me. Thankfully such times are few and far between, though as the emotional part of me never grows up such reactions as this remain ever a possibility.)*

* In terms of the following relational scripts:

• 'Please and Please' – rigid obedience and agreement that you will behave as the other demands

• 'Please and Try Hard' – risk avoidant with adherence to an abstract 'respectable norm'

▶

- 'Please and Hurry Up' – each partner attempts to earn the respect and love of the other.

- Reflect on where and when have you met or been party to the above dynamics, their gains and costs, and how you eventually extracted yourself from these relationships.

- From this exercise, what insights may be carried forward into your facilitative role?

* How might you create a guided fantasy to help your clients acknowledge their unique skills and possible real purpose in life?

5.5 Following the Muse of Imagination – Free and Associating

'Creativity' is a prime fruit of imagination and the projective level, and it is this recognition of creativity more than anything else that distinguishes Gestalt from psychoanalysis. Otto Rank (1946) was the first to forsake Freud's notions of ego, id and superego because they did not account for creativity. For him the ego had creative as well as defensive restraining forces:

> The psychological understanding of the creative type and of its miscarriage in the neurotic, teaches us therefore, to value the ego, not only as a wrestling ground of (id) impulses and (superego) repressions, but also as conscious bearer of a striving force, that is, as the autonomous representative of the will and ethical obligation in terms of a self-constituted ideal.
>
> (Rank quoted in Taft 1958, p.5)

Creativity, in Gestalt, is often seen as a positive act of aggression, *a reaching out* into the void to regenerate; be this creative reaching geared towards the construction of art or in the co-creation of relationship. Indeed, Zinker (1978) observes that creativity implies relationship. But how might consultants and coaches enrich their practice by an injection of creativity? Perls says we have to go back to basics while attuning to our core:

> Now normally the élan vital, the life force, energizes by sensing, by listening, by scouting, by describing the world – how is the world there. Now this life force apparently first mobilizes the centre if you have a centre. And the centre of the personality is what used to be called the soul: the emotions, the feelings, the spirit.
>
> (Perls 1972, p.64)

Back to the old Gestalt chestnut – lose your mind and come to your senses to create!

i) An Imaginative Group Sculpt – Being Guided by Projection

When projection begins to bite and fantasy reigns in a group, or when a lack of creative energy is in the air and discussion appears to be leading nowhere, I introduce a 'group sculpt' to explore what individuals 'imagine is happening'. In this process one individual (the director/sculptor) arranges other group members into positions (kneeling, sitting, standing, standing on chairs, moving or static) which express the group dynamic. Individuals may be positioned near or far from one another, joining hands, facing one another or back to back, in pairs or bunched in mini groups to capture best how they are seen to relate. You can further build on this representation by inviting the director/sculptor to 'shadow' each person – that is, to place their hand on the shoulder of those they've arranged and to speak out loud what they imagine that person is thinking and feeling. For example, speaking on their behalf they might say 'I'm unsure of this group and I'm playing safe by following rather than initiating'. Finally, the director places themselves in their creation and says how they themselves feel; as facilitator you might then invite participants to comment upon how the positions assigned them resonate with their own experience and to report how well the words put in their mouth represent how they 'really' feel, or to position themselves where they actually see themselves. After two or more members have performed a 'sculpt' and illustrated their imaginative perceptions, you will get a fair impression of the projections at play in the group field.

ii) Poetic and Imaginative Interventions – Facilitating via Fantasy

Although much of my time as a facilitator is spent 'grounding people' through sensory here-and-now observations, on occasion I let my imagination run free to catch an arising metaphor or image:

> 'When you spoke just then the image of a frightened deer came to mind – does this resonate with you in any way?'

> 'As you told your story, I imagined you as very small child – crying in a corner; I wonder how my image impacts you?'

> 'Inside here we're suffering in this slowly moving non-responsive group – yet outside I hear birds singing!'

> 'If this group were represented by a pool of water – how deep do you image it would be? What colour might the water take on? Would it be a large or small pool? How weed filled? Would the surface be smooth or choppy? And if there were living things in its waters – and what might these be?'

> 'If I were a meal right now – how would I taste to you and what sort of food might I be?'

> 'So if we go on as we are without changing course – where would we end up?'

At other times I have invited clients to use crayons and paper to express themselves freely and spontaneously. Sometimes I have asked people to separate out critical and nurturing messages they hold about themselves or to depict important incidents from their life on paper or in clay, by arranging stones or yet again to draw a personal badge or coat of arms. I might then ask them to reflect on their product and to consider:

- What stands out for you from this symbolic self/family portrait?

- What does this arrangement of colours/shapes/sizes/texture/positions mean for you?

- What is expected, what is new or otherwise surprises you in this self-representation?

- What pleases you and disturbs you the most in the images/formations placed before you?

- If you were to change in ways you personally desire, how would this representation shift?

- How might this symbolic self-picture need to change to be nearer the ideal or realised you?

- When you look around and see others images, which resonate with or challenge you?

At other times I've asked people to draw in the bottom left hand corner of a large sheet of paper an image, symbol, or words to describe 'where they are right now'; to then draw in the top right hand corner of their paper 'where they want to be'; and finally I ask them to draw in the centre of their page 'what gets in the way' of them travelling from 'where they are now' to 'where they want to be.' Dramatically enacting an imaginary scene or speaking aloud to an absent protagonist, these too are useful, as are expressive movement, monodrama and psychodrama – to capture projective and imagined material. At this level we are limited solely by our lack of imagination!

When employing imaginative interventions to catch the nature of a relationship, I've sometimes invited a client to consider the following:

- If your life were a play, what type of play might it be – a comedy or tragedy?

- What sort of heroic journey might you be upon if you were a character in a Greek myth?

- Bring to mind the viewpoint of various historical figures to reframe your experience. For instance, if you were Christ what might you perceive, or if you were Hitler, or yet again if you viewed the world through your mother or father's eyes?

172

Such interventions as these get at contrasting perspectives, rattle and shake personal bias and stimulate a comparison with the perspectives of others. They present and put into action the notion that perception is projection, that we only perceive that which we have first learnt to conceive and that our beliefs shape our world.

iii) Illuminating Inner Dialogue – Humanising the System

Transactional Analysis (TA) provides analytic thinking with a more social and humane face. It was devised by Eric Berne (Berne 1964) to educate his clients to the psychodynamics of relationship, thus empowering them to act as their own therapists! Sadly, much current TA has become over-prescriptive, over-regimented and over-analytic, thus losing its humanistic plot; but hopefully with relational TA on the horizon, all will not be lost.

In Berne's model, three ego states roughly equivalent to Freud's *super-ego*, *ego* and *id* are seen to relate us to the world: the *Parent* (our store of intellectual and socio-cultural teachings), the *Adult* (our store of experiential data) and the *Child* (our store of emotional memories, intuition and sensation):

- **The parent ego (super-ego):** Attends to *'life as taught'* and acts as custodian of our intellectual, cultural and social beliefs. Houses *controlling* and *nurturing* aspects of parenting and represents the conservative part of us that clings to the known, our reference to norms, accepted theories, laws, rules and traditions, rituals and customs, plus culturally defined notions of good and bad *(our orientation to social/cultural reality)*.
  * Uses words like *'should'*, *'must'* and *'because'*, acts as an internal reference for our authority and parenting of others, enshrines and copies our own parents and their values.

- **Adult ego (ego):** Attends to *'life as found'*, acts with reference to sensory and physiological perceptions, makes decisions based on reality exploration. Questions and builds up information from experimentation and testing, approaches events non-emotionally and objectively *(our orientation to physical/ sensory reality)*.
  * Uses words like *'how'*, *'where'* and *'why'*, represents the self-made reality orientated part of you.

- **Child ego (id):** Attends to *'life as felt and imagined'* and houses feelings, intuition, play and creativity. May be sub-divided into the *'the adapted child'* – parental influence within the child, *'the little professor'* – who intuitively knows best *(an echo of the adult in the child but who acts on subjective rather than objective data)* and *'the natural child'* – the repository of spontaneity, emotional expression, creativity and play *(our orientation to emotional/ transferential, projective/imaginal, and transpersonal/intuitive reality)*.
  * Uses words like *'can't'*, *'won't'*, *'wow'* and *'now'*, houses memories and

daydreams carried from childhood and pre-socialised reminiscences of being dependent and free.

So that's the theory! But within this frame is a valuable container for imaginative speculation. For instance, when a conflict or split is brewing in a group or individual, I've found it useful to explore and exaggerate the same by bringing out three empty chairs labelled 'Parent', 'Adult' and 'Child', inviting individuals out and suggesting a chair appropriate to their current stance, engaging them in dialogue while inviting them to move between chairs as their perspective/words/attitudes shift. Very quickly participants get the gist and spontaneously move themselves. Indeed, after five or ten minutes of moving between chairs exercising their ability to explore imaginatively in this way, participants become expert at locating where their attitudes originate and which sub-personality is speaking. Such action represents an imaginative leap of faith more than anything else, but when this exploration has run for a while and others have taken their turn, we can speculate on the ego that makes the decisions for those involved – plus the group's own relative ego strengths. Later we may consider the relative merits and limitations of attuning to the 'World as Taught' through the eyes of a *controlling* or a *nurturing parent*, the 'World as found' through the eyes of the *adult*, and the 'World as Felt' through the eyes of an *adapted, little professor* or *natural child* and how this pans out within the host group:

World as Taught/Learnt (Parent Ego)	*World as Found/Reasoned* (Adult Ego)	*World as Felt/Imagined* (Child Ego)
Controlling/Nurturing	Here and Now	Adapted/Professor/Natural
An authoritative position which by turns instructs, informs and nurtures others	A questioning and alert, investigating, here-and-now, reality-orientated position	An emotional and excited and intuitive position which echoes childhood

I find it valuable when entering a new group or organisation to inquire in a similar mode. Bringing the above model to mind, I impressionistically allocate a plus (+) or minis (-) to each ego – thus forming a thumbnail sketch of the group/system's personality.

Parent	**Adult**	**Child**
Controlling (+ +) Nurturing (-)	Here and Now (-)	Adapted (+ +) Professor (+) Natural (- - -)

With this imaginative sketch in place I feel better able to appreciate human influence within and upon the field. Indeed, via similar profiling in my doctorate I demonstrated how a facilitated group's personality journeyed out from Parent and Child towards a progressively stronger Adult ego (Barber 1990) during its lifetime; namely, facilitation was seen to increase reality orientation and experimentation and to grow the group up!

At root, Gestalt stands for creativity, contact and experiential wisdom founded upon the authority of the 'lived experience' – as authenticated by moment-to-moment awareness. And its purpose, well, we raise awareness through strengthening the Adult's reality orientation while working through archaic material of the Parent and Child. Our 'reality' – our phenomenology in Gestalt terms – says something about where we are in relation to our guiding dream, our inspiration, which though 'imagined' nevertheless represents part and parcel of the 'authenticity' we live (Just 2003, p.5). All we have to do to 'change' is to co-create a new reality; 'only', I say!

It is not by mere accident that the original meaning of the word 'person' is mask. It is rather recognition of the fact that everyone, always and everywhere is consciously or subconsciously playing a role, and through these roles we come not only to know each other but to know ourselves.

The creative approaches to transformation surveyed here are empowering because they put us in touch with our problems and pains, imagined and real, providing opportunity for reappraisal. But to change the body–mind is not easy for, as creatures of habit, we come to depend upon how we see the world and the narrative we live – even when we know that our vision is flawed! Yet Gestalt invites us to test the notion that if we change our mind then the world we experience will change of itself. It cautions us that when we live in the past or future we de-power ourselves and function with severely limited information gleaned from memories or fantasy-based projections of the world. The mind holds lessons of the past, the world as previously experienced and culturally taught, and remembering such things takes us into the there-and-then, far away from what is current and now.

iv) Archetypes – Universal Behavioural Blueprints?

A group or individual's review of the archetypes they shade into – universally understood symbols or prototypes with related patterns of behaviour upon which other behaviours are patterned or emulated – I have discovered, can provide a useful means for illuminating psychological blind spots and imaginative drivers. The origins of archetypes are ancient; they are present in prehistoric artwork, folklore and literature. Plato suggested that pure mental forms, collective blueprints of behaviour, were imprinted in the soul prior to its birth in the world. Building on these platonic ideas Carl Jung (1981) derived his notion of psychological archetypes, innate and universally shared prototypes. Jung treated archetypes as psychological organs, analogous to physical ones in that both were seen to be organically evolved through evolution – hence his notion of a racial unconscious. Groups of memories and interpretations associated with an archetype Jung termed 'a complex'.

In my consulting room I have a pack of archetype cards (Myss 2003) with positive (light attributes) and negative (shadow attributes) of seventy-seven archetypes. For example there is 'the Prostitute', who symbolises 'lessons in the sale or negotiation of one's integrity or spirit due to fears of physical survival or for financial gain' (Myss 2003, p.17). We prostitute ourselves whenever we sell our bodies or minds, or compromise our morals and ethics for financial gain, be that in marriage or a job that endangers our self-respect.

Have you ever sold out to people or organisations you didn't believe in, remained in employ merely for financial security? Or put another in a self-compromising position to gain power over them? If so, welcome to the prostitute within you! With the prostitute, his or her *light attributes* include accentuating the challenge of surviving without negotiating the power of his or her spirit; and his or her *shadow attributes* embrace the placing of material considerations and security above self-empowerment. Below, I've arrayed other archetypes I deem commensurate with a facilitative role:

Archetype	Light Attributes	Shadow Attributes
Detective	Transcends convention and stuffiness along with predictable behaviour	Manipulates others through duplicity
Guide	Represents the nature of the Divine in life and self	Places financial gain and control over the imparting spiritual insight
Healer	Passion to serve and repair body and mind and to transform pain into healing	Taking advantage of those whoneed help and failing to care for oneself
Exorcist	Freeing yourself and others from destructive impulses	Fear of facing your own demons
Engineer	Ability to give creative energy a practical expression and to design resolutions	Reliance on mechanistic solutions without regard for emotional consequences
Father	Talent for creating and supporting life as a positive guiding light	Dictatorial control and abuse of authority
Mother	Joy in giving birth and nurturing with patience and unconditional love	Smothering or abandoning offspring and instilling guilt for becoming independent
Messiah	Serving humanity with Humility	Exaggerated belief that we are the only means through which a cause can succeed
Trickster	Transcending convention and predictable behaviour	Manipulating others through duplicity
Warrior	Combining strength and skill with discipline of will and self-sacrifice in service of conquering the ego	Trading ethical principles for victory at any cost and indifference to the suffering of others
Rescuer	Provides strength and support to those in crisis with acts based on love without an expectation of reward	Assumes the rescued will reciprocate while keeping the rescued one needy

So which of the above psychological blueprints influence you – both positively and negatively? Where in Jungian terms does your complex constellate? Whatever we imaginatively consult, archetypes or the *I Ching, Book of Changes*, stimulants to the imagination in all forms help us meet with less familiar aspects of ourselves, spurring on our speculative imagination and creativity. Lying on the floor with eyes closed bombarded by Shamanistic drumming, Yogic meditation, being led by a guided fantasy all rattle-and-shake our conventional world and open unfamiliar doors.

So, moving out from your imaginative world – but still using it to change gear to draw nearer to a sense the void – listen to all before you and attune to your centre, for in the next chapter we explore metaphysical and transpersonal influences within facilitation.

Reflections

*In terms of our earlier discussion, imagine yourself each in turn standing in the Parent, Adult and Child, and see what emerges when you consider the question: 'So what do you most value in your role as a facilitator?'

* How do the world views below impact upon you as a facilitator?

The World as Taught/Learnt
(I value my leadership skills and how I shape and control a group, my parenting and nurture of others and giving of relevant information. And the authority I reap and claim as a respected professional who uses specialist knowledge and skill in service of others.)

World as Found/Reasoned
(I employ and value my facilitation as a tool of inquiry, a means of exploring and discovering the deeper reasons and causative agents of group-life; facilitation's also a means of developing and raising awareness to myself and my own journey of self-discovery in life.)

World as Felt/Imagined
(I enjoy the challenge and excitement of being with others and the uncertainty and chaos of group facilitation, which demands a creative, playful and emotionally expressive response from me.)

* Bring an organisation you work in to mind and impressionistically form a sketch of its personality by adding a plus + or minus – to its emerging ego states:

Parent	Adult	Child
Controlling/Nurturing	Here and Now	Adapted Child / Little Professor/ Natural Child

- What personality profile results?

- What appear to be its strengths and weaknesses?

- How might this personality be enhanced through facilitative input?

* When exploring the imaginative world of a group or team:

- At what stage and for what purpose might you perform a group sculpt?

- Which archetypes do the teams, groups and organisations you consult cluster around?

* Below are some archetypes you may associate with a client position or meet in the client-system?

Archetype	Light Attributes	Shadow Attributes
Victim	Prevents you from letting yourself be victimised or victimising others	Playing the victim for positive feedback in the form of pity plus an inability to maintain boundaries
Bully	Highlights our tendency to imitate others and helps us confront inner fears that bully us	Conceals deep fears behind verbal and physical abuse
Addict	Helps us recognise and confront addictive behaviour	Compromises integrity and honesty and allows addictive patterns to have authority over inner spirit
Seeker	Thirst for wisdom and truth where ever they are	Inability to commit to a path once found

- How might you raise the above to mind in team-building?

- Are you ever contaminated by the above positions yourself?

- Which do you like least?

Reflections upon Chapter 5

* You are invited to perform shadow consultancy for a group of close-knit consultants who are in the midst of running a change programme in a multi-national company, who are becoming increasingly concerned that they are meeting client behaviours unrelated to what is actually happening!

- How might you explain 'projection' as a possible influence within their work?

- Drawing upon the various models in this text, how might you alert this group to their own projective agendas?

- How might you help them understand the unconscious mechanisms that all too often can interfere and arrest authentic communication.

* As your shadow consulting progresses you begin to realise a good deal of this group's perception is influenced by their own projections:

- What group intervention might you make to illuminate phenomena at the projective level?

- How might you use Transactional Analysis and notions of the 'world as taught' and 'world as felt' to illustrate the probable content of projection?

- How might you work through confluence within this professional group?

- How might an intervention style modelled on 'Gestalt' help work with and work through the projective level of communication?

* You notice during subsequent sessions how resistive this group appears to be to remaining in the here and now and to maintaining good quality contact.

- How might you alert them to your emerging hypothesis and the need to establish better contact with each other and the present?

- What imaginative interventions might you suggest to help them improve their performance in this area?

* Pause to consider the following mindsets that accompany you as a facilitator:

- Before meeting a new client for coaching, what fantasies go through your mind?

- What are your fears regarding the worst that could happen?

- What do you consider to be the ideal outcomes?

In reflecting upon personal dreads, professional expectations and desires:

- What imagined events come to mind?

- What visions, mission or challenge seems to be motivating you?

- How might you best proceed in future?

In the Buddhist tradition, it's believed that there is a realm of hungry ghosts with huge appetites and throats the size of a needle. So, they're never satisfied, like the shadow with its ravenous appetite. By feeding it in small, regular amounts, the shadow doesn't need to take on a devouring attitude.

(Babbs 1991)

Chapter six

Raising Awareness to Transpersonal
and Intuitive Influences

Until we are prepared to think for ourselves and go beyond the known, our dreams will not be free to unfold.

1   The Dawning of a New Paradigm –
Accounting for Influences Beyond the Self

At the transpersonal and intuitive level we examine tacit knowledge and speculate on subtle influences which are inferred rather than known. In this chapter, more subtle influences on the 'field' are surveyed along with notions of Dharma, global resonance and higher purpose. We also look at mindfulness and meditative approaches to inquiry plus family constellations as an illuminator of the 'field's' spiritual nature.

At the more tangible end of the transpersonal continuum we find notions such as 'Nature', ecology and globalisation; at the other, we journey towards more abstract concepts of soul and spirit. But how did this continuum ever enter the territory of organisations and consulting?

Fritz Schumacher, writing in the early seventies, drew attention to the way industrialised nations were using up the natural resources – or the capital of our planet – at an unsustainable pace while contributing to global pollution (Schumacher 1973). Observing that our industrial tradition had to change, he suggested a new commercial lifestyle, one where methods of production and consumption would be designed for permanence and based on biologically sound agriculture and 'non-violent technology' – an approach that would not perpetuate violence upon people or resources. This vision of 'technology with a human face' opened the door to current ecological thinking while supporting the tailoring of production to a scale proportionate to the human condition. Where Galbraith (1967) saw investment and corporations as serving government, Schumacher saw technology serving mankind and called for nothing less than a total 'paradigm shift' (Kuhn 1962).

Today, 'paradigm shifts' are taken to have socio-cultural as well as scientific components. The world view that is currently on the wane is a mechanistic one that conceives of the universe as a mechanical system composed of rudimentary building blocks and the human body as a machine. Closely aligned to this 'old paradigm thinking' is the view of society as a competitive struggle for existence, a belief that unlimited material progress can be achieved through economic and technological growth, and more disturbingly a taking for granted that 'the female' is subordinate to 'the male' as a basic law of nature (Capra 1997). As for the 'new paradigm' pulling us into the twenty-first century, this appears to be a transpersonal and ecological conviction (see Devall and Sessions 1985) which views the world as integrated rather than a collection of dislocated parts, honours both male and female, and is deeply holistic to the degree it includes spiritual awareness (Capra 1997). From this perspective, the world is viewed as a network of phenomena that are fundamentally interdependent; the intrinsic worth of all living things is recognised along with their place as part of the whole web of life (ibid.). Field thinking no less!

Evidence for this inter-relational and holistic shift of vision is not just confined to physics (Capra 1982 and 1997) and philosophy (Roszak 1992), but is evidenced in such terms as 'transpersonal ecology' (Fox 1990) and 'eco-psychology' (Roszak 1992), which accommodates a world view where the most fine and ethereal of field conditions are seen to interrelate with the spiritual. More recently, complexity theory (Anderson 1999) has also been used to account for transpersonal influences within organisational life (Harkema and Browaeys 2003) and story-telling has been used to this end as a facilitative tool to raise awareness to spiritual influences in the workplace (Allen et al. 2002).

At the simplest of levels, 'the transpersonal' can relate to global influence, seasonal change and electro-chemical cycles that infiltrate the natural environment, while at its most complex 'things transpersonal' may be suggested to include spiritual and energetic influences beyond the ken of our senses and human understanding, subtle speculative energies that are believed to shape the universe. Largely unproven though inferred, such energies as these are suggested to exist over and above the notion of 'self'. A facilitator working holistically, attempting to account for the whole system, though they may not believe in things spiritual, nevertheless must automatically consider spiritual/divine influence and all else that informs themselves and their client's energetic field.

In the case study below, I drew upon Jungian archetypes to help me capture more subtle aspects of the client-system.

An Inquiry into Dharma –
Awakening a Team to Creativity via the Transpersonal

Some years ago I was invited to work with a management team within a multinational company facing reorganisation. In due course I met with key players, observed the team in action and arranged a day to commence team-building proper.

Although the management team seemed to get on well enough and to gentle themselves along generally in the right direction, energetically there appeared to be a general lack of vitality, focus and authentic feedback. For instance, prior to the performance of team-building proper when I joined the team for an evening meal and casual chatter, one snippet of information especially impacted me. It emerged that the Managing Director (MD) often dined rather too well at lunch and consequently all too often fell asleep during afternoon meetings. This it seemed had become something of an in-joke in the team, with other managers hinting that it was best to get the important work over with in the morning, or yet to wait until late afternoon for more pressing business. I later found out that some used this to their advantage, getting issues nodded through after lunch which at other times might have been challenged!

Treating the MD in this manner, although fuelling of humour, seemed to have acquired, informally over time, legitimate status as a way of ridiculing him and 'hitting back' in retaliation for his nit-picking and detail-chasing management style. Indeed his accountancy background and fastidious manner was widely

184

resented by those who had been 'trained to management'. This resentment was never openly broached, individually nor collectively, and so remained a covert point of contention within the team. Having gleaned this information from three team members on separate occasions in the staff club – note: a consultant is never off-duty – at the first opportunity I fed it back to the team in the presence of the MD without identifying my sources. I recollect saying something along the lines of: 'I believe this team sets people up; for example, I've heard that many here find a certain individual's detail-chasing style frustrating, but in contrast to challenging or helping him to appreciate the bigger picture, they choose to let him continue unencumbered by their counsel or feedback. It is also a standing joke that the person concerned falls asleep in meetings following lunch – but no-one challenges them. If this is so, what might be the team's motives?' No names were mentioned but all knew who we were talking about – the MD included. Over the next few weeks, the MD took lighter lunches!

Throughout this consultancy, I found myself doing a good deal of challenging, regularly holding up for examination what was seemingly being denied and increasingly speaking the unspoken. In short, I caught myself playing out the challenging energy associated with the Warrior archetype. Recognising this in myself, I began to consider the archetype I was possibly engaging in the client-system; which on reflection seemed to be one of Scholar, as knowledge was venerated, systematically collected and had to be exhaustively considered before any managerial decision could be taken. Indeed, the MD appeared to be the principle culture carrier of an over-fastidious scholarly approach, which led to speculative ideas being shunned and to a cumbersome decision-making process in which no-one could proceed without full information. Consequently, decisions tended to be excessively slow and arrive far too late – for envisioning the future and experimentation were not an option and no-one moved until the plan was watertight, but of course no plan is ever watertight within ever-changing circumstances – and reorganisation was imminent.

In my initial contact with the team, I had observed their emerging style and endeavoured to act in a culturally friendly way, building trust through evidencing my approach and sharing my reasons, thus meeting the client's Scholarly culture and going along at their pace. But now, a little later, having walked in their shoes sufficiently to embody and appreciate the prevailing field conditions at a deeper experiential level, somewhat like a cuckoo in an alien cosy nest I began to push out eggs rather than to walk softly upon the ever-present egg shells.

Becoming concentrated and focussed energetically in the manner of a Warrior, one who was persistent in the pursuit of 'truth' was not without its dangers. How long would it be, I reasoned, beneath this mantle of Warrior before I alienated myself from the larger proportion of the team; yet Warrior energy and an appreciation of the 'creative power of action' seemed the very thing the team lacked. With this caution in mind, I experimented with shifting my facilitative stance between Scholar and Warrior, the former to retain trust, the latter to role-model and introduce 'challenge' into the team.

I had initially been called to this consultation by the MD who felt – rightly, in the context of my earlier observations – that there was insufficient openness and honesty in the team. He reasoned that, with reorganisation upon the horizon, large blackholes of missing information would result unless the team bonded in a more real and authentic way. To reaffirm this initial contract, to inform more widely, to help generate commitment and especially to provide a safe container in which to frame my Warrior-inspired challenges, I suggested to the team that we might work together towards an illumination of 'what the team does well' and 'not so well' – with a view to crafting together the form future team building might take. I also shared my suspicion that the team was wrestling with the 'acquisition and ownership of knowledge' (Scholarly energy) but might possibly need to move towards an 'acknowledgement of the creative power of action' (Warrior energy). I also acknowledged how I was feeling more and more inspired to challenge their way of working, and asked them to monitor this tendency and to tell me should this feel too much at any time.

Deciding to run with the above Scholar and Warrior metaphors, we eventually settled upon collaborative inquiry based on an Appreciative Inquiry format as a way forward. This, we reasoned, would go some way to illuminating the current situation, the conditions that support people giving of their best in the workplace, while injecting more honesty and warrior energy into team culture.

In my introduction and review of Appreciative Inquiry (Bushe 1998), I outlined its progression through the following stages:

- *First, participants are asked to give a general impression of what it feels like to work in their current workplace*

- *Second, they are each in turn asked to describe a personal 'best experience' of working together when they felt at their most effective and efficient*

- *Third, they each share their own 'best experiences' while those who are listening are encouraged to remain curious and ask questions of the person sharing*

- *Forth, they are encouraged to get in touch with their own memories of similar experiences to the one being shared and to consider what it was that made this time a peak experience for them*

- *Fifth, individuals pool together the information they have surfaced to develop a consensus of the core qualities they associate with best working experiences with a view to identifying what they need to learn and build upon to integrate this experience further in the workplace*

- *Sixth, members are invited to acknowledge anything they have observed in the discussion group that has specifically helped them to become more aware of their own practice, the team, and how they might improve their work performance.*

In the weeks following the above exercise, I noticed a subtle change in the team's function – for instance, dialogue was now more inviting and accepting of difference and the communal belief system appeared to have placed 'challenge' on the agenda. Indeed, challenge was now invited. Although our Appreciative Inquiry had lasted no more than four hours in total, the potential for an attitudinal shift had seemingly been sown.

In the following meetings we evaluated gains from the above exercise. Several observations came to light:

- *Individuals felt more aware of how they were working and clear as to the conditions they needed to enhance their productivity and enjoyment*

- *Dialogue and communication between individuals who were previously distant in their day-to-day dealings were reported to be more intimate and frequent*

- *The challenge I had provided – possibly in the manner of a Blitz mentality – seemed to have fuelled a common 'we are all in it together' synergy*

- *Team ethos was believed to have improved through an injection of communal understanding.*

Over the next few weeks we went the whole hog and considered Dharma, which is to say each person's special purpose in life, how they could express their own unique talents and how they might actualise themselves in the workplace! Underpinning the concept of Dharma is the notion that we are in the world to discover our higher and spiritual self, for only through communion with our higher self are we suggested to be able to express our divinity – our true purpose, a purpose designed to make best use of our unique gifts and talents which shows us how best to serve humanity. In this regard, while the ego asks 'What's in it for me?', the higher and Dharma-informed self asks 'How might I best serve?'

In terms of putting Dharma into action, I suggested we entertain the notion that we have all been given physical form in order to express our true potentiality and to discover our unique purpose; and that if we were to run with this idea as a creative way forward, we might observe ourselves and each other at work so as to discover what exactly this might this be. Simply, we would pursue the nature of our own excellence and keep an eye open for the unique contributions we each made within the team.

I worked with this team for some eighteen months, meeting up to review the fruits of the above inquiry every six weeks or so. This consultancy more than any other reaffirmed for me that, if we don't like what's happening to us in the world, all we have to do is change our consciousness and re-frame our vision – and 'the world out there' will change for us.

Developmentally, facilitators at the transpersonal level may initially work at the projective level, unpacking erroneous perceptions; then find themselves teased from their client's projective world into one straddling imagined and spiritual influences; before being drawn further into unknown territory as the transpersonal influences they have inadvertently evoked infuse; then gradually beginning 'to facilitate them' before percolating to awareness. In this less than conscious way, transpersonal influence may be suggested to possess us before we glean a conscious appreciation of its effects. As I see field theory as a stepping stone into the transpersonal domain and believe it has a contribution to make to holistic facilitation of this more subtle kind, we examine this next.

Reflections

* In terms of the new paradigm described above, what do this stance and its philosophical position appear to be reacting against; that is to say, what intrinsic bias do you perceive in this newly emerging paradigm and what might it be ignoring or devaluing? *(Scientific positivism and 'progress' in the conventional sense are seen as too costly in human terms to be let continue unabated – but is the 'new paradigm' in danger of being somewhat idealising rather than realistic?)*

* How might this new perspective impact upon organisational culture and within teams, and how might coaches and group/community facilitators incorporate and account for this change? *(This perspective seems to be inviting us to account for the wider picture, influences over and above the self along with global and ecological influences. It is as if inter-connectedness is being considered, a view of the world where everything is taken to be interrelated and cemented by a web of complexity! Seems to be moving towards the 'energetic field' perspective we will be discussing in the next section of this text.)*

* Which of the archetypes Warrior, Magician, Hero and Scholar do you tend to evoke in your own coaching, group facilitation and organisational consultancy? *(I believe transferentially, before my clients meet me, they tend to hear of me by word of mouth – often from an enthusiastic source – and come expecting a Magician! I think once they experience me in the flesh, they symbolically see aspects of Warrior and Scholar by turns.)*

* How might a group or organisation representative of an Heroic energetic quality differ to one representative of Scholarly energy? And how might each organisation carry the seeds of its own destruction? *(I guess heroic energy might show itself in an outward, extroverted way, while scholarly energy might be more interior in character and inward facing. If I look back at the Gestalt cycle of awareness and withdrawal there might be some interesting parallels here with the above energy states.)*

.2 Travelling Through and Beyond the Phenomenological Field – Facilitating with Spirit

Field theory, for me, represents a bridge, one that integrates physical and socio-emotional energy, captures imagination and leads us towards the unknown. According to its originator Kurt Lewin (1952), it is not a theory so much as a 'way of thinking' and 'looking at the total situation', which *opens us up and un-zips perceptions.* While Lewin emphasised psychological aspects of the field, Malcolm Parlett (1991) emphasises the whole 'organised, interconnected, interdependent, interactive nature of human phenomena' and as such brings to bare a facilitative influence that looks to:

> Connections, wholes and not wholes; convergent divergent – consonant dissonant.
> Out of all a one and out of a one all.
>
> (Heraclitus in Guerrière, 1980, pp.94–5)

Parlett (1993) tells us that Lewin drew upon Maxwellian field theory in physics – which stated that unity was not due to particle or mass but rather to a 'field of force' (Wheelan et al., 1990) – an energetic blueprint that seemingly maintained the figural whole. Speculation upon the nature of this 'energetic blueprint' has of late brought quantum physics and spirit to the equation of 'field'.

Building on the Gestalt premise that perception is more than a sum of the parts, Hycner observes that a recognition of a greater reality over and above the sum total of our individual realities is a natural consequence of Gestalt's dialogical relationship; one where a facilitator through the cultivation of 'connectedness' causes us to experience in a series of 'I–Thou' moments a sense of an 'Eternal Thou' (Hycner 1993, p.91). It is hereby suggested that at times of deep intimacy we awaken a potential to be propelled into 'the transpersonal' and that a facilitator or coach becomes an instrument of the sacred when they remind us of the universe's mysteriously awesome and eternal nature. Although field theory presents us with an attractive conceptual model, the 'field' referred to is akin to an 'intelligent self-organising living form'. For example, even at the mundane everyday level we can feel the atmospheres of 'living fields' in a family, team, railway carriage or city street, as a group's electro-magnetic and biological currents, emotional micro-climates, physical energies and ripples of movement, social and cultural patterns and psychological influences all course through and around us. Interestingly, quantum physics reminds us that vibrating fields of energy are much more fundamental than matter (Sheldrake 2003), for at the quantum level there are no 'things' to study, only vibrating living relationships – and that the solidity of matter itself depends on the vibration of molecules.

Though multiple energies inform 'the field', many organisational consultants and group facilitators have begun to concentrate upon the underlying spiritual essence, which they see as a blueprint for the whole (Hycner 1993; Kennedy 1998; Hellinger et al. 1998; Wheway 1999; Sheldrake 2003; Senge et al. 2004; Kolodny 2004; Bampfield 2005). To work in a field-theoretical way, you consider events in the life-space of a group as aspects of a self-organising living whole. But what scientific evidence do we have for this?

Surfing the Internet, I discovered Roger Nelson's (2005) description of an experiment where random-number generators insulated from environmental and electromagnetic disturbance, which were placed around the world, had over the years been found to deviate from their expected numerical correlations during times of global strife, such as the death of Princess Diana, the beginning of the Kosovo conflict and the 9/11 terrorist attacks. So marked were these effects that researchers were forced to conclude that there seemed to exist an aspect of consciousness – a web of feeling – attributable to the global field!

So how do I square all this with my earlier notion that organisational intelligence is primitive and psychopathic? Well, I see differing qualities of intelligence as co-existing at different levels of the field. Conventional management training that develops sensory and social intelligence I view as largely inadequate for meaningful adaptation and change, for I deem that an appreciation and development of emotional, self and intuitive-cum-spiritual intelligence must also be included.

As to how a whole field management development curriculum geared to developing an organisation's sensory, social, emotional, projective and transpersonal intelligence might look... Here is one suggestion:

- **Developing Sensory Intelligence** (fostering observational and listening skills):
    - Developing sensitivity to the physical environment
    - Observing and attending to organisational and individual behaviours
    - Contacting and attending to sensory and physiological feedback
    - Learning about physiological needs and motivations

- **Developing Social Intelligence** (fostering facilitative inquiry and communication skills):
    - Forming and developing appropriate client–consultant relationships
    - Diagnosing and conducting inquiry into the interplay of culture and roles
    - Contracting, negotiating, facilitating and implementing suitable strategies
    - Raising awareness to managing professional, ethical and socio-cultural boundaries and rules

- **Developing Emotional Intelligence** (fostering coaching and counselling skills):
    - Illuminating historical patterns and emotional dramas that shape organisational behaviours

190

- Developing insight into the emotional needs of oneself, others, teams and large groups
- Working with and resolving conflict within oneself, others, teams and large groups
- Releasing emotional blockages, illuminating and resolving dramas

- *Developing Self-Intelligence* (fostering mindfulness and self-awareness skills):
  - Raising awareness to the effects of personal bias, fantasy and beliefs
  - Surfacing and working with individual, team and large group projections
  - Illuminating deeper motivations and meanings, developing skills in shadow consultancy
  - Identifying, challenging and working with hidden agendas

- *Developing Intuitive Intelligence* (fostering reflective and envisioning skills):
  - Illuminating and actualising your own potential and fostering that of others
  - Becoming authentic, self-witnessing and open to the unknown and unknowable
  - Valuing the self, humankind as my kind and working for the common good
  - Illuminating the higher spiritual purpose of individuals, groups, teams and organisations

Is this a fitting curriculum for consultants and coaches to work towards? And how might a holistically intelligent organisation possibly appear? I can hazard a further informed guess:

- At the sensory level an organisation such as this would pay attention to its present position and developing needs; its managers would employ sound observational, listening and action learning and research skills – *for research-mindedness amasses relevant and current data and knowledge.*

- At the social level the organisation would develop semi-permeable boundaries akin to a skin which grew to accommodate change; managers would be expert at building and maintaining relationships and would be skilled facilitators – *in this organisation, leaders empower and coach and teams make decisions.*

- At the emotional level the organisation would encourage expression and raise awareness to the emotional field; its managers would feel competent enough to work with and direct emotional energy and be able to identify historical patterns that support and hinder the organisation – *supervisors would vanish and a climate of peer support and self-empowerment flower.*

- At the projective level the organisation would raise and work with its blind spots, collusions and everything else that interfered with its creativity and adaptation; managers would employ skills of shadow consulting and realise the influence of projection upon perception – *creativity would drive process and value be seen as everything.*

- At the transpersonal level the organisation would consider its higher purposes and the value it may add to its employees and the community it serves, as well as encouraging its managers to be authentic and visionary – *profits must be earned with integrity and managers would value and encourage self-respect.*

All this is somewhat idealistic, I know, but it provides a good enough direction for me to work towards right now until something better comes along.

Over the last 50 years, Gestalt has consistently provided cutting-edge ways of understanding and working with group 'fields'. On such addition, a contrasting and very different way of contacting the field has also evolved from the family constellation work of Bert Hellinger (Hellinger et al. 1998). Although working with family systems is nothing new, suggesting we bring the family 'soul' into a room and expressing it through representatives *is*. Derived from multiple sources – Zulu ritual and Roman Catholicism, psychoanalysis and primal therapy, Gestalt and Transactional Analysis (TA), family therapy and Neuro-Linguistic Programming (NLP) – this approach is suggested to give voice to the message of soul by blending field theory with shamanism.

Family Constellations is at core an experiential process that aims to release and resolve tensions within and between people, and though largely entering Gestalt through the work of Bert Hellinger, it owes much to Alfred Adler who first coined the term and Virginia Satir who developed family sculpture.

The method involves:

- A group being led by a facilitator who encourages participants to explore urgent personal issues through the formation of a constellation

- After a brief interview, a representative for the seeker, family members or an abstract concept such as 'depression' is suggested

- The person presenting the issue chooses people from the group to be representatives and arranges these according to what feels right in the moment

- The seeker then sits down and observes

- Several minutes often elapse with representatives standing still and silent in their allocated places

- Emphasis is placed on intuition and the aim is to tune into the *Knowing Field* which is deemed to guide participants to articulate feelings and sensations that mirror those of the real family members they represent

- The facilitator may ask each representative to describe how it feels to be placed in relation to others, at which point all involved are alerted to perceive the underlying dynamic relating to the presenting issue

- A healing resolution for the issue generally involves repositioning the representatives and at the facilitator's suggestion a few spoken sentences

- If the representatives do not feel illuminated by their new position or spoken sentence, they move again or try a different sentence (the process can end before full resolution)

- In some groups the facilitator draws attention to the climax of the constellation and the seeker re-places their representative to feel what they were feeling to seek resolution

- When everything feels intuitively right, the constellation is ended.

A *healing resolution* is achieved when every representative 'feels right' in his or her place and other representatives agree, which is claimed to represent, in an abstract way, a resolution of the original issue. All the time while the constellation is unfolding, attention is drawn to configurations which generate negative feelings or sensations. It is claimed that such configurations represent *systemic entanglements* within the family of the seeker. Such *entanglements* might be unresolved trauma, illness, suicide, death, effects of war and natural disaster or yet abuse. Proponents claim that the negative legacy from such events can be passed down to succeeding generations, even though those so affected are unaware of the events illuminated. So how does this rationale grab you?

But is the soul, projection or group think the prime mover in such work? Possibly this depends primarily upon the facilitator and the ability of 'family representatives' to attune to something other than intellect, transference and imagination. This said, the main purpose of a family or team 'constellation' is to work with and, if possible, heal the system by restoring what Hellinger calls 'the rightful order of love'. Having experienced and facilitated this way of working, I can testify that when alignment happens a tangible emotional tide of relief and resonance can be felt in the room as the system finds balance. But is this of the family or the working group's need to complete? I can therefore attest to its effect even though I may doubt the rationale. But even if little immediate healing is possible, valuable insights have been reported as 'the system' is brought to greater harmony (Bampfield 2005).

Though Hellinger's original work tended towards the prescriptive, Gestalt influences to 'constellation work' dictate less how things 'should be' and explore more what intuitively feels right – in a field-sensitive way.

To work fully in a field-centred way as a group facilitator or organisational consultant demands that we attend to the interrelationship of everything; events in the life-space of a field in this light are seen as evidence of a self-organising and mutually influencing living whole. For work such as this, I believe our body provides the most sensitive instrument for picking up and sensing field in-formation, for unlike our all too often detached intellect, 'body' and 'field' work closely together to create 'our experiencing of life'. To work practically with the field in a transpersonal way, I would suggest we need to listen to how we are intuitively embodying our experience while attuning to a bodily 'felt-sense' of things, all the while letting wisdom of the field guide us.

> A felt sense is not a mental experience but a physical one. Physical. A bodily awareness of a situation or person or event. An internal aura that encompasses everything you feel and know about the given subject at a given time – encompasses it and communicates it to you all at once rather than detail by detail.
>
> (Laura Perls quoted by Gendlin 1981, p.32)

Here it is being suggested that our sensory, social, emotional, imaginative and intuitive perceptions come together in a visceral 'feeling of knowing' (Francis 2005). In this way the circle is squared as transpersonal/intuitive levels of influence are brought back into contact with the physical/sensory level.

A further component of a field approach to organisations is the premise that every member in the field has a relevant perspective to share; therefore, as primary data, all views are accurate descriptors of our co-created phenomenological reality (Maurer 2005). What is – IS. Accepting of 'what is' – in this context furthers change by supporting the Gestalt maxim that change occurs when 'one becomes what they are, not when they try to become what they are not' (Beisser 1970). The simple act of a facilitator entering a group, because the group field is constantly changing and re-constellating and 'any change in one part of the field will have an impact throughout the field' (ibid.), promotes change. This is possible because we are 'of' the field – not just in it.

Fritz Perls – the founder of Gestalt – similarly to Heraclitus emphasised the fact that we never step into the same river twice and that the sun is new every day: 'The cycle is the compact experiential reconciliation of permanence and degeneration. Man exists in the cycle or the whole' (Heraclitus in Guerrière 1980, p. 89). At root, unlike psychoanalysis which primarily emphasises homeostasis, Gestalt recognises that deconstruction is an intrinsic part of on-going creative adjustment:

> One of the many corollaries of appreciating the cyclic nature of phenomena is the perception of the void – the abyss space. It may be fertile or futile…
> It is from the void that the new emerges; it was in the deepest darkness that Moses found God; and it is when we most truly let ourselves go into the emptiness that fullness can begin to arise. The recent scientific thrill of discovering evidence that our known world emerged with a 'Big Bang' from the void (Davies, 1992, for example) echoes the human experience of a sudden insight, a figure/ground shift, a turnaround or enantiodromia

that obliterates one phenomenological world and brings another into being.

(Clarkson 1996, p.5)

Through our perception 'of the field' from 'within the field', and the interrelationship of one ever-changing field to another, we begin to register our location within a wider 'living universe'. In this, our lived connection with deeper underlying wholes, we begin to function in a way which expands us while simultaneously healing our splits; for we are no longer alone but part of an emerging greater whole.

> The final net result is that this is a whole-making universe, that it is the fundamental character of this universe to be active in the production of wholes, of ever more complete and advanced wholes, and that the Evolution of the universe, inorganic and organic, is nothing but the record of this whole-making activity in its progressive development.
>
> (Smuts 1926, p.426)

Becoming aware of previously hidden relationships we begin to appreciate and to complete patterns we were previously but dimly aware of, energised by a richer sense of belonging. Senge (Senge et al. 2004) suggests we enrich this route of contact by developing a sensitivity to:

- Sensing (seeing and perceiving things afresh)

- Presencing (opening ourselves to what is in the process of becoming)

- Realising (acting in service of what is striving to be born).

In this way, listening to the silence and paying attention in a Tantric yoga fashion – more on this later – to our senses and physicality, a facilitator or consultant attunes to what is in emergence in himself as well as in others, in the manner of a midwife, before stepping back to narrate their experiential reality. In this way we allow 'other ways of knowing' than 'the known' to enter the fray and the subliminal to come to light.

Although superficially mundane creatures immersed in the trivia of their everyday social life, digging deeper into their nature through a robust inquiring relationship, humankind has potential to touch the absolute (Chopra 1996. Through this means it is proposed we become whole – and indeed healed within a reverential relationship where we step from out the self and into the absolute. Kennedy (1998) says that Gestalt helps us open to this greater reality through:

- Recognition and relational embodiment of co-creation (a shared and focussed creativity)

- Temporality (honouring of our transient nature and our unfolding in time)

- Horizontalism (an appreciation that we are all in the same boat).

Journeying towards the spiritual; aware of the temporal nature of our lives and inquisitive about our core nature, held within the creative energy of an authentic 'I–Thou', it is suggested we travel to a different plane. But don't take anyone's word for it: experiment with what is being suggested here and evaluate the results for yourself.

Reflections

* Bring to mind a team or group in which you work – or have worked – and consider:

• How people and events are organised here into an interrelating whole

• The current influences that affect the presenting behaviour

• What is unique about this group and its culture

• What the group might manifest if it remains on its present course

• What this analysis suggests to you about the organisation or group you have in mind.

(Within the organisation I have in mind, people and events are organised around tasks and processes that the current consultancy and client-system demands. Current influences were the cost and profit margins, the availability of team members to plan and deliver, the recent and unforeseen withdrawal of a star player and the anxiety that accompanies a new venture within an untested and unfamiliar team where members have not had opportunity to bond. Money is secondary in this culture to work satisfaction and client satisfaction – which is pretty unique for a consultancy firm. The group is in the process of gelling into a team, and members openly state their commitment and investment to each other and their current client. The un-stated goals centre around achieving self-satisfaction, group satisfaction, the approval of peers and the team leader, as well as a competitive need to shine in the team leader's eyes. This is nearer a 'family' than a work-based team and I guess, from this analysis, that 'the team' might be best appreciated in familial terms with the team leader as a benevolent paternal figure around whom others compete for favour!)

* You are called upon to help a top team envisage its 10-year plan.

• How might you intervene at the transpersonal level to encourage creativity?

• How might a field approach guide you in our facilitation?

• Could you experiment with a constellation to help move a team on?

* Consider yourself in the role of a coach and reflect upon the part of yourself you exclude from the relational field, the events you inadvertently ignore or collude with.

• Now consider how different you are in the role of coach to when you are out of role.

• So what does this say about you and your facilitation?

(I think as coach I exclude my more 'psychotherapeutic self', the part of me generally attuned to 'emotional resolution' rather than 'behavioural experimentation'; though both of these are important, the contract I've co-created with my client dictates the precise nature and boundaries of my engagement, thus causing me to bracket-off what I suspect to be inappropriate. Because of this, although I recognise the influence of developmental and tranferential influences, I may ignore cathartic routes of exploration in favour of other routes. In the role of a coach or group facilitator, I think I finely attune to my client's world, almost to the exclusion of being aware of my own needs – as if I'm 'serving the process'! This is, after all, what they are paying me for! In saying this, I'm aware of how much I attend to the contract and the 'professionalism' I bring to my role. Conversely, I'm more self-serving when out of role. Still, when facilitating resistive groups, I've caught myself thinking as a facilitator how lucky they are I'm not a group member here, as I'd really 'go for it' – tell people what I thought of them, express my needs and tear down the polite defences they hide behind; that is to say, I'd be much more uncompromising and insensitive to others. I guess this describes a little of the 'facilitative shadow' I hold back in role; it is also everything I hold in check to be a person and process-centred facilitator!)

* Considering further the nature of a living field:

• What are the advantages and disadvantages of a transpersonal field-informed approach in coaching/facilitation?

• What types of consultancy or coaching lend themselves best to this approach?

• How may this approach colour your coaching and facilitation?

(I guess being encouraged to attune to 'what is unknown' and 'potentially unknowable' helps me retain a questioning stance and alerts me to the futility of attempting to find lasting answers. All consultancy and coaching I believe benefits from a research-minded stance such as this, so I am an enthusiastic supporter of looking beyond 'the known' to potential as yet unformed. As to how this colours my facilitative vision, well I've come to cherish uncertainty and the role this serves in opening up and unfreezing my own beliefs.)

▶ * In terms of family and group constellations:

- What other than 'soul' might be being constellated in these events?

- What are the limitations and drawbacks of this approach and how might you possibly use it to advantage in your consultancy?

(Strikes me that projective mechanisms may be co-creating a shared fantasy or imaginative drama, influences of transference may also inform the group and the emotions and dramas expressed may say more about the current group and its unmet needs than things transpersonal. This said, it seems a useful intervention to get at the imaginative life of a group, as long as it's not taken as 'truth' or the one and only primary reality.)

6.3 Meditative Approaches and Spiritual Laws – Surrendering to the Transpersonal?

At either end of the inner-facing continuum of 'the road to enlightenment' stand two contrasting positions. At one end are disciplined paths such as Zen and the Gurdjieff work – which attempt through rigorous structure to fracture our ever chattering mind so we might step beyond our delusions; while at the other end are such as the Hindu tradition which invites us to let desires go and to surrender to what is above us. While the Zen tradition and Gurdjieff seem to encapsulate male warrior energy focussed to a disciplined and challenging end, Hinduism appears to encourage detachment. Both perspectives, though suggestive of very different facilitative positions, have kindred goals. Both ends of the continuum are explored further below.

To Gurdjieff, a mystic and teacher in the Sufi tradition, the transpersonal was seen as best approached through a concentrated focussing of 'will'. Pre-dating Fritz Perls the founder of Gestalt, the spiritual route of Gurdjieff similarly concerns itself with how we might awaken full potential in the here and now' (Robinson 2004). While Gestalt enriches our sense of presence through mindful awareness, contact and experiential exploration, Gurdjieff stresses the need for us to integrate our heart, head and body via the disciplined use of 'self-remembering' and 'self-observation' (Gurdjieff 1973). While Gestalt invites us to attend to 'the field', our choices and perceptions of the sensory world, Gurdjieff encourages us Zen-like to create a dynamic tension fuelled by a combination of 'will', effort and physical action. But are they really so different?

In the Gestalt tradition, taking a client or group to the impasse, frustrating them to the degree they feel impaled upon the horns of a psychic life-threatening dilemma, suspending them Zen-like between impulse and resistance:

In Zen (Rinzai Zen), they talk about arousing the Great Doubt, usually via the koan. The point of Zen training is to get the mind into the state in which all alternatives to action and thought are blocked, and the intellect is not 'allowed' to comment. This leads to a climax which is referred to as being like 'a mosquito trying to bite an iron bull,' or like someone who has swallowed a ball of red-hot iron which she can neither spit up nor gulp down. Staying aware in the midst of this impasse is said to lead to a liberated state of awareness, free of self-doubt and contradiction (satori or kensho).

(Just et al. 2001)

In the Gestalt-induced 'impasse', which Perls liked to anti-existence, our meeting with nothingness and emptiness is heightened to the degree we become stuck in the throes of our own phobic avoidance: 'We are spoiled, and we don't want to go through the hellgates of suffering: we stay immature, we go on manipulating the world, rather than to suffer the pains of growing up' (Perls 1972). So here is an approach which frustrates to educate! We must break through this implosive layer if we are to acquire a new adaptation to the world. In Gestalt, clients get through this not so much via an act of will, effort and physical action, but trust in the support and contact offered by the facilitator.

Gurdjieff said in Perls' fashion that people are asleep, that we are automatic and mechanical with little or no conscience, consciousness, attention, and especially no 'will', and used the analogy of a horse, carriage and driver to illuminate the split nature of man. The 'driver' he saw as our *mind*, the 'horse' our *feelings* and the 'carriage' our *body*. The driver might know where to go but he can't communicate with the horse and doesn't know the carriage; only the horse and carriage can do anything, but they have their own wishes and preferences and take no notice of the driver who consequently has no real influence (ibid.). From this perspective 'the task of man' was essentially to become an 'objective being', the starting point for which is for us to free ourselves from our 'subjective likes and dislikes', 'tyranny of the body' and 'our neurotic needs'. 'Attention', the focusing of self's power with an 'earnest direction on the mind' is suggested as the main tool for gaining a robust will (Gurdjieff 1973). Robinson, a student of the 'Gurdjieff Work' and Gestaltist, describes beneath the first fruits of his efforts after a two-week programme:

I remember most finding myself walking down towards the Aldwich on a different level of consciousness, I was free, I was aware of the wonderful interrelatedness of everything, from ideas to the lamp-posts in the street. I was aware that I could 'see' the world differently from anyone else around me; it was a joyful, beautiful place where the world could only be the way it was, unique, vibrant and now.

(Robinson 2004)

Experiences such as this I find are not uncommon, and are often reported by participants of experiential personal growth workshops; I also recollect experiencing

199

many such states myself. I guess they arose when I felt released and freed from the self-imposed prison of my past conditioning. In the Gestalt approach, I believe we conquer a similar state through heightened awareness of ourselves in the moment. But while the Gurdjieffian way subjects you to outside pressures, Gestalt turns to our inner experiential wisdom for guidance, for we believe that 'change occurs when what is present is fully lived' and that this, 'if we take it on, is another way to enlightenment' (Wheway 1999, p.123). Simply, in experiential terms we deem 'that we are breathed, and that is the most fundamental thing' (ibid., p.128). In this context, basic awareness of oneself is seen as the first step upon the scale a transpersonal experience that travels through insight, understanding, awareness of individual 'being' and onwards to our 'being a meaningful part of the universe' (Robinson 2004).

I've a friend, a conservative intellectual type, who has attended most of my workshops but shunned with a vengeance the one entitled 'A Gestalt Inquiry into Spirituality'! He will have no truck with meditation. Yet my approach to spirituality is non-mystical while surveying the mystical, more hands on, suck it and see and experiential. As for my approach to meditation, well, in its most basic form I ask individuals, Zen-like, to 'sit down', 'shut up', 'pay attention' and 'don't fall asleep'! Unsurprisingly some people still fear letting go for fear of meeting with an experience they cannot control.

i) Meditative Approaches

While coaching seeks illumination through dialogue and the active engagement of imagination and reason, meditation generally solicits illumination via withdrawal from external and superfluous stimuli. But this is not to say they can't be harnessed together. Unlike sleep, in which we turn off our consciousness, meditation attempts to concentrate consciousness. Mindful and alert, we are encouraged to travel beyond our usual mental focus to become aware of spaces between and beyond our selves. In this way, we experiment with attempting to awaken to the presence of a greater or higher self and to phenomena over and above 'the socialised' or 'little self'. Meditative techniques I find compliment facilitation, especially when geared to intuitive inquiry or creative visualisation; they enable blinkered clients to grasp a little of what they are missing, to catch and arouse interest in the potential of 'something other' which is novel and new.

Roberto Assagioli, an Italian psychiatrist and early Freudian who founded Psychosynthesis, withdrew from psychoanalysis because he was discontented with its lack of appreciation for human potential. Deeply versed in the philosophy and spiritual practices of both East and West, he placed a very high value on human intuition, creative thought and inspiration, arguing that there was more to be gained studying the higher unconscious (super-consciousness) than the depths of 'an unconscious'. He suggested that individuals can integrate different and conflicting parts of the self via inner meditative work. Besides illuminating individual purpose and honouring our true self, he suggested meditation brought its own reward in the shape of psychological health and spiritual fulfilment. And the methods he advocated, these included creative visualisation, fantasy, free drawing, sub-personality exploration, training the will, meditation, interpersonal and group work.

Assagioli asserted that the direct experience of the self, of pure *self-awareness*, provided a royal road to spirituality, and sought through his approach to address both personal growth inclusive of personality integration and self-actualisation, as well as transpersonal development glimpsed via peak experiences. A Psychosynthesis exercise for evoking cheerfulness is described below:

- Relax muscular and nervous tension, breathe slowly and rhythmically and express cheerfulness by smiling

- Reflect on cheerfulness and contemplate its value and usefulness, especially in your own agitated world; appreciate and desire it

- Evoke cheerfulness by pronouncing the word several times

- Imagine yourself in circumstances that worry and irritate you such as being with unfriendly people, having to solve a difficult problem, being forced to do things rapidly or whilst in danger – yet nevertheless keeping cheerful

- Plan to remain cheerful all day and to be a living example of cheerfulness, to radiate cheerfulness to all and in everything you meet.

(Assagioli 1976)

Using Guided Imagery to Illuminate an Envisioned Future Self

On a workshop addressing personal development, group energy takes an inward turn and so I invite participants to consider experimenting with a more reflective learning method, one borrowed from Psychosynthesis, namely a guided meditation. As we are currently exploring Dharma and envisioning our life's purpose, I suggest this as a theme – the group are up for this and consent. I explain I will work intuitively and flow with what unfolds during the process. I suggest they begin by settling into a comfortable position, close or defocus their eyes, relax and breathe deeply... I continue 'Imagine yourself in a quiet and peaceful meadow... really attune to this scene, ground yourself in the landscape and feel at home in this place... sense the sun warm your back... feel a gentle breeze wafting across your face... listen to the sounds of birds and insects around you... Be aware that in this place you are just as you are now with all that concerns and troubles you... Bring to mind your main worries. ... Look around and see a grassy path leading to a five-bar gate, notice a continuing path that fades into the distance... Now imagine coming towards you a distant figure, someone approaching the gate to the meadow who you intuitively recognise – a version of yourself that is fully and completely realised... this is you in a robust state free of anxieties and worries, totally at home

> *in your own skin... Visualise this perfected version of you standing by the gate waiting... They beckon to you to join them... notice how you feel viewing this other you, how do they move, what aura or energy do they give out? ... See how close you can draw towards them... So what questions do you want to ask of them? ... In your own time, form your questions and listen to the answers that return' ... After about 10 minutes I continue again: 'How is this meeting resonating in your body? What impressions remain on your mind? ... How might you anchor any new learning and insight in your body–mind so it might continue to travel with you? ... How would you like to complete this meeting? ... Can you bring this newly found part back with you to this time, this room and your current life space? If not, what needs to change in your life for you to welcome this in? ... In your own time return to this room' ... Gradually people surface, stretch, open their eyes and familiarise themselves with the surroundings. I continue: 'Spend the next 10 minutes reflecting in silence on the most positive next step you could next take on your life's journey'. In plenary, we share our respective experiences, highlight what stands out and reinforce how we might bring the same to fruition. Tomorrow, we decide we will attempt to check-in first thing from the position of our realised self.*

So here we get an inkling of how Psychosynthesis captures the imagination and uses visualisation to solicit our higher nature.

Gestalt, to my mind, is itself a spiritual discipline which harnesses mindfulness bordering upon meditation to resolve inner conflict. For example, we are encouraged to face what troubles us, to invite in and gain intimacy with the fabric of our deepest forebodings, stay with experiences that disquiet us and hear the deeper message so we might, through mindful contact, dilute the energy behind our torments.

But what exactly does meditation involve and what form might it take besides guided imagery?

All the major schools of meditation seem agreed as to the posture that best cultivates a meditational state: a person sits either on the floor or a chair, maintains a straight back and lowers or de-focuses their eyes. Sometimes the heel is placed against the sacrum or the tongue rests upon the roof of the mouth. So how might this work? The mind, monkey-like leaping from branch to branch and stimuli to stimuli, is tricked by meditative approaches into awakening to something other than itself, and teased from the known into the unknown so that a new mental constellation may form.

In order to achieve a release into non-attached mindfulness, four main routes have been suggested (Rowen 1993):

- *The Way of Forms:* This approach invites us to concentrate upon a single emotionally neutral object – i.e. our breathing, a mantra (word or phrase), a mandela (a symbolic design) or to trace back our thoughts chronologically;

when we find ourselves drifting away from our meditative focus, we are asked to bring our mind back to regain mental control; this mode is geared to focussing the will.

- *The Way of Expression:* Here dancing, movement and/or loud chanting may be engaged; Tai Chi and Taoism, along with various yogic approaches, can fall into this category, as does Sufi-inspired Dervish dancing.

- *The Negative Way:* This approach attempts to eliminate and to withdraw attachment from form and expression and is designed to enable an emptying out and letting go, in the hope that by attending more and more intensely to fewer and fewer things a 'zero point' will be reached.

- *The Facilitative Way:* This approach encourages a general mindfulness, witnessing and contact with all that lies within and before us; whatever arises becomes the focus of meditative attention. Gestalt and other approaches which attune to the moment-to-moment continuum of awareness fall within this category, as do Hindu and Buddhist forms as Satipatthana, Vispassan and Mahavipassana meditation which, Gestalt-like, follow and flow with whatever is being experienced – now.

All the above paths are designed to suspend judgement and engage 'the witness within'. John Rowen (1993) suggests that the 'Way of Forms' and the 'Expressive Way' tend to be the most conservative as they hold onto existing forms. The followers of the 'Expressive Way', he believes, are very orthodox as they are often powerfully attached to a strong structure of leadership and adherence to a guru or other head of school (ibid.). As for the 'Negative Way', he suggests that social impotence results because all distinctions ebb away and there is no impulse to do anything in the world. He comes down in favour of the 'Facilitative Way' because it fosters connection, real development as well as social change. But then, as he hails from the humanistic and facilitative traditions of the Western world, he would wouldn't he!

Personally, in facilitative climates where a stilling of mind or change of gear is called for, I find a combination of meditative methods can prove useful. I am also always aware of a caution, namely, that people with weak personality structures do not fare well in meditation, for it can erode their tentative boundaries and the necessary psychic containment they depend upon. Having drummed into the reader the dangers of an over-indulged ego in the rest of this work, I now find myself paradoxically speaking on its behalf; simply, you need to have developed a strong-enough ego before you attempt to give it up.

ii) Towards a Transpersonal Reality

Advancing further into the spiritual domain we arrive at a position where quantum physics, Hindu mysticism and field theory combine forces to propose such material constructs as our physical body is 99.9% space and that there is nothing more beyond the phenomenological constructions of perception and matter than rapidly vibrating molecular patterns. When Gestalt, science and mysticism combine forces in this way, the representation of reality arrived at is one which suggests:

- We emanate from and live within a dynamically interrelating and intelligent universal field – *which supports the notion that the cosmos is innately intelligent*

- Intelligence is generalised as well as localised throughout the field, which has spiritual as well as physical manifestations which are essentially eternal in nature – *as above in the cosmos, so below in us*

- As human beings we are not separate from this unified field but rather focal points within it, foci where consciousness peaks to create and witness changing scenery – *in this sense we are intimately and energetically related to everything and everybody else*

- From this perspective we are not just our bodies or our ego or our personality, but multi-dimensional beings connected to a unified multi-dimensional field – *we are at this moment concentrated and focused within a physical–social–emotional–projective–intuitive multi-dimensional and spiritual experience*

- Within this context, matter is a phenomenon of consciousness and reality is a phenomenological creation we construct from perception – *for we tend to perceive that which we have first learned to conceive*

- As matter arises from localised impulses of intelligence which emanate from a universal underlying energy field and as we ourselves are aspects of this energetic field, we can by conscious intent influence its laws to trigger space-time events – *being intimately connected to the cosmos we house a potential to affect its laws.*

(Chopra 1996)

Interestingly, when we ponder the existence of a spiritual or transpersonal level of phenomena for us to engage, we are challenged to let ourselves be guided by forces beyond our understanding and ken. This runs counter to the physical level of experience where everything can be touched and checked out; counter to the social level where theories and beliefs fill our information gaps; counter to the emotional level where emotions structure experience for us; counter to the projective level where imagination fills the spaces. Guided by the wisdom of insecurity and trusting to the emerging process we are hereby tantalised into a more global and universal appreciation which suggests:

- If we accept the stance that 'the cosmos is innately intelligent' then we must consider everything naturally has meaning and purpose and nothing ever happens by accident; even though we may not be able to perceive structure and meaning from our individual vantage point – *as facilitators and coaches we need therefore to let the innate intelligence of the person or group work for us*

- Because 'as above in the cosmos, so below in ourselves' we enter into a dialogue with the cosmos itself when we fully connect to a person, group or organisation – *facilitators need to go with the flow to understand the seasons, organic un-folding and natural movements of the universe within ourselves and client-systems*

- As 'we are intimately and energetically related to everything and everybody else' our respect should extend to reverence of all that surrounds us – *for everything and everybody is travelling upon their own sacred journey*

- Because we 'are at this moment concentrated and focused within a physical–social–emotional–projective–intuitive experience' we should shun simplistic solutions and to attend to this – *our multi-faceted nature in our facilitative role and in the group's dynamics*

- As 'we perceive that which we have first learnt to conceive' we need to realise that we are dealing with a symbolically co-created reality rather than a cause-and-effect series of tangible facts – *for in the 'real world' beyond our senses there is just stimuli awaiting organisation*

- 'Being connected to the cosmos' and housing 'a potential to effect its laws', our facilitation and organisational consultation has the potential to become an empowering process – *one that illuminates the interconnectedness of the individual, group and universe.*

Activating the above, a Gestalt practitioner shifts from an 'I–Thou' relationship towards a reverential 'Thou–Thou' one, wherein we explore the divine nature of our lived experience. Simply, the mundane practical engagement we enjoy from day to day is transformed into something sacred. Relationship, in this sense, at its best is sanctified by a shared authentic presence and facilitation becomes an act of spiritual illumination.

iii) Engaging Spiritual Laws

Delving deeper into the Vedic tradition from whence many of the aforementioned spiritual notions emanate, we are drawn back again to the notion that certain aspects of mind (emotions, feelings and desires), our spirit (un-manifest potential) and soul (higher self) reach us through the medium of a *causal-body* which is suggested to exist in eternity beyond time and space. In this light, the higher purpose of facilitation may be suggested to be one of bettering our connection to our mind, spirit and soul.

As to how we might better attune to the universe's spiritual nature, Deepak Chopra (1996) suggests that the spiritual world opens up when we tune to certain universal laws. Below, these laws cited are presented for your examination; but don't swallow them un-chewed, rather approach them as working hypotheses to take out for a test drive. Then again, why bother? Well, if your facilitation is truly holistic everything deserves consideration – initially! Throw them out by all means, but only after you've played with them long enough to have experientially put them to test. Conversely, for those of you who are more sceptical and armoured against the 'new age' mentality you had best consider what is being said and develop a critique so that you may better argue against it, for like it or not the ideas transmitted by Deepak Chopra and other new-age gurus – though fashioned some four thousand years or more ago and little understood – are already well and truly established in many walks of organisational life! Get out there more, folks!

In Chopra's highly influential work *The Seven Spiritual Laws of Success* are described core laws of life, laws that shape material existence: 'Law is the process by which the unmanifest becomes manifest; it's the process by which the seer becomes the scenery; it's the process through which the dreamer manifests the dream' (Chopra 1996, pp.3–4). From this perspective the physical world is realised by non-material means governed by so-called spiritual laws which are as much a part of you as the cosmos:

- The Law of Pure Potentiality: *'The source of all creation is pure consciousness ... pure potentiality seeking expression from the un-manifest to the manifest'* (Chopra 1996, p.7)

- The Law of Giving: *'The universe operated through dynamic exchange ... giving and receiving are different aspects of the flow of energy in the universe'* (ibid., p.25)

- The Law of Karma or Cause and Effect: *'Every action generates a force of energy that returns to us in like kind... what we sow is what we reap'* (ibid., p.37)

- The Law of Least Effort: *'Nature's intelligence functions with effortless ease... with care-freeness, harmony and love'* (ibid., p.51)

- The Law of Intention and Desire: *'Inherent in every intention and desire is the mechanics for its fulfilment... intention and desire in the field of pure potentiality have infinite organising power'* (ibid., p.65)

- The Law of Detachment: *'In detachment lies the wisdom of uncertainty... in the wisdom of uncertainty lies the freedom from our past, from the known, which is the prison of past conditioning'* (ibid., p.81)

- The Law of Dharma or Purpose in Life: *'Everyone has a purpose in life ... a unique gift or special talent to give to other'* (ibid., p.93).

Is this a crazy projection or something worth considering? Though all this may feel a little off-beam and superfluous, or indeed a step too far for many readers who merely want to improve their facilitative skills, I would remind you that holistic facilitation requires you to suspend judgement. I am at this juncture challenging you to do this, now. So, though running the risk of adding insult to injury I further invite you to consider the facilitative interventions Chopra's 'laws' support – namely, that you invite people to:

- Reflect upon how they, as an intrinsic part of the universe may better tune in to the intelligence of nature through the practice of non-judgement

- Give a gift of attention, a smile, or a sense of presence to others in their life and to open themselves in turn to such simple gifts of life as sunlight, company and joy

- Witness the choices they make in the moment, to contemplate the consequences of each and every choice they make, and to look within to ask their heart for guidance

- Practice acceptance, to take responsibility for their own situation and its problems while endeavouring to be non-defended in word and deed

- Consider their desires, to raise them to consciousness and then to surrender them, and in this way trust in the plan the universe has for them through the practice of moment to moment awareness

- Commit themselves to detachment, to accept their uncertainty and to open themselves to all possibilities

- Pay attention to the still-small voice of spirit within them, to rise to mind their own unique talents and to ask on a daily moment-to-moment basis 'How can I serve and what can I give to help my fellow human beings?'

Nothing too new age and esoteric in the above, I hope, just good solid Gestalt-friendly suggestions! Interestingly, at one level, it might be suggested that these laws boil down to an efficient and effective use of everything suggested in this text: that we strive to become reflective and non-judgemental; interested and giving; witnessing and intuitive; accepting and responsible; trusting to the moment; open to uncertainty; intuitive and caring. So how might coaching and consulting at this level of engagement appear?

Francis (2005) reminds us that Martin Buber has suggested that when a person is in touch with the 'grand will': 'Then he intervenes no more, but at the same time he does not let things merely happen. He listens to what is emerging from himself, to the course of being in the world; in order to bring it to reality as it desires' (Buber 1980, p.59). Facilitation at this level, similarly to quantum physics, treats 'fields' and 'energy' as the primary reality over and above matter and involves balancing intuition with creative attention:

> In business decision-making, the convention (although not always the reality) is that we explicitly preference 'hard data' over 'soft skills', and favour logical, practical, controllable approaches over the contextual, contingent and relational. There are benefits of course, but there are also personal, social and environmental costs. Technological decision-making processes that are predicated upon individualist, reductionist, analytical principles alone seem to improve parts while compounding problems for

the greater wholes upon which those parts depend. The outcomes are never sustainable and invariably damaging in the longer term. By way of contrast, developing practical approaches to 'working with the field' involves focusing attention on the client, the situation and the consultant as a virtual system in relationship. It means becoming more aware of what the field offers and of how to capitalise on the emergent qualities of fields. It means fostering the conditions under which field phenomena such as intuition and coincidence can arise, so that we are not just field-informed but can be field-forming – becoming much more receptive to what is trying to emerge naturally, 'but also' artfully co-creating from emergence.

(Francis 2005, p.31)

So here we have it, a facilitator here energetically tunes into 'the whole', conjures up emerging vision and, like a shamanistic guide, encourages people to remain with their core questions and issues until fresh meanings percolate to awareness. Work of this nature requires a good deal of personal development if a practitioner is to avoid the grandiosity. 'Ordinariness' is an asset in this context.

iv) Heuristic Inquiry and Researching Intuitively

While field theory invites us to look outwards and Jungian archetypes encourage us to look inwards, whilst Gurdjieff pushed us towards an energetic breakthrough and meditation invites us to stop the world by stepping between our thoughts, and while Chopra asks us to engage universal laws, all for a glimpse of the transpersonal, the heuristic model of research described here invites us to mine mindfully into the authority of our lived experience. Indeed, to my mind, Gestalt is heuristic inquiry par excellence. If my therapy, coaching or consultancy doesn't enliven the phases and in-dwelling meditative processes described below by Moustakas (1990) I deem it a failure:

- *Initial engagement*: first, I invite participants to immerse themselves in deep personal questioning of what precisely they wish to focus upon in our facilitative inquiry, so as to discover and awaken an intense interest, relationship and passion in what might be facilitated

- *Immersion*: second, I invite participants to live, sleep, dream and merge with the awakening themes and their personal questions to the extent they embody and become them, so that they may appreciate intuitively from the inside their intimate effects

- *Incubation:* third, I invite them to allow inner workings of intuition to clarify and extend their understanding of their quest, while waiting the tacit knowing that percolates to conscious from a deep well of subconscious inner experience

- *Illumination*: forth, I invite my participants to review the data acquired from their own experience and that of others in order to identify tacit hidden meanings and/or an integrating framework that might be further tested and refined until it forms a comprehensive fit with experience

- *Explication*: fifth, I invite participants to attempt to put to examination what has been awakened in consciousness and to familiarise themselves with the layers of meaning that surround the phenomenon they are exploring, inclusive of its universal qualities and deeper meanings, in order to create an appreciation of its phenomenological whole

- *Creative synthesis*: sixth, I invite participants to form a creative synthesis or gestalt of the investigative theme and the opposing ideas and arguments for and against a particular proposition, with a view to appreciating the real significance of what they are actually experiencing, inclusive of knowledge, passion and presence.

(Moustakas 1990)

So here is a holistic route inclusive of deep meditative reflection to help us to shape the chronology of facilitative inquiry into our own transcendental experiences.

In the following case study, a few snippets drawn from my research diary of the more significant reflections of a heuristic inquiry into the difference between therapy and coaching is offered as an example of meditative self-reflection.

Heuristic Inquiry as a Meditative Mode of Self-Supervision and Facilitative Inquiry

Insights Arising from the Orientation Phase of my Inquiry:

(Initial engagement) – *'I realise I used to see coaching as a pale reflection of therapy. As "feelings" were not kosher in the business community I suspected therapy had been dressed up as coaching! That coaching was a ruse. Later in my career I saw coaching as an educational intervention. But at root, such was my therapeutic bias that I deemed coaching at worst a superficial scratching of the surface and at best akin to training. Since this time I have noticed a more positive value creeping in – proportionate to the degree I have reviled therapy's elitism and begun to appreciate coaching's "normalising" of the helping relationship.'*

Insights Arising from the Identification Phase of my Inquiry:

(Immersion) – *'I am now mining deeper into my history by reviewing how I first became a coach, or rather identified with 'being' one. I remember teaching on an MSc in Change for several years which drew to its number many consultants and organisational change agents. "Coaching" was a term they introduced me to. It had a performance-centred and prescriptive connotation. I remember a definition of*

---

coaching that said it was designed "to help both business executives and individuals set and achieve their goals" – and baulking at this definition. Coaching and therapy appeared to me as different as chalk and cheese, and I looked down on coaching. While therapy was holistic, coaching seemed to remain largely focused within the world of "facts" the so-called "real world". … When I started to teach coaching some years later I felt at home with Timothy Gallwey's (2001) description of coaching as the art of creating an environment through conversation and a way of being, one that facilitates the process by which a person can move toward desired goals in a fulfilling manner. As the cultural field caught up with my Gestalt biases I settled more fully into becoming a coach. In this phase of my inquiry I began to identify the wider field conditions, while noting my transition from being highly suspicious of coaching to becoming socialised into it – my transition from therapist to therapist–coach. This phase of inquiry wasn't immersion so much as bombardment as I reflected on the issues while driving, talking to colleagues, walking the streets and upon the toilet – whenever my attention tuned out of the here and now! The fuse of deep reflective inquiry was lit and would not go out'.

Insights arising from the Exploration Phase of my Inquiry:

(Incubation) – *'Writing two or more months well within the process intuitions still percolate thick and fast. l realise I often forget when I'm a coach or therapist, and after the initial orientation and identification phases of the client–practitioner relationship just respond to what is surfacing. Yet there is nevertheless a qualitative difference. Therapy is more regular, more holding, more intimate and intense; coaching a little more objectified, socially and culturally defined and contractual. I am more likely to be surprised in therapy, to meet with confusion more powerfully, to feel at the mercy of processes I am but dimly aware of, to be led by my uncertainty and by influences over and above me – it is more spiritual. And coaching, well I guess I feel more educational, clearer in my intention and more useful in a practical, male, action-based and problem-solving way!'*

(Illumination) – *'As I review everything I'd previously written about coaching and therapy, rummage through teaching notes and speak to past and present clients, especially those who moved from coaching into therapy or came for therapy after first experiencing me as a tutor, fresh connections arise. The momentum behind this inquiry is again quickening; as if a research-minded witness has awakened and will not rest. Both during and after client contact I find myself reflecting "How similar is this act of coaching to therapy?" and vice versa, plus "How different or alike are my interventions in these areas?" I'm beginning to suspect that within the <u>pre-contract phase</u> in coaching and therapy alike, word of mouth referral from current or past clients is the usual point of entry. In the <u>orientation phase</u> of the coaching relationship a good deal of talk prevails, verbal exchange being the norm, while in therapy emotional silences figure large. During the <u>identification phase</u>, coaching clients ask many questions and give an abundance of work-related* detail – they seem eager to impress, justify and to be understood. Therapy clients, conversely, seem more prepared to feel their way – don't know how I can help but seem relieved to be talking about their issues – and relieved to be heard. Re the contract we work to, I notice coaching clients are apt to meet irregularly or bi-monthly, while therapy clients meet regularly and often weekly. The duration of sessions also varies, a coaching session can be one to three hours long and may include my observing events in the workplace; individual therapy is usually one hour and in the therapy room. Some coaching sessions take place on the phone, while all therapy is face to face. In the _exploration phase_ of coaching clients continue to demonstrate a need to over-inform me and focus on specific events – they strive to understand intellectually and to be intellectually understood. Therapy clients listen and wait and speak of general and unfocussed themes as if haunted by intangibles – they strive to accept their experiences emotionally. In the _resolution phase_ as we debrief upon our time together, in coaching our journey of discovery is readily discernible and easily described. The journey through therapy is less tangible and more resistive to verbalisation. As for _post-contact_, coaching clients regularly return as new challenges arise in their life, while therapeutic clients rarely return. In this review I sense a tacit model of coaching and therapy forming, a sort of emergent framework I can take forward for discussion with others, something to put to test and check out against the on-going experience of co-researchers.'

(Explication) – 'To appreciate better the phenomenological ground being surfaced in the relational phases of coaching and therapy, and to get at their contrasting natures, I pour my findings into a comparative framework for circulation to others. Discussing my findings with others in workshops and after coaching sessions, plus with ex-clients, meant my research now informed my facilitative interventions and stimulated group inquiry. Having gone some way to distinguish how coaching and therapy differed and being alerted by the above feedback, I turned to the respective facilitative presence each demanded. Using John Heron's (2001) "Six Category Intervention Analysis" model I profile my facilitative style. Certain general comments fielded from clients of my workshops also gave me food for thought: "I would advise participants coming to your workshops to go with an open mind and heart and be prepared to make contact with all that you know, not just what you think you know. This connection will enable you to use your own intuitive power to benefit fully both yourself and others". Overall, my suspicions were supported re a tendency to be more educative and authoritative in coaching and less so in therapy. As suspected I was seen as highly challenging of blind spots but supportive of the person. At later stages of coaching, confronting seemed to retain its frequency but supportive and cathartic interventions increased, supporting the notion that coaching might edge into more therapeutic territory over time. As therapy progressed facilitation was perceived as more confronting and informative, suggesting it might approach the normalising territory of coaching before it ended – possibly as the client began to "take back transference"? This supports the thesis that my facilitation *brings what is out of awareness into awareness in both modalities; that my coaching eases into therapy and my therapy eases into coaching. Painting in broad brush-strokes it seems true to say that my facilitative style tends towards the "authoritative" in workshops, is fairly evenly balanced in coaching and is primarily facilitative in therapy. I guess Gestalt in its loosening of the social world and attention to the whole does much to arouse a client from unconscious incompetence (where they see no reason to change and are unaware of the options) to conscious incompetence (where they are awakened to new challenges of learning), then onwards to a stage of conscious competence (where they feel encouraged to practice new skill or entertain a different reality) and thus to a stage of unconscious competence (where they can integrate a new way of being). It appears to me that this process is primarily experiential and non-verbal in therapy and more cognitive in coaching?'*

Insights arising from the Resolution Phase of my Inquiry:

(Creative synthesis) – *'Here I performed field analysis of coaching and therapy focussing upon Parlett's (1991) principles of organisation, contemporaneity, singularity, changing process and possible relevance to encapsulate my findings. This field analysis confirmed my suspicions that I've a tendency to be more educative and authoritative in coaching and less so in therapy. As suspected I was seen as highly challenging of blind spots but supportive of the person. At later stages of coaching confronting seemed to retain its frequency but supportive and cathartic interventions increased, supporting the notion that coaching might edge into more therapeutic territory over time. As therapy progressed, facilitation was perceived as more confronting and informative, further suggesting it might approach the normalising territory of coaching before it ended – possibly as the client began to "take back transference"? This seemed to support the budding hypothesis that my facilitation brings what is out of awareness into awareness in both modalities; this notion of facilitation becoming more supportive and confronting in the longer term was also supported in the workshop setting. … What I've begun to suspect is that field conditions sculpt the natures of coaching and counselling. Individuals walk in attuned to different realities, presenting different needs and expecting different things. My Gestalt-informed approach and presence feeds positively into this mix. What is then co-created shapes what results. As the facilitative inquiry and relationship matures my default facilitative style high in supportive, challenging and catalytic interventions eventually emerges. So what might I do differently? Nothing! But I am now mindful of what I do and my biases are more gently held. In this summary I feel I've arrived at an approximation of "my truth". Writing up my research and having its findings accepted for publication in a major professional journal completed this final phase of my inquiry.'*

(Barber 2011)

v) Freeforming – A Synthesis of Zen and Gestalt and Aikido

Freeforming was created by Peri Mackintosh from a synthesis of Vipassanna meditation, Rinzai Zen, movement and dance, spontaneous theatre and mime, plus most importantly Aikido and Gestalt. Leaning into the present moment and spontaneous mindful movement are the foundation of this approach.

At the start of Freeforming sessions we might sit meditatively, following our breathing and emptying our minds in Zen fashion, or we might just engage in free-form movement to illuminate non-verbally where we are right now. We may work in pairs or as a group discover through spontaneous movement how we might best intuitively meet together. We may form small groups to see what moving sculpture evolves or come together as a large group meeting one another with eyes closed and focusing on smells. Some sessions may last ten minutes, others half an hour. Afterwards, we reflect on what we are aware of now.

I wrote up the following in a reflective journal just after my first experience of Freeforming:

> Joining with others, drawing awareness to my body and moving in synchronisation with their movement I felt differing paces and sequences of movement spontaneously arise. My actions flowed out from the patterns around me, joined with and broke away, I acted into emotions that arose and complimented these with sounds. When the group was involved, a moving sculpt of group energy emerged as individual patterns gave way to communal ones... What is Freeforming? A kinaesthetic-led pattern for meeting; an experiment in controlled confluence and self-awareness; experimenting with falling into the field and self-expression; a medium for exploring and maintaining creative indifference; a dance between subjectivity and objectivity; becoming field led and field informed; a way of becoming the field; surrendering intellect in favour of co-emergence in couples, small and larger groups; massaging towards the edge of 'now'; searching for the meeting point and sensing the in-between; responsive responding; cultivating Zen moment to moment awareness while allowing yourself to experience organic co-creation?
>
> (Macintosh and Barber 2011)

At root, Freeforming is a process-centred cultivating of 'a-ha' learning moments, but more 'acting into' than martial in terms of Aikido; more performance informed than starkly an authentic encounter; more playful than psychotherapy; more tacit and inconclusive than conclusive! Personally, I recognise Freeforming's potential for developing intuition; sensitising those who are intellectually and bodily armoured and as a medium for acquiring mindfulness and tacit knowing. In sum, Freeforming is a contact meditation, a dynamic co-creational awareness practice. The focus is upon connective awareness and a 'meeting of minds' without words. The creative challenge is one of maintaining a fluid continuity of connective awareness by attuning to your body and the rhythms of your fellows. Freeforming is improvisational, experimental and playful, and in service of Gestalt provides another route to a vividly heightened awareness of being alive to the moment.

In 'Gestalt training terms' the purpose of practice is threefold. Firstly it enables a dialogic relationship without language, which encourages inclusion. Secondly it brings a practitioner's attention into the here and now while interrupting ruminative thinking. Thirdly it can help connect isolated aspects of ourselves by opening us to fresh ways of being and relating. A modified example of this approach adapted for a master's programme into coaching and consulting is described below.

A Transpersonal Intervention within a Business Master's

Shortly after a Freeforming intensive, I did a half day on Gestalt within a coaching and consulting MSc. I had introduced the notion of de-constructing 'reality as taught' so as to let new experience in, and started my session by inviting the group to sit in silence for five minutes to explore how we interacted with and used 'silence'. I then invited participants to form pairs and to gaze into each other's eyes, to observe what arose to distract their reception of the one before them, and to monitor how shyness, laughter, fear of intimacy etc. got in the way of connecting with others. We then took it in turns being led with eyes closed by a seeing partner who guided us around the parkland outside the classroom. This was followed by an invite to close our eyes and form a group in the centre of the lawn – in silence. After 20 minutes, I invited participants to enact a spontaneous sculpt – just move together as intuition and the play of the group dynamic took us. Later we formed a circle with arms linked and debriefed our experiences. People felt relieved and rested, out from their busy heads and much calmer than before. One burst into tears, remembering a previous group experience that got out of hand, though this experience was very different she said, so gentle and holding and safe. I next invited participants to walk back in slow motion to their class, to breathe in and sense and feel what happened to them when they returned to the organisational energy field. Some felt the loss of childhood, the armouring of her previous openness. We worked further upon where in our body we 'sensed' the group, what muscles we tensed, where we focussed our consciousness and awareness, what memories returned to us here, what social rules we were re-enacting, what we imaginatively projected out on others, most important of all what our soul was learning today! We ended with me demonstrating Gestalt as field-led emergent coaching with a volunteer, then facilitating a closing plenary into how and what we had learnt today.

(Macintosh and Barber 2011)

Reflections

* In terms of the Gurdjieff approach, how might you set about maximising a person's attention and effort in the moment, and what do you consider the implications are for group facilitation and contracting inner inquiry of this nature with clients? *(I'm aware of a more challenging and confronting approach in evidence here, as if in a Zen-like way permission is given to frustrate others into heightened awareness. I can't envisage being contracted to work at this level as a coach, but am fully aware of situations in a therapeutic setting where this has occurred. I guess for me, the contract is with the 'unconscious' in therapy and with the 'conscious self' in coaching. What are your ideas here?)*

* Reflect upon the philosophy suggested by Chopra:

1. The source of all creation is pure consciousness... 2. The universe operates through dynamic exchange... 3. Every action generates a force of energy that returns to us in like kind... 4. Nature's intelligence functions with effortless ease... 5. Inherent in every intention and desire is the mechanics for its fulfilment... 6. In detachment lies the wisdom of uncertainty... 7. Everyone has a purpose in life.

• What coaching intervention might you make to capture the essence of each of the above laws?

* Using the following principles of heuristic inquiry –

• *Initial engagement*: deep personal questioning

• *Immersion*: merging with the awakening themes

• *Incubation:* allowing inner workings of intuition to extend understanding

• *Illumination*: reviewing the data acquired from experience

• *Explication*: putting to examination what has been awakened in consciousness

• *Creative synthesis*: forming a creative synthesis of the investigative theme

– consider how you might structure a collaborative inquiry into either group facilitation or the process of coaching. *(There seems to be in evidence here a complimentary developmental cycle that might be placed within the orientation-to-resolution cycle discussed earlier in this text. It strikes me that I might encourage group members to stay with a developing theme between sessions, to carry it around and to keep a diary of the thoughts, feelings, fantasies and dreams that arise relating to the same. I might then encourage group members to share their findings and to consider what this means for them, individually and collectively, and to form a working hypothesis to carry in and test out in their life.*

6.4 A Speculative Map of Transpersonal Influences – Integrating Soma and Soul?

Although it is impossible to understand and map such as 'the fertile void', the generative force of the universe, my trawl trough the various mystical and spiritual texts, notably Hindu and Taoist sources, has led me towards the following tri-partite synthesis (see **Figure 3**):

- The **Causal Body** is said to be the eternal portion of ourselves, to exist beyond time and space and to house *spirit energy* (pure un-manifested potential) plus *soul energy* (the source of our Higher self) and *mind energy* (emotional feelings and desires); energy from this level is suggested to fuel the archetypes of mystic, saint, guru and master (representative of phenomena nearer to the unchanging eternal now or the Tao).

- The **Subtle Body** is seen to have existence in time but not in space, to house our *ego* (mental and intellectual awareness) plus our *intellect* (ideas, beliefs and concepts); mental energies of this level may be suggested to influence the archetypes of magician, teacher, shaman and artist (an energetic level nearer to Chi the energetic shaper of form).

- The **Physical Body** – exists in both time and space and houses our *energetic field* (electro-magnetic energy) plus the *material field* (cellular structure and sensory perception); earthly influence from this level may be suggested to fuel the archetypes of warrior, scientist and pragmatist (material form and the power of physical action).

Through the notion of a 'Causal Body', we start to grasp a little of why Taoists claim we can't talk about the Tao, for the 'real Tao' isn't a concept that words can describe nor a physical entity open to the senses, but rather something that existed before there were words, objects or even the universe itself – yet is still an integral part of ourselves:

> All Chinese philosophy has tried to unify Heaven, Earth and mankind, the sublime and the mundane, the material and the spiritual. The Chinese have always tried to integrate man and nature, knowing that man and nature are not two things, two separate entities, but are always one.
>
> (Forstater 2001, p.19)

We can never step out of the human field we are biologically framed within and can never be other than of the universal field we co-exist within. The 'felt' part of the Tao, represented in the Chinese term 'Chi', is taken to be an inherent energy that permeates and organises existence, a shaper of 'fields'. Tao in this light is the potential out of which all things physical and spiritual evolved – the primal 'fertile void' – while Chi is more akin to the energetic blueprint that gives 'form' a shape.

Figure 3.　Experiential Levels of Energy

CAUSAL BODY – TAO?

(SPIRIT and SOUL)

TRANSPERSONAL/INTUITIVE – Reality as intuitively guided (Listening to the Void/Nourishing Soul?)

Intuitive and symbolic influences which relate us to the universe and help us to hear its message; altered states of consciousness; near-death experiences; visions and divine guidance

- *What greater purpose do I serve here?*
- *What am I here to learn?*

⇩　　　　　　　　　　　　　　　　　　　　　　　　　⇧

SUBTLE BODY – CHI?
(EGO and INTELLECT and MIND)

PROJECTIVE/IMAGINATIVE – Reality as imagined/projected (Integrating the Shadow/Unconscious?)

Internal meanings and images we thrust out upon the world; life as a mirror or reflection of the self; our unconscious at work upon and within us; artistic and poetic creations

- *Which part of me is engaged or disengaged right now (intellect/heart/image/role)?*
- *What part of me am I denying right now (my relationship to my shadow)?*

EMOTIONAL/TRANSFERENTIAL – Reality as emotionally enacted (Recreating an Emotional Past?)

Emotional patterns and prior learning carried into the present; family dynamics and memories binding us to the past; when memories use us and take us over

- *What past dramas are impinging upon the present (transference)?*
- *What relational dance am I being drawn into here (counter-transference)?*

SOCIAL/CULTURAL – Reality as intellectually constructed (Attachment to the World as Taught?)

Negotiating a self in relation to others; acquiring a role in the intellectually taught world maintained by language, culture, social norms and beliefs

- *What are the social rules or professional values I work to here?*
- *What community or group shapes my behaviour right now (profession/culture)?*

⇩　　　　　　　　　　　　　　　　　　　　　　　　　⇧

PHYSICAL BODY – FORM?
(ENERGY and MATTER)

PHYSICAL/SENSORY – Reality as physically sensed (Physically supporting ourselves?)

Experiencing ourselves as a sensory being living in a physical world; life as a series of sexual and survival instincts, the animal within us; impulses and needs; body as self

- *What information am I gathering from my senses right now?*
- *What do I need to better ground myself in my physical being?*

In relation to our emerging model, the 'Causal Body' is nearer to Tao, the 'subtle body' to Chi and the 'physical body' to 'physical form'.

So why bother with all this? Well, because at the transpersonal level we struggle to get to grips with what are essential 'unknowns' and are caused to speculate upon the unverifiable, I am attempting to create a guide to help us appreciate a little of the complexity at play. This map – Figure 3 – and the notions it enshrines are my attempt at using a metaphor to catch a metaphor!

But what good is the notion of soul to the modern world?

> Contemporary society worships at the altar of functionalism. Concepts such as process, method, model and project have come to infiltrate our language and determine how we describe our relation to the world. The recovery of soul means the rediscovery of Otherness; this would awaken again the sense of mystery, possibility and compassion. Stated philosophically, being could find expression in doing.
>
> (O'Donoghue 1997)

It is always hard to read terms such as 'heaven' and 'soul' without being re-stimulated into attitudes of mind seeded by the church, religion or our earliest conditioning, but what I'm hoping to convey is something of the unknowable quality of existence; the mystery and complexity of the whole universe in which we function; a universe most scientists agree has no beginning nor end and seems to be expanding in all directions into never-ending space! In this context, our 'causal' and 'subtle' bodies plus other notions of spirit may be seen as poetic devices to capture states of experience that are nigh indescribable and impossible to define or to convey in conventional terms:

> The unifying force of all life phenomena which is suggested by Heraclitus is physis. The river water symbolizes the one physis or life force. Physis was first named by the pre-Socratic Greeks as a generalised creative force of Nature (Guerrière 1980). It was conceived of as the healing factor in illness, the energetic motive for growth and evolution, and the driving force of creativity in the individual and collective psyche.
>
> (Clarkson 1991, 1996)

There are times facilitating a group when I find myself in a heightened state of awareness, in a zone where everything seems to interrelate with everything else, wherein I seem able to flow in tune with a reality where my interventions intuitively hit the target and I 'intuitively know' what needs to happen next. It's as if I'm in touch with a finer energetic connection than usual – I'm in the zone! At such times, physically, I am often aware of warm currents of energy flowing down the side and back of my neck and experience a sensation that feels as if a warm viscous fluid is being poured into me at the back of my head. I don't label this experience in any way but rather just let myself stay with the phenomena without allowing my imagination to blow it out of proportion or my intellect to locate it in 'the known'.

'Staying with' emerging phenomena, witnessing, letting experience inform us, remaining non-judgemental and open, heightening moment-to-moment awareness – all these good old Gestalt notions contribute to transpersonal facilitation. And what makes me believe an experience is a transpersonal rather than a fantasised, imagined or transferential one? Well, I can never be sure, but there seem to be some distinctive and qualitative differences.

For instance, transference evokes earlier emotional energy along with memories of times long past; fantasy-driven material projects out imaginative movie-like material upon the world; while the transpersonal feels less emotionally and imaginatively and internally generated and rather more like 'being guided by something external'. Indeed, I would go so far as to suggest that transpersonal experiences seem also to encapsulate aspects of 'love' plus a sense of connection and being at one. So now to love!

> Sanskrit has ninety-six words for love, ancient Persian has eighty, Greek has three, and English one
>
> (Master Park 1995)

Reading this, I am caused to consider the damage the English language has done to me.

i) The Nature of Love

Love in Juddu Krishnamurti's view is less an emotion born of man than *a core condition of the universal field*, 'a pathless land', something that man cannot come to through any creed, ritual, philosophic knowledge or psychological technique (Holroyd 1991). Krishnamurti suggests we must empty the mind to experience 'love', for 'when these things disappear, when these things don't occupy your mind and when the things of mind don't fill your heart, then there is love' (ibid., p.104). True love, in this context, doesn't come into being through a realisation of the self but, with a surrender or 'death of the self'; for it is not a creation or motivation of the ego, nor yet an activity of self, as it can't be practised nor cultivated and doesn't seek results. He therefore concluded that as long as the mind is arbiter, there is no love. Love in this light is not brought into existence by the object of desire and likewise the turbulences within a loving relationship are not caused by love so much as by conflicts of the self, for in a truly loving relationship there is no barrier between the observer and the observed, and you can only look on another in this way when there is love. Love here is being suggested to emanate from the 'causal level' of our existence beyond space and time.

Personally, I believe love to be the absence of fear, a resounding 'yes' to life; fear says 'no' while love says 'yes'! When loving, I feel connected, supported and intimately connected to the universe. When fearful, I am most isolated and alone. Years of working therapeutically with clients have taught me that below the layer of social games, under our protective cultural and gamey mask, and deeper still below the underlying level of distress this disguises, beneath all this – at the core

219

is love. Within the most damaged and seemingly wretched of individuals, a loving in-born nature seems to remain.

At the transpersonal and intuitive level, love is approached poetically to raise the spirit and enlighten our sense of self. It is comparable to a bird on the wing – not meant to be caught nor encased. It is freely given, so the more you try to contain or control it – the more you destroy it. A bird in the sky and on the wing has freedom, space, joy and adventure. It is in a creative dialogue with the vastness of nature. The same bird in a cage will superficially appear the same but it will not be the same bird. A golden cage is still a cage! Love is unlimited and balks at limitation; it is formless and constrained by form. Capture your loved one, imprison them in a golden cage and they will come to resent you. To love is to fly together.

> It is tenderness that makes you vulnerable, that makes you open, that makes you sensitive to the mysterious world that surrounds you.
>
> People who are not tender, who are hard like a rock, go on missing life.
>
> Life passes them by; it cannot penetrate them, they are impenetrable.
>
> Life is a joy for those who are tender, soft, loving, compassionate, sensitive.
>
> (Osho 1995)

Rogers (1967) reminds us that unconditional love is an essential ingredient of facilitative excellence. All this has interesting ramifications for facilitation and a facilitator's sense of presence, for if we are to invite love into our facilitative relationship we will need to step out of the way to let it flow in. In this context, conversely, standing outside a person-to-person relationship, putting ourselves in the spectator position or adopting an objective, professionally informed role may prevent our endeavours from being loving. This is not to say we need to lose ourselves or flow into and become confluent with our clients, but that we need to set up relational spaces and ego-less conditions that allow love to pour in naturally.

ii) Gestalt as Relational Tantric Yoga?

Tantric practitioners focus upon our dance between polarities, stipulating that these must be understood and healed before we can maximise our full potential. Like Gestaltists they are alive to paradox, pursue 'immediacy' and 'being', are trained to maintain a sensory focus and schooled to authenticity; they also stress experiential rather than intellectual or theoretical knowledge. So what then is Tantra?

> Tantra is a path of expressing the fullest vitality of our life force in each moment. This means returning over and over to the present moment where we can feel and sense all the information that flows through us. Then we can respond to our experience, rather than being reactive to what is emerging. The only way to do this is through our awareness in the present.
>
> This choice for living is fierce, surrendering to the flow of everything we can feel and learning to attune to sensing more of our connectivity

with all. And by the way, feeling is not to be confused with emotionality when our emotions keep us attached to something that is not real.

So in Tantra we start with the body's intelligence and wisdom. We are consciousness embodied. We are 'light beings' in that all of matter is vibrating, but at different rates or frequencies. Light, sound and colour are all on a continuum of faster vibration, whilst our apparent concrete reality is vibrating at slower speeds creating the appearance of density. Our cells hold all our memories and through our bodies we have access to all the information of the universe. Our bodies give us the food for our choices allowing the mind to contribute as a supporting partner.

(Welch 2011)

Tantra practitioners believe the universe is fundamentally interconnected and whole. They see enlightenment as 'the capacity to become conscious of our connection to all of Being' and work to expand mindfully the capacity to reconnect with the larger reality of which we are all a part. To boost consciousness and connectivity, Tantric practitioners cultivate moment-to-moment awareness, sensory responsiveness and manage their emotional reactivity through non-attachment:

The Tantra path is one of learning to discern and experience the subtle realms that surround the individual body and our resonance with all realms of energy and consciousness that exist. As we open up and allow our vulnerability to sensitize us we begin to become more radiant, vital and alive; we become more of our truest potential as expansive beings… But the paradox of the Tantric path is that it is only by letting go of Ego (in the Eastern sense of any grasping to our beliefs about our identity) that we can experience our true, constantly shifting, and endless nature.

(Welch 2011)

Tantric cosmology views sexual energy as a crucial life force. They also believe that chakras, spinning vortexes of energy, connect us to the universe and are the foundation of our creative energies:

- Seventh Chakra (root of spine): our foundation, base and connection to Earth

- Sixth Chakra (pubis): sexual dynamo and our creative life force

- Fifth Chakra (navel): our will

- Fourth Chakra (the heart): our master chakra

- Third Chakra (throat): communication and expression

- Second Chakra (between eyebrows): the third eye our intuition

- First Chakra (top of head) access to universal consciousness and connection to the heavens.

Though I have no commanding belief in the existence of chakras, I can testify to experiments with participants where we focussed attention upon the head, heart and navel to explore presence. In these exercises it was interesting to note changes of voice tone, breathing rate and the sense of being grounded that accompanied such experiments. This reminds me of an observation Fritz Perls made, namely that in bodywork anything above the waist relates to expression, and anything below to support. So the jury is out for me on this one!

Below is an example of Tantric-informed interventions within a workshop examining 'presence':

Training the Intuition in a Workshop on Presence and Contact

After negotiating ground rules and refining the learning agenda, I invited participants to form pairs, sit facing each other and take turns in describing every minute movement they saw on their partner's face – 'I'm aware of you swallowing, breathing shallowly, blinking, moving your head to one side, smiling, breaking eye contact…' – whilst the person being described sat passively receiving the observations. After five minutes, participants changed roles and, after ten minutes, de-briefed, paying particular attention to how it felt to be observed and to pay intimate attention. Shyness, shame, feelings of being invaded or invading the other, feeling held and supported, temperature changes – all were reported.

Next, as it appeared I had caught the group's interest, I invited them to remain in pairs and gaze into one another's eyes, and practice each in turn, giving and receiving full undivided attention; following 5–10 minutes of this, individuals de-briefed and shared any subtle difference of presence they experienced when in the respective roles of 'giver' and 'receiver'.

As interest continued to grow I extended this investigation into contact, inviting individuals to place their left hand on the other's chest, over their respective hearts, and to practise connecting on-verbally by sensing the subtle the connection between them. Again after 5–10 minutes each pair debriefed. By this time I noticed that eye contact was steady and regular, breathing deep and slowed; concentration profound and robust.

Lastly, I encouraged participants to focus upon their breathing while remaining in heart-to-heart communication, but add a visualisation; as they breathed out, they should picture a subtle energy pulsing from their hearts, along their arms and into the other's heart – a heart-to-heart connection. Then, with their inhale, to breathe their partner into their own heart!

Following these exercises, individual and group energy was noticeably different. During plenary I was struck by the relaxed attentiveness of the group, its quality of connection, the settled postures and degree of thoughtfulness evidenced in feedback. As if the general business and customary anxiousness I associated with this group had dissolved, leaving behind it more grounded individuals attuned to 'being' rather than 'doing'. As if energy were more focussed and individuals far more present than before.

With Tantra, this text has squared the circle. We started with raising awareness to physical phenomena and have now come full cycle to integrate spirit with physicality.

iii) Summary

In transpersonal terms, if I were to choose a key idea to stand as a symbol for the Gestalt approach to facilitation, one that permeates this work, it would be 'a love of experiential truth and the quest for authenticity'. Thin-skinned and sensitised to themselves and their clients, Gestalt facilitators in the unforgiving light of authenticity realise that they cannot facilitate what they haven't experienced or do not know, for the dialogical approach of Gestalt's deep and forever interpersonally deepening nature shows up such flaws. It is a rare and somewhat disturbed client, in my experience, who goes counterintuitive to the extent of allowing a facilitator to take them further than the facilitator has been themselves, as most of us have our own internal crap detector which whizzes wildly when a bogus, inexperienced facilitator enters the scene. Many of my interventions at the transpersonal level move between imaginatively exploring objects that stimulate the intuition and staying with emerging silence, waiting for inspiration. Such interventions as these seek to go beyond the known and to open us up to a non-verbal dialogue with the void.

At the last, authenticity is a product of a lifetime's learning, it stems from a deep commitment to 'what is' and is born of ego surrender and dissolution of any need to impress or gain ascendance over others. Indeed, Gestalt has been suggested to work to the same ends as the meditative practices of Theravadan Buddhism (Kolodny 2004). What Buddhists term 'hindrances' to enlightenment have been seen to have their counterparts in the Gestalt notion of 'blocks to contact', mechanisms that take us away from the present moment. Both Buddhism and Gestalt teach us to recognise hindrances when they arise and show us a way to return to present-time awareness.

Translating the Buddhist lesson into Gestalt terms, when our awareness is full and steady and our habitual resistances do not interrupt our moment-to-moment contact, we are able to appreciate ourselves and our lives more clearly. Available to 'what is', 'both in the immediate sense of what is true in the given moment, as well as in the larger sense of "the truth of things"' (Kolodny 2004, p.96), we develop a skilful means 'for noticing and "dwelling in" our actual experience before labelling and meaning-making set in' (ibid., p.96). Buddhist and Gestalt traditions alike rely on insight and intuitive knowing rather than the kind of analysis that accompanies attempting to figure things out. And the nature of self-insight and awareness that arises of itself from opening ourselves to the moment, well, this I have personally found to be penetrating and deeply cleansing, and all we have to do is to invite it in.

In terms of its transcendental qualities, Gestalt's transpersonal nature owes much to Field Theory (Lewin 1952) with its multiple laminations of holistic reality; the cultivation of an 'I–Thou' relationship (Buber 1980) which facilitates a meeting with the divine through authentic contact; and attention upon what is unfolding now which awakens us to the moment. In this regard, Gestalt has much in common with Zen, which emphasises heightened concentration upon present experience so as to achieve 'a-ha illumination', plus Taoism, which suggests we must surrender our ego in order to enrich our contact and be one with the universal field that runs through and around us. As one of the oldest Taoist/Zen sayings reminds us, acceptance is key to our spiritual awakening:

> The Perfect Way is only difficult for those who pick and choose;
> Do not like, do not dislike: all will be clear.
>
> (Seng-ts'an quoted in Suzuki 1950, p.24)

Such impersonal godliness as this is sometimes hard for a Western mind to grasp, but should come as second nature to a Gestalt practitioner alive to the ever-fluid moment and the intelligent self-constellating field.

Fritz Perls acknowledged his indebtedness to Zen (Perls 1947) and Joseph Zinker, who spent much time with Gestalt's founding father, observed of his teacher:

> What hasn't survived about Fritz – is his presence. He was like a Zen master who taught you by… smearing himself all over you, in the most powerful way. He made you sit up.
>
> (Zinker interviewed by Barber 2001, p.30)

Note how this image of Gestalt is far from the watered-down, institutionalised and sanitised clinical 'professional presence' taught to many Gestalt psychotherapy trainees.

In Gestalt, Zen and Taoism alike, we are encouraged to empty our mind, to 'lose our heads and come to our senses' so that with an open mind and heart we might be guided by what is vibrant, alive and unfolding. Gestalt's attention to what is in process of becoming and dissolving, the breathing in and out of the fertile void, has been compared to going with the flow of Yin and Yang (Woldt and Ingersoll 1991) – twin forces of emergence and dissolution. Tao-like, Gestalt practitioners further contend that if we go with the flow and innate intelligence of the relational field, all the resources we need to proceed will be revealed (Zinker 1978). By stopping the course of our mind and through a loosening of the psycho-social mechanisms that hold our phenomenological world together, Gestalt encourages something other to flood in. In this light, Gestalt-influenced education, akin to Zen, is less like filling a bucket and more like lighting a fire.

As agents of inquiry, Gestalt, Tantric Yoga, Zen and Taoism alike invite you into experiential engagement. But once in contact, what do you do next? Well, you might begin to explore the following hypotheses – which belong to no single spiritual tradition yet seem to underpin them all:

1. We live in a phenomenological world shaped by individual consciousness, which itself represents a manifestation of the divine ground/field from whence everything is drawn and has being.

2. We as human beings are capable of discovering this divine ground/field by experiential engagement, especially when we are subject to experiences that are designed to bypass our ego and to awaken to the intimate relationship between the knower and the known.

3. We possess an eternal self which co-exists alongside a socially constructed phenomenological self, and that this aspect of our dual nature may be awakened through 'shocks' or 'a-ha experiences' which confront us with new gestalts relating to this, our core nature.

(Adapted from Aldous Huxley's introduction to *The Song of God: Bhagavad Gita*, trans. Swami Prabhavananda and Christopher Isherwood, 1951, p.li quoted in Boldt 1993)

So with the above to mind, begin an inquiry into your own core nature.

In sum, Gestalt, as a spiritual way, leads us towards a deconstructed, ever-reconstellating but practical transpersonal view of the world which propounds that:

- The 'past' and 'future' don't exist unless I create a memory or image of them in 'the present' – *therefore 'the present' is the source of both the 'past' and 'future'*

- Everything we need is here right now – *therefore 'the present' is the focus of our ultimate power and the beginning and ending of time*

- 'The mind' creates a personal universe – *therefore 'awakening' must entail the realisation that we are simultaneously the creator, object and witness of the play of conscious awareness*

- The whole time–space continuum is focussed in 'the present' – *therefore all possibilities co-exist simultaneously here and now*

- 'The self' is a co-creation and is culturally maintained – *therefore what stands between us and our self-actualisation-cum-enlightenment are our creations*

- We are the authors of our life – *therefore we have the potential to change our lives by changing our beliefs*

- We create possibility through 'imagining ourselves into an experience' – *therefore we can dissolve our limitations by surrendering our thoughts and 'experiencing ourselves' out of it.*

The obstacles in your path to becoming a facilitator of excellence are fundamentally the same as those identified by Yoga as frustrating spiritual development, namely: ignorance, ego, desire and attachment, hatred, anger and fear. Could becoming a facilitator perhaps be a spiritual path? You will at the very least be enlivening 'life as learning'; endeavouring to expand your everyday awareness; integrating all you associate with body, spirit and mind and serving others while hopefully realising yourself. You will be pure consciousness on a journey of discovery – for awareness is one!

> Learn to live with awareness. Take this into your daily life. Acknowledge special awareness moments. This is the true beauty of living.
>
> (Corrigan 2011, p.55)

Reflections

* Central to many transpersonal approaches of change is the notion of Dharma, the illumination of a person, group or community's special purpose and the expression of its own unique talents. With this in mind:

- What are your special talents as a coach, consultant and facilitator?

- What do you do best and get the most pleasure out of in your work?

- Ideally, where do you really want to be as a coach and/or group facilitator?

(I believe my flexibility plus the breadth and depth of the holistic model that is informing me does much to enrich my facilitation. I especially enjoy the cut and thrust of working through the angers and rejections of hostile groups that come my way; it is as if with nothing to lose I feel freed in the heat and energy of the moment to be fully myself and fully authentic; inspired as it were! I think I work best under pressure, tested and generally rising to the occasion. As for where I want to be, I think I'm here now! Working with a range of challenging clients – both individual and corporate, within a range of different territories – within business and academic settings while straddling education, coaching, consultancy and therapy – learning about myself and the human condition I feel fully satisfied.)

* In relation to Figure 3:

- How might notions of the physical, subtle and causal bodies inform your coaching style?

- How might you go about facilitating at the 'causal level' – indeed, is this possible?

- What verbal and non-verbal interventions might be made at the 'subtle level'?

- What verbal and non-verbal interventions might be made at the 'physical level'?

- What case would you make for there being nothing to facilitate at the causal level?

* Classic polarity pairings in the Tantra system include:

  - Earth and heaven
  - Yin and yang
  - Feminine and masculine
  - Consciousness and embodiment
  - Being and doing
  - Diffuseness and centredness
  - Emotionality and directionality
  - Soul and spirit
  - Individual and the collective/communal
  - Separation and connectivity
  - Earth and air
  - Sensation and perception
  - Duality and non-duality
  - Subject–object and unified consciousness
  - Emotionality and feeling
  - Body intelligence and mental cognition/rationality
  - Wisdom and compassion
  - Relative and absolute realities.

- So, which of the above polarities haunt your life?

- Which impact upon your professional life and within your offering of facilitation?

- Where might the middle ground or creative point of balance be within the various polarities you have identified as influencing you?

Reflections upon Chapter 6

* You are invited to help a team of enlightened managers to inquire into how they might make their company 'a fit home for the human spirit' and to enable them to review notions of spirituality they might explore within their practice:

• How might you set about co-designing with your clients a series of activities geared to raising awareness to the role 'notions of spirit' play in their working lives?

• How might you safeguard becoming ungrounded, impractical or fey in your facilitation?

• How might you design a day's inquiry into the field conditions that have led to the present contract and the expectations riding upon the same?

* Eventually a weekend workshop into 'the role of spirituality in the workplace' is requested, which you decide to facilitate in the manner of a collaborative inquiry structured around investigative cycles where 1) themes are suggested by the team, 2) strategies for the exploration of themes are decided, and 3) the group debriefs in plenary the outcomes and findings of their investigations.

• Which concepts of the text might you draw from to inform a workshop geared to the above agenda?

• How might you employ field theory to illuminate the transpersonal influences managers themselves are co-creating within the workshop?

• What meditative approaches might be used as a research tool to inquire into your client's desired theme?

* Towards the close of the workshop, participants request follow-up activities to experiment with back in the workplace:

• What work-based explorations might you suggest for your clients, post-workshop?

• How might you inquire into the fruits of your workshop and your own facilitative contribution?

* Imagine yourself in a state of personal fulfilment and contemplate how you will feel, what you will be doing, the people and the creations you will invest your energy within:

• If indeed you were to achieve this state, what words would best describe you in this imagined state of self-actualisation?

▶ * Now consider where you are now on your journey to this realised place and how you might travel in life to draw nearer to this self-fulfilled position:

- Work back from this imagined time and place, in which you envision yourself as self-actualised, and imagine the stages you went through to get there. (When you return to where you are now – you will have your plan.)

The soul is many things, linked to the realm of sense by what is lowest in us, linked to the intelligible realm by what is highest. For each of us is an intelligible cosmos.

(Chevalier and Gheerbhant 1994)

Integration
and Synthesis

When you simply obey the commands of your heart,
Thoughts of sorrow and joy do not arise.
There's just no alternative to acting as you do,
And you accept this as your destiny.

(Chuang Tzu)

Chapter seven

A Final Synthesis

The only thing that makes life bearable is the ever-present uncertainty of not knowing what comes next, the joy of a future that remains thankfully unknown. Just imagine how it would be to know every outcome, to be able to predict with certainty the result of every strategy – what a living Hell. Yet this is what the business community all too often expects of leaders and consultants!

Reflections upon the Journey so Far –
A Final Brainstorm!

So where have we arrived on our facilitative journey through this text thus far? We have been exposed to a developing facilitator–client relationship with its differing degrees of engagement from 'pre-contact' to 'post-contact', while operating alongside is a gentle progression through ever-deepening 'sensory' and 'social' engagements which hopefully generate an appreciation of our more hidden 'emotional', 'imaginative' and 'intuitive' realities. Drawing from a multiple stream of influences, I have attempted to demonstrate how we might construct 'skilful contact' with an external reality informed by our 'presence and being', a state developed out of an inner reality informed by a lifetime of personal growth and experiential learning. From my illumination of this vantage point and my working in a Gestalt way, I hope you have gleaned the importance of positioning yourself within an 'authentic relationship' while remaining mindful of the contractual obligations and idealisations that inform our role as a facilitator. In **Figure 4** I have attempted to portray the holistic field in which a Gestalt facilitator is embedded, plus the essential conditions that inform our getting in touch with 'now'.

In the last analysis, this work invites you through the cultivation of 'awareness' and 'active experimentation' to welcome change and to support others to get in touch with a similar place. Listening to your uncertainty and guided by the wisdom of insecurity, strong in your vulnerability as a fellow traveller alongside others, you are invited in your facilitative role to illuminate the human condition. This is the essential message of Gestalt, that 'becoming the whole of what we are' frees us from attempting to 'be this' or trying to 'do that'. Alive to ambiguity and paradox, attuned to our own vulnerability, we are better able to develop the sensitivity necessary to be guided by the 'embodied intelligence' that emanates from ourselves and the field we facilitate within. A field that is all the while facilitating us! This is the experiment that Gestalt invites us to undertake. So set about engaging your own explorations, develop your own sensitivities, collect your own data and allow this model-cum-metaphor to lead you into new facilitative territory and competence.

The *Reflections* suggested at the end of this section, with a bit of luck, will refresh what has gone before, assist you in assessing where you are now and help evaluate the influence this text might have already wrought upon the range and expression of your facilitative style.

Finally, to help ground much of what has been discussed in this text in practice, I have added an all-singing, all-dancing case study of a consultancy I facilitated over a three-year period, which initiated an academic–commercial partnership to deliver an MSc in Change within the host organisation to enhance personal and team development plus cultural change. This warts-and-all study had moments of the highest highs and the lowest lows! Hopefully I have caught

Figure 4. The Holistic Facilitative Field

External Field Influences

Developing & Co-creating a Facilitator–Client Relationship

Pre-Contact ⇨ Orientation ⇨ Identification ⇨ Exploration ⇨ Resolution ⇨ Post-Contact

Psychologically preparing for an imagined future & reflecting upon the options	*Forming a relationship & developing trust & an appreciation of how we might work*	*Forming an agenda & purpose & co-creating a mutually satisfying way of working*	*Collaboratively inquiring into the identified issues & addressing the mutually agreed agenda*	*Evaluating outcomes & results while working to a mutually satisfactory closure*	*Reflecting upon the experience as a whole & integrating its learning*

⇩　　　　　⇩　　　　　⇩　　　　　⇩　　　　　⇩

Unfolding Perceptions & Self/Co-constellated Influences

Sensing ⇨ Thinking ⇨ Feeling ⇨ Imagining ⇨ Intuiting

Getting a 'sense' of the other & acclimatising to their physical bio-energetic presence	*Building a relationship & social contract in which to focus effort & purpose*	*Investing emotionally & committing to a mutually agreed plan of action*	*Co-creating & testing hypotheses arising from engagement in the field*	*Reflecting upon the learning & experiential wisdoms*

⇩　　　　⇩　　　　⇩　　　　⇩　　　　⇩

How we physically, socially, emotionally, imaginatively and intuitively engage & connect

⇩

Contact and Sensitivity

NOW

Presence and Being

⇧

My embodied physical–sensory, socio-cultural, emotional–transferential, projective–imaginal & intuitive learning

⇧　　　　　　　⇧　　　　　　　⇧

How I professionally relate to the Contractual Relationship	*How I am informed through the Idealised Relationship*	*How I work from within the Authentic Relationship*

Appreciating Formed and Unfolding Influences

Internal Field Influences

something of the living drama of Gestalt consulting with its multiple levels of address and field-led foci.

I hope you have found my models and case studies illuminating and will use them to tread with expanded awareness into an enriched facilitative role, and in the yin sense, I hope you remember to allow yourself to be guided by the inner intuitive voice of what is at heart facilitating you.

Deep within every life, no matter how dull or ineffectual it may seem from the outside, there is something eternal happening. This is the secret way that change and possibility conspire with growth. John Henry Newman summed this up beautifully with the idea that to grow is to change and to be perfect is to have changed often. Change, therefore, need not be threatening; it can in fact bring our lives to perfection.

(O'Donoghue 1997, p.164)

Holistic Consulting in Action –
An Illustrative Case Study

The Consultant's Gestalt Mindset –
Transpersonal Considerations of Change

To motivate and develop personnel while fostering a co-operative team spirit presents a major challenge for business communities of the twenty-first century (Waitley 1995; RSA 1995; Barber 2002). This case study sets out to examine the gains and challenges of using a Gestalt-informed peer-learning community within a commercially based master's to nurture personal development. On ancient maps in locations where danger was thought to exist, the traveller was warned 'here be dragons'. This account raises awareness to the organisational dragons that await Gestalt-inspired change agents.

Gestalt in a Zen-like way invites us to concentrate upon and to heighten our attention on the moment so that we might be 'enlightened to what is' rather than caught in mental ruminations and judgements. To paraphrase a well-known Zen/Taoist maxim, sustain from a definitions of things as being 'this' or 'that' and follow what is 'now' and currently emerging, for by making something 'good' we simultaneously define what is 'bad'; do this and all will become clear. But our ego and very identity rest on a collection of enduring self-beliefs, and we know how hard is it to loosen our self-image to 'get out of the way of ourselves' to perceive a greater more complex whole. Yet this is the primary task of a Gestalt consultant, group facilitator or coach. Endeavouring to leave our ego outside the room is the transpersonal aim we aspire to, so we might awaken to a greater whole and see more clearly the contextual field in which we and others are embedded. This invitation to look out on the world anew, to question what has become unquestionable is as difficult teaching fish to see water! But a necessary and essential task if awareness is to be deepened and broadened. Long before 'mindfulness became a buzz-word' Gestalt practitioners were endeavouring to cultivate the same in an attempt to raise personal and community consciousness and to foster choice. Though Taoism and Zen, akin to Humanism, suggest that the divine is within all things and everything should be treated with respect, we are nevertheless cautioned that this is not a gentle way:

> From Japanese bushido, or 'way of the warrior', we learn three keys for making aggressive energy serve our creative visions: be present, be concentrated, and be strong.
>
> (Boldt 1993, p.63)

▶ Fritz Perls acknowledged his indebtedness to Zen (Perls 1947) and Joseph Zinker, who spent much time with Gestalt's founding father, has observed of his teacher:

> What hasn't survived about Fritz – is his presence. He was like a Zen master who taught you by... smearing himself all over you, in the most powerful way. He made you sit up.
>
> (Zinker interviewed by Barber 2001, p.30)

Note how this image of Gestalt is far from the watered-down, institutionalised and sanitised clinical 'professional presence' taught to many Gestalt psychotherapy trainees.

In Gestalt, Zen and Taoism alike, we are encouraged to empty our mind, so that with an open mind and heart we might be guided by what is vibrant, alive and unfolding now. Gestalt's attention to what is in process of becoming and dissolving, the breathing in and out of the fertile void, has been compared to going with the flow of Yin and Yang (Woldt and Ingersoll 1991) – twin forces of emergence and dissolution. Tao-like, Gestaltist practitioners further contend that, if we go with the flow and innate intelligence of the relational field, all the resources we need to proceed will be revealed (Zinker 1977). In Western terms, Gestalt is spiritual in a Quaker way, in that you are encouraged to clear your chattering mind and wait for the spirit/field to inform you. By stopping the course of our mind and through a loosening of the psycho-social mechanisms that hold our phenomenological world together, Gestalt encourages something other to flood in. In this light, education, in the Gestalt mode, akin to Zen, is less like filling a bucket and more like lighting a fire.

In summary, akin to Zen and Taoism, Gestalt invites you to conduct experiential inquiry into everything around and within you, and seeks to seed a similar mind-set in the client-system. Raising awareness to the whole experiential field in this way broadens perception so that all and everything is up for question, and was previously taken for granted can be rattle-and-shaken and reappraised. You, your clients, the organisation are in this way all subject to investigation as to their true nature plus the influence each exerts upon the other. As in research, methods and modes of inquiry are subject to investigation as much as what results. Gently yet persistently, individuals are encouraged to awaken from complacency to learn anew. To this end individuals and the client-system are invited and educated into the skills of co-operative inquiry to research 'what is happening' and 'what they are contributing' - now. Setting about their everyday business individuals take this newly acquired research-mindedness with them, engage personalised learning contracts they have earlier refined with their peers, who incidentally, are co-opted to help keep the communal spirit of peer learning and inquiry alive. In this vein, participants mindfully attended to themselves, the learning of others and the field conditions they are both co-creating and embedded within.

Individuals of the Gestalt-informed peer-learning community described in this study, in plenary group and learning sets regularly attended to what was unfolding – now – and were in this way encouraged to put to test the worth of the above notions. Later in this study, two models, the fruit of its facilitative inquiry, are presented for consideration.

Therapeutic Community and Field Theory – Seeds of the Gestalt Peer-learning Community

The Therapeutic Community (TC), a social model of care associated with mental health and group analysis (Pines 1983), in a like manner to field theory (Lewin 1952) and Gestalt emphasises the wider community context to which the individual relates. Focusing upon the systemic energy/field of the immediate community, it attempts to shape group culture through the injection of 'democratic decision-making', 'efficient communication', 'experimentation' and 'reality confrontation' (Rapoport 1960). Underpinning this approach is the working hypothesis that an individual's pathology is related to stressful environments, deficient group leadership and low morale (Jansen 1980). This implies that disease is to be found not only in our physiological body but also in our 'socio-cultural' and 'organisational' bodies, our wider holistic field, which can similarly benefit from therapeutic and healing intervention.

In my view, the 'culture of enquiry' a Therapeutic Community creates goes much deeper in terms of developing social and emotional intelligence than the learning company (Pedler et al. 1997) or the peer-learning community described by Heron (1974). Indeed, it houses many of those qualities we have more recently begun to associate with such trends as Servant Leadership (Spears 2002), which amongst other things stresses: getting in touch with the inner voice and seeking to understand what one's body, spirit and mind are communicating; empathy; healing and the search for wholeness; a commitment to fostering awareness; convincing others rather than coercing compliance through positional authority; nurturing the ability to dream great dreams; intuition; stewardship and holding what is deemed valuable in trust for others; commitment to growth and building community. All of which are enhanced by a Gestalt climate.

My first encounter with the Therapeutic Community occurred at the Henderson Hospital in the early 1970s. In order to replicate a Therapeutic Community experience, rotation was encouraged between small analytic groups, experiential workshops, seminars, cooking and cleaning groups, plus a large community group some 30-to-40 strong. This latter experience, where the community came together to reflect long and deeply upon the processes in which it was engaged, produced many Zen-like moments (i.e. when silence and impasse would suddenly give way to spontaneous insights and learning). Indeed, the Group Analytic method of following the emerging group process and describing the group flow via metaphor, I found out later had much in common with Gestalt. I was particularly impressed by the blend of intellectual and experiential learning stimulated through the healthy antagonism of psychoanalytic approaches and humanistic psychology, one analytic and containing, the other exploratory and socially engaging. Two contrasting ends of the human inquiry continuum were in this way brought together.

Following my attendance on the Therapeutic Community programme cited above, as an educator interested in 'community' and affective education (Krathwol et al. 1964), I experimented with integrating Rapoport's (1960) principles of Therapeutic Community practice to my teaching, with the following effects:

> Content was still transmitted and students still sat exams, but we paused more often to reflect upon 'what we were doing' and 'how we were doing it'. Simply, we began to examine the social cement that held us together. As a consequence, energy rose, learners seemed to show greater emotional commitment and my teaching gained a 'real life' feel and a social inquiry edge.
>
> (Barber 1996, p.242)

But there was still something missing. My analytic bias seemed to venerate the teacher's authority while infantilising the student. A little later, as Director of the Certificate in Therapeutic Community Practice, I had opportunity to experiment further. Becoming increasingly frustrated with what were taken to be analytic givens, such as the necessity of transference, I began to feed phenomenological inquiry and field theory into the Therapeutic 'Educational' Community through the medium of Gestalt. Gestalt's emphasis on dialogue, the creation of authentic relationships and holistic phenomenological inquiry, helped loosen the group analytic foundation in two ways:

> i) It brought field theory (Lewin 1952), with its holistic vision, and phenomenological inquiry into the frame to support open experimentation rather than the workings of a mysterious 'analytically inspired' unconscious, so that what were previously taken to be 'analytic givens' now become 'working hypotheses for testing'.
>
> ii) It countered the pathological orientation of psychoanalysis, where the facilitator remains distant and opaque so as to invite transference (emotionalised prior learning) and in its place promoted a facilitative transparency which encouraged quality person-to-person contact,

authentic dialogue and collaborative inquiry within the present, in contrast to a fixation upon the effects of the past.

I subsequently refined this tailoring of Gestalt to peer learning at Surrey University when facilitating the group strand of the MSc in Change Agent Skills and Strategies (Barber 1996), a two-year, part-time master's programme where students in the first year explore change and developmental processes and in the second year rehearse the same under guidance. This model, along with the MSc in Change was transported into the organisational consultancy described below as a vehicle for culture change and healing.

Into the Dragon's Lair –
Organisational Resistance to Change

Following a well-received two-day experiential workshop on group facilitation within a large telephone-marketing consultancy in central England, the company's founder and chairman approached me with a view to developing his organisation further. As most staff, including the major power holders, had been personally recruited by him in the 1980s through facilitated seminars which incorporated a potent mixture of group encounter and charismatic spirituality, he exercised enormous political power and personal control within company life and thus had the 'authority' to recruit me to his creation.

As discussions progressed, an off-campus, company-based master's in change was suggested but negotiations were not smooth sailing. The University saw the company's eagerness to get things under way as pushy and careless, and the company saw the University's slow, over-careful response as faint-hearted. Bear in mind the company's culture emphasised 'will' and it was commonly believed that if you wanted something desperately enough you would get what you desired. Due to the University's caution, the company became increasingly agitated and demanding and the University, largely in retaliation, became nit-picking and legalistic with regard to its own contractual arrangements and guarantees. This resistance, I suggest, is symptomatic of the cultural dynamic explored below.

Gestalt-informed consultants often see organisations as living fields which sometimes become stuck within a 'sensation–withdrawal cycle' (Critchley and Casey 1989) and suggest that all living things, organisations included, may be diagnosed and facilitated towards health through an attention and address of the following phases:

Sensation (sensory feedback from the self and environment)

Awareness (alertness to feelings and needs)

Mobilisation of energy (raising motivation for need fulfilment)

Excitement (engagement of physiological energy)

Action (behavioural enactment)

Contact (meeting with an experience of satisfaction)

Withdrawal (natural completion and rest).

Taking this model as a framework for understanding the unfolding dialogue between my client/commerce and the University/academia led me to suspect that University culture in general, and the department to which I was attached in particular, had seemingly become stuck between 'awareness' and the 'mobilisation of energy'. When teams or organisations are stuck at this point, there is much intellectual rumination but little action, for fear of unleashing powerful emotions which would threaten or overwhelm the existing intellectual controls. Projecting blame and holding onto hurts and angers is seen to be the norm in these so-called 'knowing-and-angry organisations' (Critchley and Casey 1989). Organisations representative of minority groups commonly exhibit these symptoms, and the author's department, promoting such fringe activities as experiential learning and Humanism on a predominately engineering and technological campus, fitted neatly into this category.

Still, persistence, flexibility and remaining in dialogue won out in the end, for after a prolonged period of floating in limbo and mounting frustration, realising it was impossible to supply the securities being demanded from the University, I forced the pace by re-framing the proposed off-site master's as an on-going field experiment. To the University, experimentation was kosher even if partnership was not, and this re-framing was enough to sanctify and seed a fledgling commercial–academic partnership.

Within six months, interviews were completed and a commercially based MSc was under way with a cross-section of 24 participants from executive, middle-management and the shop floor.

Awakening Dragons – Fostering an Educational Dialogue

In the introductory three-day block of the commercially based master's, within a palatial commercial building where the cognitive agenda was to raise awareness to the nature of learning and our affective task was to bond as a peer-learning community, participants and tutors began to evolve a way of being together. At the start of each day, we spent 30–90 minutes – depending upon the nature of the emerging issues – seated in a community circle raising attention to current individual and community learning needs, while reflecting upon the dynamics we co-created together. This process was often akin to group meditation, with long silences and an eventual surfacing of conflicts and frustrations. It also provided opportunity for tutors to role-model resolution of the same through timely facilitation and processing. Following this attunement and community checking-in process, we generally set about planning how we would address the academic content of the day, including mini lectures, experiential experiments, self-directed activity and assignment preparation. At the close of the day participants came together as a plenary group to debrief, share evaluations and celebrate gains, and to say their goodbyes.

As to the general content and curriculum of the peer-learning community's check-in and plenary, this tended to cluster around the experiential levels:

i) **Reflecting upon Physical–Sensory Phenomena:** *[Gathering and attending to sensory information – developing sensory intelligence]* Learning to observe and listen: attending to the environment; focusing upon what is presented; identifying physical support systems; differentiating between thoughts and feelings and observations; developing awareness and sensitivity to our physiological needs

ii) **Reflecting upon Social–Cultural Phenomena:** *[Relating and understanding the cultural context – developing social intelligence]* Learning about how we socially and intellectually structure and relate: forming rules and roles; informing others; prescribing; reflecting in a critical way; defining the purpose and task; building a learning community; creating a safe environment; meeting relational needs

iii) **Reflecting upon Emotional–Transferential Phenomena:** *[Expressing and directing emotional energy – developing emotional intelligence]* Learning about our emotional responses and patterns: understanding and expressing feelings; releasing blockages of emotional energy; reviewing how our present relates to our past; raising awareness to family scripts; releasing ourselves from the presenting past

iv) **Reflecting upon Imaginal–Projective Phenomena:** *[Exploring and integrating imagination with the self – developing self-intelligence]* Learning about the hidden self: identifying our sub-personalities; illuminating inner motives and ego defences; unpacking how imagination informs us; exploring our persona and ego needs; undoing projective identifications and control dramas; raising the shadow

v) **Reflecting upon Intuitive–Transpersonal Phenomena:** *[Becoming and speculating upon potential beyond the self – developing* *spiritual intelligence]* Learning about how and where we belong: valuing ourselves and others; becoming authentic and identifying core values; developing holistic vision; illuminating your life's purpose; awakening to wisdom above and beyond the self; relating ourselves to the cosmos

Within this first three-day meeting, a good deal of old scores and resentments surfaced. Recorded in field theory terms, clustered around questions surfaced by Parlett (1991) and divided into subheadings of 'external impressions', 'my internal reactions' and 'possible future action', my notes of the time record the following:

'a) <u>How are people and events organised here?</u>

External Impressions:

- Historically, a core group of people appear to have lived, loved, fallen in and out of love and been friends for what seems like forever in this community.

- Some of the longer serving members of the community appear to take it on themselves – and be looked to by others – to police the community rules.

- Community members, being familiar with 'other people's stuff', tend to ridicule or laugh at those who act characteristically and/or true to the company stereotype.

- To be female in this organisation seems to confer a stronger position from which to emotionally bully others.

- Some individuals seem to need to overstate their difference to avoid being swamped by the group.

My Internal Reactions:

- Shock at how punitive some women of this community are permitted to be, almost as if they have divine protection or a permit to abuse.

- Surprise at the carefulness of the men.

Possible Future Action:

- Facilitate an all-male and an all-female group in a fishbowl setting?

- Investigate further the male and female stereotypes this culture produces?

- Look at the role 'sex' plays as a competitive and/or controlling tool?

- Examine how male and female roles in the community keep each other trapped?

b) **What influences of the present field explain current behaviour?**

External Impressions:

- A highly competitive group with strong players for power and dominance.
- Powerful members make long speeches rather than enter into dialogue with others.
- Tendency to 'tell people how it is' rather than enquire.
- Competition for attention and air-time.

My Internal Reactions:

- With so much being said it is not easy to be heard or to enter gently into the group.

Possible Future Action:

- Encourage attention and more sensitive listening and role model same?
- Facilitate exercise in deeper levels of listening with the heart as well as the ear?

c) **What is unique about the present field?**

External Impressions:

- A gifted group of individuals who are potential stars in their own right.
- The organisation seems genuinely to value people and appears to offer opportunities for individuals to maximise their potential.
- Senior management appears person centred and caring.
- People appear to want a 'quick fix' and actionable skills rather than mindfully and carefully to acquire the same.
- This is a 'people pleasing culture' (quote).
- Individuals openly share their personal and transpersonal beliefs.
- Individuals can be very loving and caring of each other.
- Some individuals are very committed to the organisation and some appear trapped within it.

My Internal Reactions:

- I find this group very easy to like.

Possible Future Action:

- Monitor and draw attention to the community's development?

d) What is in the process of becoming?

External Impressions:

- If the quieter members are permitted to stay quiet and the noisier ones noisy, the community will split into activators and those who hold hidden resentments and hurts.

- If things go on as they are a 1960s encounter group could become the norm.

My Internal Reactions:

- I was aware of letting this run this time round to get at the emerging pattern, so as to see the organic form this group co-creates.

- I was fascinated by how sophisticated and yet naive the community could be.

Possible Future Action:

- Gently encourage the quieter ones to speak and noisier ones to hold back?

- Challenge each individual to break their usual group pattern?

- Let the pattern run until the community sorts itself out?

- Facilitate an event that illuminates the emerging pattern?

- Combine the above approaches?

- Go with the trend and run an encounter group?

e) What am I blind to or excluding at this time?

External Impressions:

- I sometimes came out more strongly then I intended when policing the ground rules of striving to be authentic, respecting others, or in focusing the group upon what was happening 'now'.

- Conflict seemed to be held onto until near the end, when all manner of grievances arose as time was conveniently running out.

- A tendency for senior community members to swing a little between depending and rebelling against authoritative facilitation.

My Inner Reactions:

- Having an acute sense of impatience when – in a personal, biased way – I felt that 'time', or 'my time' was being squandered.

- I believe the undertone of my communication was 'life is too short for us to waste playing out the usual rescuer–victim persecutory dramas you play out to get attention here'.

- Held back my power to let others develop their life dramas.

Possible Future Action:

- When the group is stronger, state clearly the ground rules that I am prepared to live-or-die for and invite challenge?

- Be less patient with repetitive deflective behaviour that appears to be getting nowhere?

- Challenge the resistances?

The above describes the baseline from which the community began. In the interests of openness, the above field analysis was circulated and discussed in our next meeting, and subsequently verified as resonant with the experience of others. Hopefully, from my description you can begin to appreciate the emotionally expressive nature of this company, with its encounter-like 'tell it like it is' character and competitive 'I want to be a star' culture.

Interestingly, returning to Critchley and Casey's organisational categorisation, this description equates with that of the 'hysterical organisation' interrupted between sensation and awareness:

> Organisations stuck here are in sharp contrast to the suppressed organisation – instead of denying feelings, these organisations go overboard with their feelings and much of their time is taken up with experiencing and expressing sensation. Where they fail is in extracting any sort of sense from this welter of sensation – they have plenty of excitement but they do not know what it means for the organisation's health... Many such organisations get stuck because, by and large, they enjoy the experience of sensation.
>
> (Critchley and Casey 1989, p.6)

Another feature essential for an understanding of this company is the emotional dependence individuals felt towards the chairman.

The chairman, having originally drawn the working community together, retained an immense personal following because of his earlier facilitative role. Indeed, in the 1980s Heelas (1987) compared the company to a cult, and even now, the chairman took very seriously indeed his obligation to provide

248

individuals with unsolicited developmental experiences. For instance, he would often advance or demote people depending on his whim. But as with all intimate relationships, a large degree of transference proliferated. Sometimes he became so trapped within the parental role that he enacted with gusto a 'beneficent parent' one minute and a 'punitive parent' the next. So personally felt were the dynamics that neutrality was rarely in the equation. He was either loved or rejected – or loving and rejecting – by turns. No doubt this was as exhausting for him as it was for others, yet, on the plus side, this intense emotional climate was generally felt by all involved to be generative of a good deal of interesting drama. The company was his stage and he commanded the leading role.

In regard to the company's earlier history and cult-like nature, it is illuminating to read a participant's account of the start to his 'usual' working day, written in his subsequent master's dissertation. He observes that a Zilgeon gong – the large sort found in orchestras – was sounded by each person prior to each morning's 'cleaning ritual':

> Some people just hit it, others make it reverberate and the sound just grows and grows like rolling thunder. We now begin the ritual of cleaning. For the next ten minutes we will silently clean our work area and any other part of the building we are allocated. Everyone has their own spray can of Pledge and a J cloth. … The idea here is that we experience creating our own space. … This cleaning is like all the showy effort you see in a theatre to prepare for the performance, which is not a bad analogy because during the day, it is a show.
>
> (Pollecoff 1998, p.56)

Following the cessation of cleaning, again sounded by the gong, a countdown to the working day was enacted:

> Over the years the countdowns have grown more elaborate. And the movements you make whilst singing grow more complex, as a step or facial expression is added. Although there are favourites and stalwarts like 'Match of the Day' or 'Hawaii Five O' ('Book him Danno') they change by the day. Today is the 'Flintstones' Countdown'.
>
>> Phoners – meet the phoners
>> They're a modern working family
>> When you're – with the phoners
>> You'll go down in history.
>> Do Da Dada Da Dada Da
>> Da Da Da Da Dada Do
>> [Everyone does a twist, during this bit]
>> …Ten, Nine, Eight, Seven, Six, Five, Four, Three, Two, One…
>
> (Pollecoffe 1998, pp.57–8)

The above account gives further support to the notion that this was a dramatic, histrionic company. In this light, systemically, what the University offered in terms of emotional containment and reflectivity, the company obviously needed; and what the company displayed in terms of emotional expression and creativity – possibly the University needed? But then what organisations 'need' and what they 'want' is rarely the same thing.

Sitting in the Fire – Commercial Threats to Community Learning

Two months into the programme, when academia and commerce had grown more accustomed to each other, a period of stability ensued; but then, everything has its seasons. Some eight months into the programme, a number of interesting challenges arose:

> **Event 1:** A doctorate student acting as a bridge tutor between the University and organisation accepted a lucrative full-time position to spread peer learning throughout the company at large. *(Having a commercial background, she had been least resistive to an academic–commercial partnership and had been my closest tutorial ally during the programme's gestation. Though she would still service the MSc, she was now more 'company' than 'University'.)*

> **Event 2:** The chairman, who had invited me in, sold the company and upped and left. *(The retirement of the chairman evoked within the company a response not unlike that of a trusted parent deserting his family: emotional distress on all sides was deep and long-lived, with individuals swinging between adoring and rejecting, gratitude for the past and fear of the future.)*

> **Event 3:** The author was invited to heal the organisation following the chairman's departure. *(This took the form of communally working through the waves of shock and grief that were occasioned by the chairman's leaving; and although offering rich insight into the company's culture, this re-surfaced issues of inclusion and exclusion in the tutorial team.)*

The organisational field now began actively to threaten the learning community. A few weeks after the chairman's departure, the author was invited into the centre of the peer community and heatedly quizzed about the nature of his relationship with him: 'Are you still in contact with X?' 'Do you report back to him about us?' etc. Though uncomfortable at the time, this regular surfacing, airing and resolution of hidden and imagined agendas helped to maintain community hygiene. X, the retiring chairman, had evolved a divisive culture where one group warred with another, while all the while he remained powerful and special. By contrast, within the master's programme, teacher and student alike were seen as accountable to the peer-learning community and held to account. Indeed, community meetings under the influence of Gestalt, at this time, intensified our experience and the transitional process in the Zen-like way:

Accumulation: In Zen this initial phase of creativity is seen to come to the fore as one follows an idea or vision that enables a build-up of energy, which in turn may be focused in a specific direction or on a particular theme.

Saturation: In the second phase, immersion and absorption are seen to take over as interest grows and the theme is absorbed, to the degree that it takes over the whole of your attention. Indeed, in extreme cases you now dedicate your life and give it over freely to the chosen direction. One tries at this time to assimilate with the intellect, but the intellect is foiled and you are thrust into further immersion. Here there is saturation in creative vision, as intensity builds and, no matter what, you still adhere to your vision.

Explosion: The work now becomes a thing in itself, whole and complete, which has its own life and now uses you. In this context, life simultaneously becomes a meditation and an art form of the integrated theme.

(After Boldt 1993, pp.105–6)

There were many Zen-like explosions. The peer community, in this way constantly awakened, kept us in contact with our discomfort and forced us to change. The community's dynamic, akin to the company's, like a holograph, appeared to mirror its current impasse and growing destabilisation as management changes and a company takeover got under way. Finally pressures from the organisational field began to fragment communication and threaten the timely return of course assignments to the degree. I circulated the following letter to participants:

While I am accepting – and sympathetic to the fact – that commercial pressures and overseas postings make part-time study difficult, I interpret my role as Director of the external MSc as one where I am employed by you (my clients) and the conjoint partnership of the University and the commercial funding body to bring the MSc to a successful conclusion. ... I am holding you to your contract with yourself, your company and myself, to meet the requirements of the MSc programme. ... You may choose to feel alerted; supported; told-off; patronised or cared for. Whatever reaction and whatever you feel is fine, just as long as we open further dialogue.

The above missive was received positively by all – bar one – as a supportive tutorial act. It also says masses about the anxieties I and the tutor team entertained with respect to commercial pressures swamping the academic boundaries; the fine balance between policing deadlines and maintaining personal support; plus the demands of an off-campus course that felt at great psychic as well as geographical distance from the University.

So What Really Changed?

At the end of the taught component of the course, prior to writing up their dissertation, an evaluation day was organised. The community decided to approach this evaluation in the manner of a collaborative action-research inquiry (Lewin 1946) through recurring cycles of:

i) Clarifying and planning – contemplating and raising awareness to the purposes and structure of inquiry

ii) Engaging and observing – experientially engaging, giving ourselves over to the energetic field while observing the processes of investigation

iii) Integrating and debriefing – meditating upon the value and meaning of the information raised.

On the evaluation day I was commissioned to record events, to write up and to circulate an account to the community. I also requested – and was granted – permission to publish what transpired. The following is constructed from verbatim field notes of the time.

In the check-in to the evaluation day, participants began sharing how they had changed:

'This experience has opened up an appreciation of the options'; 'provided therapeutic insight and an intense working through of personal issues in a relatively short space of time'; 'awakened me to "being" as well as "doing"'.

In relation to the cult-like culture of the company it was also noted that the programme had:

'encouraged life changes and de-construction of previous notions of the self... [and] exerted a collective effect upon the organisation – by way of setting people free from their history'; 'There have also been many major life changes such as marriage; babies being born; changes of employment's; movement out of the organisation – events that were less common previously'.

In terms of learning, not only did awareness appear to have been enhanced but there was tacit evidence for an emotional working through and a re-evaluation of self and relationships:

> 'a healing process; I have become more softer, and questioning of what I'll do with the rest of my life'; 'Clearer as to what is mine and what are other's processes that affect me'; 'Feel much more compassionate'; 'I don't need to be angry and bullying; which I did to others as they did to me to avoid being controlled'; 'I'm more angry and upset than before, as if it's peeled the layers off. My quality of energy is different now. More aware of organic rather than imposed change now'.

Standing back from content to examine the developing relational dynamic, the process of moving from mundane physical and social levels of engagement to more emotionally empowering and intuitive levels of communication paralleled a similar process to that of the workshop days.

Regarding the method of inquiry we would use, it was suggested we adopt a 'fishbowl' format. This necessitates a circle of six chairs being placed in the centre of the larger community group, of which participants fill five chairs but leave one empty. Should someone walk in, another must leave, so as to keep an empty and inviting chair. Through this process, speakers regularly alternate. Only five people are active at any one time, others may enter and the whole community is party to discussion. With this holding structure in place, attention now turned towards the healing effects of the learning community within the company:

> 'Emotions are more accessible now and our personal quality of life (within the organisation) has improved; for example, we can now say no'; 'This course has helped me integrate difficult experiences of the past (within the company), and helped me develop confidence'; 'Before the MSc I didn't feel qualified as a human being. So many years of negative feedback. I now value my humbleness and skill in working with people here'; 'The course resonated with the healing and family-organisational therapy; feel more whole as a human being'; 'I've reinvented myself and my career on this course, and learnt the importance of beingness and being ourselves'.

Bear in mind, as this company had once been compared to a cult (Heelas 1987), it was perhaps from this legacy that individuals felt themselves freed. This aside, keeping the affective educational domain to the fore while building models and intellectual understanding appeared to have permeated back into the workplace:

> 'The self and peer assessment felt very rich, and is starting to be integrated into the organisation more now'; 'Peer groups are still meeting and have generated peer sets within the company'; 'Tutors as

peers in one sense, but recognisable authorities in another – was well handled and provided a good role model.'

There was perceived to be an immense difference in boundaries between business and education, to the degree a warning is proffered to all humanistic educators who wish to tend their wares in a commercial culture:

'Boundaries in a business context are usually positive and un-negotiable. Educational ones were more humanistic and person-centred, and this may have given some people permission to break them'; 'There is also the difference between business being action driven and academia being reflective. Developing an attitude to work and life that is inquiry based was not easy with commercial pressures in your face.'

This theme was developed by exploring how cynical business and organisational values infiltrated the learning community:

'Trying to get away with it – fake it until you make it'; 'After all, we are good sales people who market things. Be, do, have – are all part of our culture'; 'Front was part of our survival, and the articulation of needs was not strong here. The greater cause of work always came before people and the group. We did not share needs for fear of looking stupid'; 'What is unique in this group, its earlier history of growing- up together through personal growth seminars, fed us with family stresses'.

Later in the day, we returned again to how the educational community had affected organisational culture:

'My doing and acting is now balanced by encouragement to reflect'; 'Greater sensitivity in the organisation towards people and their needs'; 'Changes to the company have been in our completing and working through the old culture, which enabled us to put a full stop to our previous conflicts'; 'Facilitated cultural change with the new company takeover and helped us re-create our culture'; 'We have re-committed to values we once held dear; such as person-centredness and growth'.

Re the 'hysterical culture' earlier described:

'We have moved from a panicky culture to one more accepting of new people'; 'the course kept us sane through a very organisationally traumatising time. The course helped to build-up our new culture'; 'This group processed something for the organisation, and took this back again resolved in part. The old way had reached the end of the road and the course gave the company a new direction. Look how the company has doubled in size since the MSc began!'; 'We now have a new lease of life, structure and capability for sustaining people-centred values that provide support and in turn influence our client relations. Increased skills means increased charge-out rates to clients'.

In the final minutes, participants shared their appreciation of the inquiry process. What began as a rather mechanistic and intellectual task was observed to have transformed into a richly experiential, contemplative and flowing process – as is usually the case, I note, when people are encouraged in a Gestalt container to be reflective 'human-beings' rather than over-busy 'human-doings'.

Taking this case study's earlier description of the community in the initial meeting as a baseline, there appeared to be less dependence, less distress reaching out from the past, less competition – as the 'stars' now appeared less in ascendance and the community was self-facilitating. I speculated that learners in a Gestalt-informed peer-learning community, in feeling more seen, heard and cared for, have possibly less need to politically and emotionally act out their distress.

Individually and on mass, the community personality had seemingly shifted from an over-concern with individual and competitive ego-survival to a more spiritual/transpersonal stance, as was evidenced in such comments as:

> 'I've become more softer and questioning of what I will do with the rest of my life'; 'I now value my humbleness'; 'feel more whole as a human being'; 'I've reinvented myself… and learnt the importance of beingness and being ourselves'; 'Feel much more compassionate'; 'My doing and acting is now balanced by encouragement to reflect.'

Organisationally, there seemed also to have been many qualitative changes:

> 'Peer groups are still meeting and have generated peer sets within the company'; 'Emotions are more accessible now and our personal quality of life (within the organisation) has improved'; 'Greater sensitivity in the organisation towards people and their needs'; 'Changes to the company have been in our completing and working through the old culture, which enabled us to put a full stop to our previous conflicts'; 'Facilitated cultural change with the new company takeover and helped us re-create our culture'; 'We are re-committed to person-centredness and growth'.

But was Change a Phoenix or a Death Knell?

From the foregoing inquiry it would appear substantial gains were made in developing individuals in areas of self and spiritual awareness, via fostering higher-level motivation and a greater sensitivity to others. The person-valuing culture of the learning community appears to have also supported individuals through the hiatus of a change of company ownership and done much to heal trauma of the past, while simultaneously building individual resilience.

Reflecting upon the ability of a peer-learning community working in a Gestalt way to facilitate organisational change, it is suggested there was transfer of learning from the course community to the organisation, that individuals developed and that the wider organisational culture was in part changed. Regarding the feasibility of a learning community – within the framework of a master's programme serving to promote personal and spiritual development, quality supervision and organisational renewal – participant feedback attests to a degree of success.

A year after the master's, all bar one of the programme's participants had left the company. All except one who left in the first block completed the taught component of the course to achieve a post-graduate diploma. Five-sixths gained a master's and two have since progressed to doctorate study – all this from a cohort who were primarily without a first degree and came via a non-traditional route of academic entry.

After the chairman's departure, the company's original culture was obliterated as it doubled and then trebled in size. As over-expansion plus a drive to replace 'the old' with 'the new' led to redundancies, most course participants chose to leave and start up their own companies or work free-lance. So was this experiment an organisational phoenix or a death-knell? I guess the answer to this question depends upon whom you perceive to be the 'real client'. Was it the original organisation, the newly forming organisation, the chairman or the learning community? Personally, I believe it was the latter. Recent evidence from on-going conversations and an informal appreciative inquiry (Cooperrider and Srivasta 1987) conducted in a conference setting suggests it challenged the personal and institutional patterns – remnants of the earlier cult culture that kept people stuck – and gave them the strength to leave their institutional home. Indeed, some set up successful companies and took many of their colleagues with them.

Personal Learning

So what have I learnt from this experience? First, I have come to realise the truth of Gestalt's paradoxical nature of change, that it is better to raise awareness and to build-in community support than to aim to change something or somebody directly. Second, I appreciate the wisdom of Stapley's (1996) observation that change agents have responsibility for 'relating to the emotional and cognitive state' of a client-system, and should see themselves as parent-like, temporarily sustaining a holding environment wherein clients can be facilitated beyond unhelpful methods of thinking and behaving – and indeed supported while they deal with the anxiety and uncertainty that accompanies change. As a supportive container, a Gestalt-informed peer-learning community seems to have performed this function excellently. Third, I came to recognise that organisations make collective demands on the individual that infiltrate and subjugate them to a 'collective consciousness' which 'sucks them into the personality structure of the group', with the consequence that when the organisational field is threatened the individual also becomes threatened. From this perspective, a change agent, romantically, represents a St. George-like archetypical figure, a slayer of dragons who struggles to release the organisation's grip on individuals and to release his 'still small voice' and reflective wisdom. Gestalt influence was a powerful ally here. Fourth, I realise I had in hindsight, intuitively rather than mindfully, put in action Nevis's Gestalt principles of organisational development and proven through hands-on practice their effectiveness:

- Learning occurs best through a focus on the process of interaction rather than content

- Change in systems occurs only if members of the system are themselves actively involved in the change process

- People in organisations have potential for solving their own problems

- prime task of organisational development is to facilitate an understanding and utilisation of the organisation and its member's potential

- A climate of openness and trust is essential for a healthy work environment

- A feedback and action research model of consulting is the best route to organisational learning and change

- Change is the responsibility of the client not the consultant

- The small group is a highly effective unit for change.

(Adapted from Nevis 1997)

Finally, I came to realise the importance of continually clarifying 'contractual' and 'idealised' levels of communication within the community, while fostering a dialogue with the 'authentic level' (Greenson 1967) and the core truths of all concerned.

Reflections upon Chapter 7

In terms of being holistic and focused upon field-led inquiry, how do you rate yourself with respect to:

• Showing interest in tacit ways of knowing and in generating knowledge by dialogue?

• Taking an interest in the 'how' much more than the 'what' of emerging material?

• Focusing on the whole of experience inclusive of internal and external influences?

• Emphasising the authority of the person and their phenomenological experience?

• Attending to what is unique as well as what is general in the facilitative field?

• Championing the authority of what is experienced moment-to-moment?

• Retaining flexibility so that new avenues of exploration may emerge?

• Enquiring within the frame of an authentic and intimate relationship?

• Exploring the inter-relatedness and interdependence of phenomena?

• Endeavouring to educate and to develop all involved?

• Honouring 'being' rather than 'doing?

• Retaining an eclectic and fluid stance?

In relation to nurturing a climate for growth and learning, how effective are you at:

• Helping to elicit and clarify purpose in a democratic person-sensitive way?

• Taking responsibility for setting the initial culture and trust for exploration?

• Endeavouring to give to each individual the attention they warranted?

• Responding to intellectual content and emotional expression?

• Raising awareness to the options in a take it or leave it way?

• Endeavouring to cultivate and embody a genuine presence?

• Taking the initiative to share your thoughts and feelings?

• Accepting and acknowledging your limitations?

- Acting as a flexible and transparent resource?

- Performing collaborative and holistic inquiry?

- Negotiating the focus and content?

In terms of multiple levels of experience, how effective a facilitator are you at:

- Engaging the physical–sensory environment and illuminating sensory intelligence?

- Responding to the social–cultural environment and illuminating social intelligence?

- Holding emotional–transferential energy and illuminating emotional intelligence?

- Surfacing the imagined–projective ('shadow') and attending to self-intelligence?

- Locating intuitive–transpersonal qualities and attending to spiritual intelligence?

Regarding the client–facilitator relationship, how well do you handle the following phases:

- Orientation: laying the groundwork for communication?

- Identification: focusing upon mutual interests and needs while identifying a unifying theme?

- Exploration: engaging with the client's energy and interest and exploring their unfolding issues?

- Resolution: debriefing for insight and completion and raising awareness to the outcomes?

I invite you to consider the following scenario:

On the third meeting of a group, which you have been contracted to facilitate upon the theme of 'preparing for change', a mood of superficial agreeableness arises and prevents movement towards the agenda you are contracted to address. Rambling remarks, evasive comments and other general time-wasting behaviours begin to proliferate and take over. Over coffee you hear that a member of the team has been sacked and begin to suspect that the earlier, over-polite behaviour was due to people protecting themselves from feelings of anger and distress. After coffee, as the group recommences, you notice the same cocktail-like atmosphere return. What do you do?

▶

1 Do nothing

2 Ask the participants if they are satisfied with how the group is developing today

3 Join in with whatever they are discussing

4 Try to draw them into a more meaningful discussion

5 Suggest they get down to real feelings

6 Be aggressive yourself – criticise the group for pussy-footing around

7 Ask how they feel about what has been going on

8 Say how you are feeling

9 Share similar experiences in your life

10 Ask why everybody is being so polite

11 Ask what they think may be going on in the group today

12 Describe the group mood of politeness

13 Say that there seems to be an unspoken agreement among the members to be polite

14 Suggest that all this politeness is a reaction against the anger of previous meetings

15 Encourage them to relate this to what is happening in their lives outside the group

16 Lead into a discussion of their family relationships and past experiences

17 Encourage them to use the situation to consider behaviour they may wish to change

18 Use a non-verbal procedure to get at the underlying feeling

19 Use a role playing or psychodrama procedure.
(After David Kennard, undated)

In terms of the above imaginative scenario:

• Which of the above interventions would you choose and which would you never ever use?

• And why not?

• Which of the above interventions seem to you more group analytic in style?

From of old there were not two paths.
'Those who have arrived' all walked the same road.

(Zen saying)

Bibliography

Ackoff, R.L. (1981) *Creating the Corporate Future*, Wiley, New York.

Allen, J., Fairtlough, G. and Heinzen, B. (2002) *The Power of the Tale: Using Narratives for Organisational Success*, John Wiley, Chichester, UK.

Anderson, P. (1999) 'Application of Complexity Theory to Organization Science', *Organization Science*, Vol. 10, No. 3, Special Issue, May–Jun. 1999, pp.216–32.

Aronson, E. (1976) *The Social Animal*, Freeman, San Francisco, USA.

Assagioli, R. (1976) *Psychosynthesis: A Manual of Principles and Techniques*, Hobbs & Dorman, New York.

Attwood, M., Pedler, M., Pritchard, S. and Wilkinson, D. (2003) *Leading Change: A Guide to Whole Systems Working*, Policy Press, Bristol, UK.

Auster, R.E. (1990) 'The Interorganisational Environment: Network Theory, Tools, and Applications', in *Technological Transfer*, ed. R. Williams and D. Gibson, Newbury Park, CA: Sage.

Babbs, J. (1991) 'New Age Fundamentalism', Chapter 4 in Zweig, C. and Abrams, J., *Meeting the Shadow: The Hidden Power of the Dark Side of Human Nature*, Tarcher, Los Angeles, USA.

Bampfield, J. (2005) in conversation with the author.

Barber, P. (2011) 'An Inquiry into Gestalt Coaching and Therapy', *AMED Journal of People and Organisations*, Summer 2011.

Barber, P. (2006) *Becoming a Practitioner-Research: A Gestalt Approach to Holistic Inquiry*, Middlesex University Press, London.

Barber, P. (2006a) 'Keeping Psychotherapy Trainees in "Their Place" – How Training Institutions Stifle Love and Breed Compliance', submitted to the *International Gestalt Journal*.

Barber, P. (2005) 'Group as Teacher: The Gestalt Informed Peer-Learning Community as a Transpersonal Vehicle for Organizational Healing', *International Gestalt Review*, USA.

Barber, P. (2005a) 'The Shadow-side of Leadership – The Stifling of Creativity and the Fostering of Collusion in Training Organisations', *Organizations and People*, Vol. 12, No. 1.

Barber, P. (2003) 'Gestalt: A Prime Medium for Holistic Research and Whole Person Education', *British Gestalt Journal*, Vol. 11, No. 2, pp.78–90.

Barber, P. (2002) 'A Dialogue with Holism & the Soul', *Organisations & People*, Vol. 9, No. 1, pp.2–8.

Barber, P. (2002a) 'Self Development within Experiential Groups – a Gestalt Perspective', *Self & Society*, Vol. 30, No. 2.

Barber, P. (2002b) 'Coaching & Consulting: A Dialogue with Holism & the Soul', *Organisations & People*, Vol. 9, No. 1.

Barber, P. (2002c) 'Gestalt: A Prime Medium for Holistic Research and Whole Person Education', *British Gestalt Journal*, Vol. 11, No. 2.

Barber, P. (2001) 'The Present Isn't What it Used to Be', *British Gestalt Journal*, Vol. 10, No. 1.

Barber, P. (1999) *Consultancy Relationships*, Management Consultancy Business School Publication, Chinor, Oxford

Barber, P. (1998) 'Working Transparently with Transference: An Action Research Approach to Therapy (Part 2)', *British Gestalt Journal*, Vol. 6, No. 2.

Barber, P (1997) 'Through the eyes of a Client and Therapist: An Action Research Approach to Therapy (Part 1)', *British Gestalt Journal*, Vol. 6, No. 1.

Barber, P. (1996) 'The Therapeutic "Educational" Community as an Agent of Change: towards a Lewinian Model of Peer Learning', *International Journal of Therapeutic Communities*, Vol. 17 (8) pp.242–52.

Barber, P. (1992/1998) 'Care Communication', in Hinchcliff et al. (eds), *Nursing Practice & Health Care*, second edition, Edward Arnold, UK.

Barber, P. (1990) 'The Facilitation of Personal and Professional Growth through Experiential Groupwork and Therapeutic Community Practice', Doctoral thesis, Department of Educational Studies, University of Surrey.

Barber, P. and Dietrich, G. (1985) 'Responding to Authority', in *Caring for People with Mental Handicap*, ENB & Learning Designs publication, UK.

Barber, P. and Mulligan, J. (1998) 'The Client–Consultant Relationship', Chapter 4 in Sadler, P. (ed.) *The Management Consultancy Industry*, Kogan Page, London.

Barrett, G. (2004) 'The Theatre of Gestalt – The Drama of Therapy', *Renewal*, No. 4, December.

Bassett, G. (2004) 'The Theatre of Gestalt – The Drama of Therapy', *Renewal*, No. 4, e-journal of Gestalt in Action, Redhill, UK.

Bates, A.L. and Barber, P. (2004) 'A Transpersonal Reflections on Humanism and the Nature of being Human', *Renewal* (e-journal), Vol. 1, No. 1, gestaltinaction@msn.com.

Bates, A. and Barber, P. (2004) 'Dangersin Forgetting Our Humanistic Roots', *British Gestalt Journal*, Vol. 13, No. 2.

Bateson, G. (1972) *Steps to an Ecology of Mind: Collected Essays in Anthropology, Psychiatry, Evolution, and Epistemology*, University of Chicago Press.

Beisser, A. (1970) 'The Paradoxical Theory of Change', in Fagan, J. and Shepherd, I.L. (eds) *Gestalt Therapy Now*, Science & Behaviour Books, Inc., Palo Alto California.

Benedetti, J. (1998) *Stanislavski and the Actor*, Methuen, London.

Bennis, W. (1987) *On Becoming a Leader*, Perseus, USA.

Bennis, W.G. and Shepard, H.A. (1956) 'A theory of group development', *Human Relations*, 9, 415-37.

Bennis, W., et al. (2002) *Focus on Leadership: Servant-Leadership for the 21st Century*, John Wiley & Sons, New York.

Bentley, T. (2001) 'The Emerging System: A Gestalt Approach to Organisational Interventions', *British Gestalt Journal*, Vol. 10, No. 1, pp.13–19.

Berne, E. (1964/1978) *Games People Play: the Psychology of Human Relations*, Grove Press, USA.

Bettelheim, B. (1969) *The Children of the Dream*, Macmillan, London & New York.

Bettelheim, B. (1960) *The Informed Heart*, Penguin, Harmondsworth.

Bion, W.R. (1968) *Experiences in Groups*, Tavistock Press, London (first published 1961).

Bly, R. (1988) *A Little Book on the Human Shadow*, HarperOne, Collins, UK.

Bohm, D. (1984) *Wholeness and the Implicate Order*, London: Ark Paperbacks (original work published 1980).

Boldt, L.G. (1993) *Zen and the Art of Making a Living*, Penguin/Arkana, London.

Boud, D. and Walker, D. (1998) 'Promoting Reflection in Professional Courses: the Challenge of Context', *Studies in Higher Education*, 23 (2) pp.91–206.

Bowen, M. (1978) *Family Therapy in Clinical Practice*, Jason Aronson Inc, Northvale, NJ.

Brammer, L.M., Shostrom, E.L. and Abrego, P.J. (1989) *Therapeutic Psychology: Fundamentals of Counselling and Psychotherapy*, Prentice-Hall International Publications, Eaglewood Cliffs, New Jersey.

Brockbank, A., McGill, I. and Beech, N. (2003) 'Reflective Learning: What is it Exactly?', *Organisations & People*, Vol. 10, No. 2.

Brownell, P. (2004) 'Perceiving You Perceiving Me – Self Conscious Emotions and Gestalt Therapy', *Gestalt!* Vol. 8, No. 9.

Buber, M. (1980) *I and Thou*, Scribner & Sons, New York, USA.

Bunker, B. and Alban, B. (1997) *Large Group Interventions: Energising the Whole System for Rapid Change*, Jossey-Bass, San Francisco, USA.

Burke, W.W. (1987) *Organizational Development: a Normative View*, Addison-Wesley, USA.

Bushe, G.R. (1998) 'Five Theories of Change Embedded in Appreciative Inquiry', presented at the 18th Annual World Congress of Organisational Development, Dublin, 14–18 July 1998.

Capra, F. (2002) *The Hidden Connections – A Science for Sustainable Living*, Harper Collins, London.

Capra, F. (1997) *The Web of Life: a New Synthesis of Mind and Matter*, Flamingo, Harper

Capra, F. (1982) *The Turning Point*, Simon and Schuster, New York.

Cartwright, D. and Zander, A. (eds) (1968) *Group Dynamics – Research and Theory*, Row, Peterson & Co, USA.

Carter, J.D. (2000) 'Unit of Work', in *Gestalt Workbook*, Gestalt Institute of Cleveland, Organization and Systems Development Training Program, pp.99–103.

Chevalier, J. and Gheerbhant, A. (1994) *A Dictionary of Symbols*, Buchan-Brown translation, Blackwell, London.

Chidiac, A.M. (2011) 'To Infinity and Beyond… the Hot Seat: Musings on Twenty-eight Years of Changes in the Gestalt Approach to Groups', *British Gestalt Journal*, Vol. 20, No. 1, pp.42–51.

Chopra, D. (1996) *The Seven Spiritual Laws of Success*, Bantum Press, Transworld Publishers, London.

Clarkson, P. (1996b) 'The archetype of physis: The soul of nature – our nature', *Harvest: Journal for Jungian Studies*, 42 (1): 70–94.

Clarkson, P. (1995) 'The Soul of Gestalt – Gestalt as Qualitative Research', workshop paper delivered at UK Gestalt Conference, Cambridge.

Clarkson, P. (1993) '2,500 Years of Gestalt: From Heraclitus to the Big Bang', *British Gestalt Journal*, 2 (1), pp.4–9.

Clarkson, P. (1991) 'New perspectives in supervision', address delivered at conference of British Society for Supervision Research. Clune, N. (1999) *The Coming of the Feminine Christ*, Amarita Publications, Brighton.

Coffey, F. and Cavicchia, S. (2005) 'Revitalising Feedback – An Organisational Case Study', *British Gestalt Journal*, Vol. 14, No. 1.

Collins, D. (1998) *Organisational Change: Sociological Perspectives*, Routledge, London.

Cooper, C.L and Mangham, I.L. (1971) *T-Groups: a Survey of Research*, Wiley-Interscience, London.

Cooperrider, D.L. (1990) 'Positive Image, Positive Action: The Affirmative Basis of Organizing', in Srivasta, S. and Cooperrider, D.L. (eds) *Appreciative Management and Leadership*, Jossey-Bass, San Francisco, USA.

Cooperrider, D.L. and Srivasta, S. (1987) 'Appreciative Inquiry in Organisational Life', in Pasmore, W. and Woodman, R. (eds) *Research in Organisational Change and Development*, Vol. 1, Greenwich, CT: JAI Press, USA, pp.129–69.

Corrigan, M. (2011) *Your Quest for a Spiritual Life: Based on Patanjali's Yoga Sutras*, O Books, Winchester and Washington.

Critchley, B. and Casey, D. (1989) 'Organizations Get Stuck Too', *Leadership and Organizational Development Journal*, Vol. 10, No. 4.

Dale, A. (1998) in conversation with the author.

De Board, R. (1978) *The Psychoanalysis of Organizations*, Tavistock, London.Deering, A., Dilts, R. and Russell, J. (2003) 'Alpha Leadership: Value Through Values', *Organisations & People*, Vol. 10, No. 2.

Deering, A., Dilts, R. and Russell, J. (2002) *Alpha Leadership: Tools for Business Leaders Who Want More from Life*, John Wiley & Sons, Chichester.

Derrida, J. (1976) *Of Grammatology*, Baltimore, MD: Johns Hopkins University Press.

Dethlefsen, T. and Dahlke, R. (1990) *The Healing Power of Illness*, Element, Brisbane.

Deutsch, M. (1960) 'The Effects of Cooperation and Competition upon Group Process', in Cartwright, D. and Zander, A. (eds) *Group Dynamics – Research and Theory*, Row, Peterson & Co, USA.

Devall, B. and Sessions, G. (1985) *Deep Ecology*, Peregrine Smith, Salt Lake City, USA.

Douglas, T. (1985) *Understanding people gathered together*, Tavistock publications, London.

Edelwich, J. and Brodsky, A. (1980) *Burn-out*, Research Press, New York.

Egan, G. (1994) *Working with the Shadow Side: a Guide to Positive Behind the Scenes Management*, Josey-Bass, San Francisco.

Enright, J. (1980) *Enlightening Gestalt Waking up from the nightmare*, Pro Telos, Mill Valley, CA.

Etzioni, A. (1964) *Modern Organizations*, Prentice-Hall, Eaglewood Cliffs, NJ.

Fisher, D. and Torbert, W.R. (1995) *Personal and Organisational Transformation*, McGraw-Hill, London.

Flood, R. (1990) *Liberating Systems Theory*, New York: Plenum Press.

Forstater, M. (2001) *The Spiritual Teachings of The Tao*, Hodder & Stoughton, UK.

Foucault, M. (1982) 'The subject and power', in *Michel Foucault: Beyond Structuralism and Hermeneutics*, ed. H. L. Dreyfus and P. Rabinow, New York: Harvester Press.

Fox, W. (1990) *Toward a Transpersonal Ecology*, Shambhala, Boston, USA.

Francis, T. (2005) 'Working with the Field', *British Gestalt Journal*, Vol. 14, No. 1 pp.26–33.

Freud, S. (1936) *Ego and the Mechanisms of Defence*, Hogarth Press, London.

Freud, S. and Breuer, J. (1895/2000) *Studies on Hysteria*, translated by Strachley, J. Basic Books, Perseus & Hogarth Books, USA.

Friedman, M. (1989) 'Dialogue, Philosophical Anthropology, and Gestalt Therapy', based on a panel discussion on 'Dialogical Gestalt', 11th Gestalt Conference, in *British Gestalt Journal*, Vol. 13, No. 13, pp.7–40, 1990, GPTI publication.

Fry, R.E. and Kolb, D.A. (1979) *Experiential learning theory and learning experiences in liberal arts education*, in S. Brooks and J. Althof (eds), *Enriching the liberal arts through experiential learning*, Jossey-Bass, San Francisco.

Galbraith, J.K. (1967) *The New Industrial State*, Princeton University Press, New Jersey.

Gauthier, P. (1980) 'Psycho-education as a Re-education Model: Theoretical Foundations and Practical Implications', Chapter 10 in Jansen, E. (ed.) *The Therapeutic Community*, Croom Helm Ltd, London

Gendlin, E. (1981) *Focusing*, Bantum, New York.

Geust, D. (1992) 'Right Enough to be Dangerously Wrong. In Search of Excellence Phenomenon', in Salaman, G. (ed.) *Human Resource Strategies*, Sage, London.

Green and Moscow (1986) *Managing*, cited without full reference in Collins, D. (1998) *Organisational Change: Sociological Perspectives*, Routledge, London.

Greenson, R. (1967) *The Technique and Practice of Psychoanalysis*, International Universities Press, New York.

Guerrière, D. (1980) 'Physis, Sophia, Psyche', in Sallis, J. and Maly, K. (eds), *Heraclitean Fragments: A Companion Volume to the Heidegger/Fink Seminar on Heraclitus*, Alabama: University of Alabama Press, pp.86–144.

Gurdjieff, G.I. (1973) *Views from the Real World, Early Talks of Gurdjieff as Recollected by his Pupils*, Routledge & Kegan Paul, London.

Gurdjieff, G.I. (1973a) *Life is real only then when 'I am'*, Routledge & Kegan Paul, London.

Gurdjieff, G.I. (1979) *Meetings with Remarkable Men*, Routledge & Kegan Paul, London.

Hackman, J.R. and Oldham G.R. (1980) *Work Redesign*, Addison-Wesley, Reading, MA.

Handy, C. (2003) 'Seven Metaphors on Management', book review in *Organisations & People*, Vol. 10, No. 3.

Handy, C. (1993) *The Age of Unreason*, Century, London.

Handy, C. (1991) *Gods of Management: The Changing Work of Organisations*, Century, London.

Harkema, S. and Browaeys, M. (2003) 'Innovation and Culture Revisited: A Conceptual approach Based on Complexity Theory', *Organisations & People*,

Vol. 10, No. 1.Harris, J. (2005) 'A Gestalt Approach on Working with group Process', Manchester Gestalt Centre webpage, mgc.org.uk.

Harris, J.B. (1999) 'Gestalt Learning and Training', *British Gestalt Journal*, Vol. 8, No. 2.

Harris, J.B. (1998) 'Does Gestalt Need a Theory of Group Development?', unpublished paper.

Harrison, R. (1995) *The Consultant's Journey*, McGraw-Hill, Developing Organisations Series, London.

Harvard Business Review (2006) 'Breakthrough Ideas for 2006 – a compilation', February pp.35–67.

Harvey-Jones, J. (1988) *Making it Happen. Reflections on Leadership*, Collins, UK.

Hawkins, P. (1980) 'Between Scylla and Charybdis: Staff Training in Therapeutic Communities', Chapter 13 in Jansen, E. (ed.) *The Therapeutic Community*, Croom Helm Ltd, London.

Haywood, S. and Cohan, M. (1990) *Bag of Jewels*, In-Tune Books, Avalon Beach NSW, Australia.

Heelas, P. (1987) 'Exegesis Methods and Aims', in Clarke, P. (ed.) *The New Evangelists: Recruitment, Methods and Aims of New Religious Movements*, London Ethnographic Press, pp.17–41.

Heider, J. (1985) *The Tao of Leadership*, Wildwood House, Aldershot, Hants.

Hellinger, B., Weber, G. and Beaumont, H. (1998) *Love's Hidden Symmetry: What Makes Love Work in Relationships*, Zeig Tucker & Theisen, New York.

Heron, J. (2001) (5th ed) *Helping the Client – a creative practical guide*, SAGE publications, London.

Heron, J. (1999) in conversation with the author.

Heron, J. (1998) *Co-Counselling Manual*, South Pacific Centre for Human Inquiry, 11 Bald Hill Road, R.D.1 Kaukapakapa, Auckland 1250, NZ.

Heron, J. (1990) *Handbook for Leaders*, HPRG Publication, School of Educational Studies, University of Surrey.

Heron, J. (1989) *The Facilitator's Handbook*, Kogan Page, London.

Heron, J. (1988) 'Impressions of the Other Reality: a Collaborative Inquiry into Altered States of Consciousness', Chapter 9 in *Human Inquiry in Action: Developments in New Paradigm Research*, Reason, P. (ed.), Sage Ltd, London.

Heron, J. (1981) 'Experiential Research Methodology', in Reason, P. and Rowen, J. (eds) *Human Inquiry, a Sourcebook of New Paradigm Research*, Chichester, Wiley.

Heron, J. (1974) *The Concept of a Peer Learning Community*, Human Potential Research Project, University of Surrey, Guildford.

Herrick, N.Q. and Maccoby, M. (1975) 'Humanizing Work: a Priority Goal of the 1970s', in Davis, L.E. and Cherns, A.B. (eds), *The Quality of Working Life*, Vol. 1. The Free Press, New York.

Herzberg, F. (1966) *Work and the nature of man*, Holland, Cleveland, OH.

Higgins, J. (2009) *Images of Authority: Working within the Shadow of the Crown*, Libri Press/Middlesex University Press, Oxford/London.

Hinshelwood, B. (1989) *What Happens in Groups*, Free Association Books, London.

Holmes, A. (2002) *The Chameleon Consultant: Culturally Intelligent Consultancy*, Gower, UK.

Holroyd, S. (1991) *Krishnamurti: The Man, the Mystery and Messages*, Element, Dorset.

Huczynski, A.A. (1993) *Management Gurus: What Makes Them and How to Become One*, Routledge, London.

Hycner, R. (1993) *Between Person & Person*, Gestalt Journal Press, New York.

I Ching (1968) *I Ching, or Book of Changes*, Baynes, C. and Wilhelm, R. translation, Routledge & Kegan Paul, London.

Jansen, E. (1980) *The Therapeutic Community*, Croom Helm Ltd, London.

Jarvis, P. (1992) *Paradoxes of Learning: On Becoming an Individual in Society*, Jossey-Bass, California.

Jarvis, P. (1985) *The Sociology of Adult and Continuing Education*, Croom Helm, Beckenham.

Jones, M. (1952) *Social Psychiatry, a Study of Therapeutic Communities*, Tavistock, London.

Josephson, E. and Josephson, M. (eds) (1972) *Man Alone: Alienation in Modern Society*, Dell Publishing Company, New York.

Jung, C.G. (1981) *Archetypes and the Collective Unconscious*, Princeton University Press, USA.

Just, B. (2003) 'Gestalt Therapy as Literature: A Brief Introduction to the Trans-theoretical Genre', unpublished paper.

Just, B. (2002) 'Authenticity Workpoints', *Australian Gestalt Journal*, 6, 1, pp.87–101.

Just, B. (Undated) 'Gestalt Therapy as Literature', unpublished paper.

Just, B., Feldhaus, B. and Bearinger, O. (2001) 'Impasse', *Gestalt!*, Vol. 5, No. 2, Early Fall.

Kahn,C. (1987) *The Art and Thought of Heraclitus*, Cambridge University Press, New York.

Kanter, R.M. (1985) *The Change Masters: Innovation for Productivity in the American Corporation*, Simon & Schuster, New York.

Kaufman, S.A. (1993) *Origins of Order: Self-Organization and Selection in Evolution*, Oxford University Press, Oxford.

Kennard, D. (1984) in conversation with the author.

Kennard, D. (Undated) working alongside the author.

Kennedy, D.J. (2003) 'The Phenomenological Field', *British Gestalt Journal*, Vol. 12, No. 1, pp.76–87.

Kennedy, D.J. (1998) 'Gestalt: A Point of Departure for a Personal Spirituality', *British Gestalt Journal*, Vol. 2, No. 7, pp.88–98.

Kepner, J. (2003) 'The Embodied Field', *British Gestalt Journal*, Vol. 12, No. 1, pp.6–14.

Kernberg, O.F. (1996) 'Thirty ways to destroy the creativity of psychoanalytic candidates', *International Journal of Psycho-Analysis*, 77, 5: 1,031–40.

Klein, M. (1983) *Discover Your Real Self*, Hutchinson, UK.

Kline, N. (1999) *Time to Think: Listening to Ignite the Human Mind*, Ward Lock, London.

Koffka, K. (1935) *Principles of Gestalt Psychology*, London: Kegan Paul, Trench.

Kohler, W. (1947) *Gestalt Psychology*, Liveright Paperbound Edition, New York, 1970.

Kohler, W. (1922) 'Some Gestalt problems', in Ellis, W.D. (ed.) *A Source Book of Gestalt Psychology*, London: Routledge and Kegan Paul Ltd., 1938.

Kolb, D.A. and Fry, R.E. (1975) *Toward an applied theory of experiential learning*, in C. Cooper (ed.), *Theories of group processes*, John Wiley & Sons, NY.

Kolodny, R. (2004) 'Why Awareness Works – And Other Insights from Spiritual Practice', *British Gestalt Journal*, Vol. 13, No. 2.Krantz, J. (2001) 'Dilemmas of Organisational Change: A Systems Perspective', in Gould, L., Stein, M. and Stapley, L. (eds) *The Systems Psychodynamics or Organizations*, London: Karnac Books.

Krathwol, D.R., Bloom, B.S. and Masia, B.B. (1964) *Taxonomy of Educational Objectives: The Classification of Educational Goals. Handbook 2: Affective Domain*, Appendix, David McKay Co, London, pp.176–85.

Kuhn, T. (1962) *The Structure of Scientific Revolutions*, University of Chicago Press, USA.

Kvale, S. (1992) *Psychology and Modernism*, Sage, London.

Lawrence, R. (2002) *Little Book of Yin & Yang*, Thorsons, UK.

Lazarus, R.S. and Lazarus, B.N. (1994) *Passion & Reason: Making sense of our emotions*, New York: Oxford University Press.

Lewin, K. (1952) *Field Theory in Social Science*, Tavistock, London.

Lewin, K. (1946) 'Action Research and Minority Problems', *Journal of Social Issues*, 2, 34–6.

Lewis, M. (1992) *Shame, the exposed self*, New York: The Free Press.

Lippitt, L.G. and Lippitt, R. (1978) *Consulting Process in Action*, University Associates, La Jolla, CA.

Macintosh, P. and Barber, P. (2011) 'Freeforming – Connecting Without Words', in Brownell, P. and Stevens, C. (eds) *Innovations in Gestalt* – accepted for publication.

Main, T.F. (1980) 'Some Basic Concepts in Therapeutic Community Work', Chapter 1 in Jansen, E. (ed.) *The Therapeutic Community Outside the Hospital*, The Richmond Fellowship, Croom Helm, London.

Main, T. (1946) 'The Hospital as a Therapeutic Institution', *Bull. Menninger Clinic*, Vol. 10, p.66.

Maister, D., Green, C. and Galford, R. (2000) *The Trusted Advisor*, Free Press, New Year.

Margerison, C. (2003) 'Memories of Reg Revans 1907–2003', *People & Organisations*, Vol. 10, No. 2.

Maslow, A. (1967) *Toward a Psychology of Being*, 1st published 1962.

Master Park (1995) 'The Way to the Truth', internal publication, Chun Do Sun Bup.

Maturana, H. and Varela, F. (1975) 'Autopoietic Systems: A Characterization of the Living Organization', *Bio. Computer Lab. Research Report* 9.4, University of Illinois, Urbana.

Maurer, R. (2005) 'Gestalt Approaches with Organisations and Large Systems', Chapter 13 in Woldt, A.L. and Tolman, S.M., *Gestalt Therapy: History, Theory, and Practice*, Sage, California, USA.

Mayo, E. (1933) *The Human Problems of an Industrial Civilisation*, Macmillan, New York.

McLeod, A. (2003) *Performance Coaching: The Handbook for Managers, HR Professionals and Coaches*, Crown House Publishing, Carmarthen.

Meltzer, D. (1992) *The Claustrum: an investigation of claustrophobic phenomena*, Clunie Press, Perthshire.

Menzies Lyth, I. (1988) *Containing Anxiety in Institutions. Selected Essays Vol. 1*, Free Association Books, London.

Menzies Lyth, I. (1960) 'Social Systems as a Defense Against Anxiety: on empirical study of the nursing service of a general hospital', *Human Relations*, 13: 95–121.

Merton, R.K. (1968) Social Theory and Social *Structure*, The Free Press, New York.

Mitroff, I.I. and Kilmann, R.H. (1978) *Methodological Approaches to Social Science, Integrating Divergent Concepts & Theories*, Josey Bass, San Francisco.

Moreno, J. (1999) *Acting Your Inner Music: Music Therapy & Psychodrama*, Barcelona Publishers, Gilsum NH, www.barcelonapublishers.com.

Moreno, J.L. (1951) *Sociometry, Experimental Method and the Science of Society. An Approach to a New Political Orientation*, Beacon House, New York.

Morgan, G. (1997) *Images of Organisation*, Sage, London.

Morrell, M. and Capparell, S. (2001) *Shackleton's Way: Leadership Lessons from the Great Antarctic Explorer*, Viking Press, New York.

Moustakas, C. (1994) *Phenomenological research methods*, Sage, London.

Moustakas, C. (1990) *Heuristic research: design, methodology and application*, Sage, Newbury Park.Moxley, R.S. (2002) 'Leadership as Partnership', in Bennis et al., *Focus on Leadership: Servant-Leadership for the 21st Century*, John Wiley & Sons, New York.

Mulligan, J. (1999) in conversation with the author.

Mulligan, J. (1993) *The Personal Management Handbook*, Warner Books, Little, Brown & Company Ltd, London.Muna, F.A. (2003) *Seven Metaphors on Management: Tools for Managers in the Arab World*, Gower, UK.

Myss, C. (2003) *Archetype Cards*, Hay House Inc, Carsbad, CA.

Naisbett, J. and Aburdene, P. (1985) *Re-inventing the Corporation*, Warner, New York.

Nelson, R. (2005) 'Correlations of Continuous Random Data with Major World Events', http://noosphere.princeton.edu.

Nevis, E. (1997) 'Gestalt therapy and organization development: A historical perspective', *Gestalt Rev.*, 1: pp.110–30.

Nevis, E. (1996) *Gestalt Therapy: Perspectives and Applications*, Gestalt Institute of Cleveland Book Series, Cleveland, USA

Nevis, E.C. (1987) *Organisational Consulting*, Gestalt Institute of Cleveland Press, New York.

Nicholson, J. (1977) *Habits*, Macmillan, London.

Nixon, B. (1998) *Making a Difference: Strategies and Real Time Models to Transform your Organisation*, Gilmour Drummond Publishing, Cambridge.

O'Donoghue, J. (1997) *Anam Cara: Spiritual Wisdom from the Celtic World*, Bantam Press, Transworld Publications, London.

Osho (1995) *The ABC of Enlightenment: A Spiritual Dictionary of the Here and Now*, Element Books, Harper Collins, London.

Owen, M. (2001) *The Magic of Metaphor*, Crown House, Camarthen.

Palmer, P. (2004) *A Hidden Wholeness – The Journey Towards an Undivided Life*, Jossey-Bass, San Francisco, USA.

Parlett, M. (1997) in conversation with the author.

Parlett, M. (1993) 'Towards a more Lewinian Gestalt Therapy', *British Gestalt Journal*, Vol. 2, No. 2, pp.11–14.

Parlett, M. (1991) 'Reflections on Field Theory', *British Gestalt Journal*, Vol. 1, No. 2, pp.69–81.

Pascale, R. (1991) *Managing on the Edge*, Penguin Books, London.

Pascale, R. and Athos, A. (1986) *The Art of Japanese Management*, Warner Books, New York.

Peck, M.S. (1993) *A World Waiting to be Born – the Search for Civility*, Rider, London.

Peck, M.S. (1987) *The Different Drum: Community Making and Peace*, Touchstone, New York.

Pedler, M. (1996) *Action Learning for Managers*, Lemos & Crane, London.

Pedler, M., Burgoyne, J. and Boydell, T. (1997) *The Learning Company: a Strategy for Sustainable Development*, 2nd Edition, McGraw Hill, London.

Peplau, H. (1952) *Interpersonal Relations in Nursing – A Conceptual Frame of Reference for Psychodynamic Nursing*, G.P. Putnams & Sons, USA.

Perls, F.S. (1977) 'Comments on the New Direction', in Smith, E.W. (ed.) *The Growing Edge of Gestalt Therapy*, Citadel Press, New Jersey, USA.

Perls, F. (1972) *In and Out the Garbage Pail*, Bantam Books, New York.

Perls, F.S. (1947) *Ego, Hunger and Aggression*, Allen Unwin, London.

Perls, F.S., Hefferline, R.F. and Goodman, P. (1994) *Gestalt Therapy: Excitement and Growth in the Human Personality*, Gestalt Journal Press, Highland, NY, first published by Julian Press, NY, 1951.

Perry, J.W. (1976) *The Far Side of Madness*, Spring Publications, Dallas, USA.

Peters, T. and Waterman, R. (1982) *In Search of Excellence*, Harper and Row, New York.

Phillipson, P. (2002) *Self in Relation,* Gestalt Journal Press, Gouldsboro, USA.

Pines, M. (ed.) (1983) *The Evolution of Group Analysis*, Routledge and Kegan Paul, London.

Pollecoffe, M. (1998) 'Mythos – A Journey in Search of the Soul of an Organisation', unpublished MSc thesis, Department of Educational Studies, University of Surrey, Guildford.

Polster, E. and Polster, M. (1973) *Gestalt Therapy Integrated: Contours of Theory and Practice*, Brunner-Mazel, New York.

Preston, J. (2005) 'A Revolt in the Classroom', *Sunday Telegraph, Review*, 3 April.

Pugh, D.S., Hickson, D.J. and Hinings, C.R. (1984) *Writers on Organizations*, Penguin Books, 3rd Edition, Harmondsworth, London.

Randall, R. and Southgate, J. (1980) *Cooperative and Community Group Dynamics: or Your Meetings Needn't be so Appalling*, Barefoot Books, London.

Rank, O. (1989) *Art and Artist: Creative Urge and Personality Development*, W.W. Norton, New York, first published 1942.

Rank, O. (1936) *Truth and Reality*, New York: Norton.

Rapoport, R. (1960) *Community as Doctor*, Tavistock, London.

Reason, P. and Goodwin, B. (1999) 'Toward a Science of Qualities in Organizations: Lessons from Complexity Theory and Postmodern Biology. Concepts and Transformation', *International Journal of Action Research and Organizational Renewal*, 4.3, 1999, pp.281–317.

Reason, P. and Rowen, J. (1981) *Human Inquiry: a Sourcebook of New Paradigm Research*, John Wiley & Sons, Chichester.

Revans, R. (1982) *The Origins and Growth of Action Learning*, Chartwell Bratt, Bromley, UK.

Revans, R. (1971) *Developing Effective Managers*, Praeger, New York.

Ribeiro, J.P. (1997) 'Comparative study of therapeutic factors from the process among four Gestalt therapy groups', in P. Clarkson (ed.), *Counselling Psychology Integrating Theory, Supervised Practice and Research*, Routledge, London.

Rice, A.K. (1958) *Productivity and Social Organization*, Tavistock, London.

Robbins, H. and Finley, M. (1997) *Why Teams Don't Work – What Went Wrong and How to Make it Right*, Orion Business Books, London.

Robinson, J. (2004) 'Experiences of the Gurdjieff "Work" & Gestalt Psychotherapy – A Sympathetic Review', *Renewal*, No. 4, e-journal of Gestalt in Action, Redhill, UK.

Rogers, C. (1967) *On Becoming a Person*, Constable, London.

Rogers, C. (1962) 'The Interpersonal Relationship: The Core of Guidance', *Harvard Educational Review*, 32, No. 4, pp.416–29.

Rogers, C. (1957) 'The Necessary and Sufficient Conditions of Therapeutic Personality Change', *Journal of Consulting Psychology*, 21 (2): 95–103.

Rose, A.M. (ed.) (1977) *Human Behavior and Social Processes: An Interactionist Approach*, Routledge and Kegan Paul, London.

Roszak, T. (1992) *The Voice of the Earth*, Simon & Schuster, New York, USA.

Rowen, J. (1993) *The Transpersonal: Psychotherapy and Counselling*, Routledge, London.

RSA (Royal Society of Arts) (1995) *Tomorrow's Company*, copies available from RSA (T) 0171 839 1641.

Salaman, G. and Thompson, K. (1973) *People and organisations*, the Open University Press.

Saner, R. (1999) 'Organisational Consulting: What a Gestalt Approach Can Learn from Off-Off Broadway Theatre', *Gestalt Review*, Vol. 3, pp.6–21.

Saner, R. (1990) 'Manifestations of stress and its impact on the humanitarian work of the ICRC delegate', *Polit. Psychol.*, 11:4.

Saner, R. (1989) 'Die Logik des Zerfalls: Arthur Schnitzler und das Wiener fin-de-siècle' [The logic of decomposition: A. Schnitzler and Vienna's Fin-de-Siècle], Radio DRS, Switzerland, 20 February.

Saner, R. (1984) 'Culture bias of Gestalt therapy made-in-USA', *Gestalt Theory*, 6.

Schneider, S. (1988) 'National vs. corporate culture: Implications for human resource management', *Human Res. Manage.*, 27:2.

Schumacher, E.F. (1973) *Small is Beautiful: a Study of Economics as if People Mattered*, Blond & Briggs.

Schuster, J. (2002) 'Servant-Leadership and the New Economy', in Spears, L.C. (ed.), *Focus on Leadership – Servant-Leadership for the 21st Century*, John Wiley and Sons, New York.

Scott, D. and Usher, R. (1999) *Researching Education: Data, Methods and Theory in Educational Enquiry*, Cassell, London.

Senge, P. et al. (2004) *Presence: Human Purpose & the Field of the Future*, SoL, Cambridge MA.

Shaw, M.E. (1971) *Group Dynamics: the psychology of small group behaviour*, McGraw-Hill, New York, USA.

Sheldrake, R. (2003) *The Sense of Being Stared At*, Hutchinson, London.

Shohet, R. (2005) 'The Work of Parker Palmer', *Self and Society*, Vol. 32, No. 6, pp.37–41.

Simmons, M. (1993) 'Creating a New Leadership Initiative', *Management Development Review*, Vol. 6, No. 5.

Simmons, M. (1996) *Leadership and Gender*, Gower, London.

Simmons, G.F. (2003) 'Managing Cultural Diversity in Technical Professions', book review in *People and Organisations*, Vol. 10, No. 2.

Skynner, R. (1989) *Institutes and How to Survive them*, Methuen, London.

Smuts, J. (1926) *Holism and Evolution*, Macmillan and Co, London.

Spears, L.C. (2002) 'Tracing the Past, Present, and Future of Servant-Leadership', in Spears, L.C. and Lawrence, M., *Focus on Leadership: Servant-Leadership for the 21st Century*, John Wiley & Sons, New York.

Spears, L.C. and Lawrence, M. (eds) (2002) *Focus on Leadership: Servant-Leadership for the 21st Century*, John Wiley & Sons, New York.

Sperry, L. (2004) *Executive Coaching: The Essential Guide for Mental Health Professionals*, Brunner-Routledge, New York

Sperry, L. (1996) *Corporate Therapy and Consulting*, Brunner-Mazel, New York.

Stacey, R. (1992) *Managing Chaos: Dynamic Business Strategies in an Unpredictable World*, London: Kogan Page.

Stapley, L.F. (1996) *The Personality of the Organization: a Psycho-Dynamic Explanation of Culture and Change*, Free Association Books, London.

Spinelli, E. (1992) *The Interpreted World: An Introduction to Phenomenological Psychology*, Sage Pubs, first published 1989.

Suzuki, D.T. (1950) *Living by Zen*, Rider, London.

Taft, J. (1958) *Otto Rank: A Biographical Study Based on Notebooks, Letters, Collected Writings, Therapeutic Achievements and Personal Associations*, Julian Press, New York.

Tao te Ching (1976) *Tao te Ching*, Ta-Kao, C. (trans.), Unwin Paperbacks, London.

Trist, E.L. (1981) 'The Socio-Technical Perspective', in van de Ven, A. and Joyce, W.F. (eds), *Perspectives in Organizational Design and Behaviour*, Wiley-Interscience, London.

Tuckman, B.W. (1965) 'Developmental Sequence in Small Groups', *Psychological Bulletin*, 63.

Vaysse, J. (1980) *Toward Awakening, An Approach to the Teaching Left by Gurdjieff*, Routledge & Kegan Paul, London.

Waitley, D. (1995) *Empires of the Mind*, BCA, London/NewYork.

Weber, M. (1947) *The Theory of Social and Economic Organization*, translated by A.M. Henderson and Talcott Parsons, The Free Press, NY.

Welch, K. (2011) 'Tantra Reflections', *Renewal*, No. 25, Summer.

Wheatley, M. (1992) *Leadership and the New Science*, San Francisco: Berrett-Koehler.

Wheelan, S.A., Pepitone, E.A. and Abt, V. (1990) *Advances in Field Theory*, Sage, London.

Wheway, J.K. (1999) 'Spirituality and Selfhood', *British Gestalt Journal*, Vol. 8, No. 2, pp.118–29.

Whiteley, J.S. and Gordon, J. (1979) *Group Approaches in Psychiatry*, Routledge and Kegan Paul, London.

Whyte, W.H. (1960) *The Organization Man*, Penguin.

Willett, J. (1977) *The Theatre of Bertolt Brecht*, Methuen, London.

Wilmot, J. (2005) 'Psychology for Teachers', *Self and Society*, Vol. 32, No. 6, pp.31–6.

Wilson, P.J. and Chesterman, D.K. (2003) 'Schools of Leadership', *People & Organisations*, Vol. 10, No. 3.

Woldt, A. and Ingersoll, R.E. (1991) 'Where in the "Yang" has the "yin" Gone in Gestalt Therapy?', *British Gestalt Journal*, Vol. 1, No. 2, pp.94–103.

Woldt, A.L. and Tolman, S.M. (2005) *Gestalt Therapy: History, Theory, and Practice*, Sage, California, USA.

Yalom, I.D. (1975) *The Theory and Practice of Psychotherapy*, Basic Books, New York.

Yontef, G. (1996) 'Gestalt Supervision', *British Gestalt Journal*, Vol. 5, No. 2, pp.92–102.

Yontef, G.M., (1993) *Awareness Dialogue & Process*, Gestalt Journal Press, Highland, New York.

Zinker, J. (2001) 'The Present Isn't What it Used to Be: A Gestalt Encounter with Joseph Zinker', an interview by Paul Barber, *British Gestalt Journal*, Vol. 10, No. 1, pp.29–37.

Zinker, J. (1998) *In Search of Good Form*, Analytic Press, USA.

Zinker, J. (1978) *Creative Process in Gestalt Therapy*, Vintage Books, New York.

Zweig, C. and Abrams, J. (1991) *Meeting the Shadow: The Hidden Power of the Dark Side of Human Nature*, Tarcher, Los Angeles, USA.

May you experience the yin of peace.
May you experience the yang of love.

(Lawrence 2002, p.158)

AUTHOR BIOGRAPHY

Paul has co-designed and delivered courses in Therapeutic Community Practice, master's degrees in 'Change Agent Skills' plus 'Management Consultancy' and has taught, examined and advised on several Doctorates in Psychotherapy. As a facilitator he applies a holistic model derived from Gestalt, Taoism, Humanism and Group Analysis to coaching and organisational development. He is a Fellow of the Roffey Institute, a Visiting Professor in the Department of Work-Based Learning at Middlesex University and at Nova Sud (Serbia), and currently advises and examines on the Practitioner Doctorate in Psychotherapy and Doctorate in Public Works at the Metanoia Institute. The sister volume to this text, *Becoming a Practitioner–Researcher: A Gestalt Approach to Holistic Inquiry*, is also published by Libri Publishing.

Address for correspondence: gestaltinaction@msn.com
Website: www.gestaltinaction.com